THE LANDMEN

How They Secured the Trans-Alaska Pipeline Right-of-Way

Armand C. Spielman and Michael D. Travis

PO Box 221974 Anchorage, Alaska 99522-1974
books@publicationconsultants.com—www.publicationconsultants.com

ISBN 978-1-59433-608-9
eISBN 978-1-59433-609-6
Library of Congress Catalog Card Number: 2016934077

Cover photograph credit to Erik D. Mundahl

Maps by Eric Stratton, StrattNat Productions, Anchorage, Alaska

Manufactured in the United States of America.

Dedication

To the men and women who secured the land to build the Trans-Alaska Pipeline System. The authors especially recognize Jay Sullivan and his right-of-way team, Land Field Services, John Knodell of Exxon Corp., Harry Brelsford of Alyeska, and Quinn O'Connell of Connole & O'Connell. Because of their relentless work, Alyeska Pipeline Company now operates a marvelously engineered facility across Alaska.

Michael Travis is also the author of

El Gancho

A saga of an immigrant family's journey out of Mexico

Melozi

A Teen's Search for A Summer Job Lands
Him An Adventure In The Alaska Bush

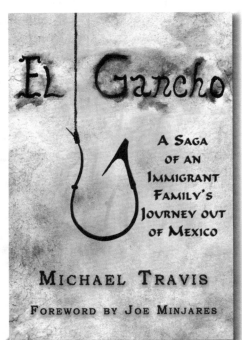

Acknowledgments

The basis of this book was developed by countless interviews between Michael Travis and Armand Spielman. In addition, many people provided crucial details about acquiring the right-of-way (ROW) for the pipeline and Haul Road corridors. The authors are grateful for their interest and contributions to this story. They are listed in alphabetical order along with a short note about their participation.

Daniel Beardsley—Dan provided many intricate details of procuring ROW and inside stories about working at Land Field Services

Marthy Johnson—Marthy skillfully edited this story.

Warren Krotke—Warren assumed Armand Spielman's position when Armand resigned from Alyeska. Warren provided specifics about the last months of ROW acquisition for TAPS.

Al Olsen—Al worked as an appraiser for the Alaska Department of Natural Resources. He discussed the valuation of the Valdez Marine Terminal.

Patty McNamee—Patty is an archivist with the National Archives and Records Administration in Seattle, Washington. She researched and found BLM records pertaining to land agreements with Alyeska.

Peter Nagel—Peter is a Senior Landowner Reality Specialist with the Alyeska Pipeline Service Company. Peter researched company files to clarify details for the authors.

Robert Ylvisaker—Bob was a tremendous resource for the authors. As executor of Jay Sullivan's estate, he had the trust of Jay's and Nancy's children. The family loaned Bob many special photographs and documents that helped the authors write this story. Bob also provided the authors with many stories about working at Land Field Services. He read a draft of the story to ensure its accuracy.

Michael Travis especially thanks his beautiful wife Barby for encouragement. She enjoyed meeting Armand and agreed that his story must be told.

Armand C. Spielman and Michael D. Travis

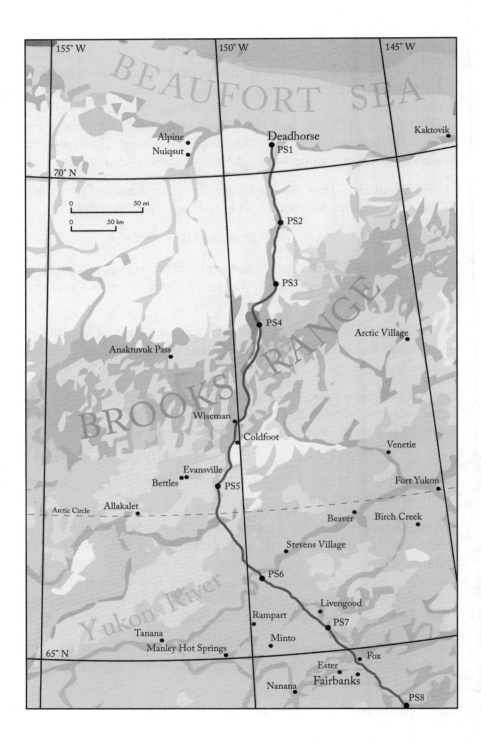

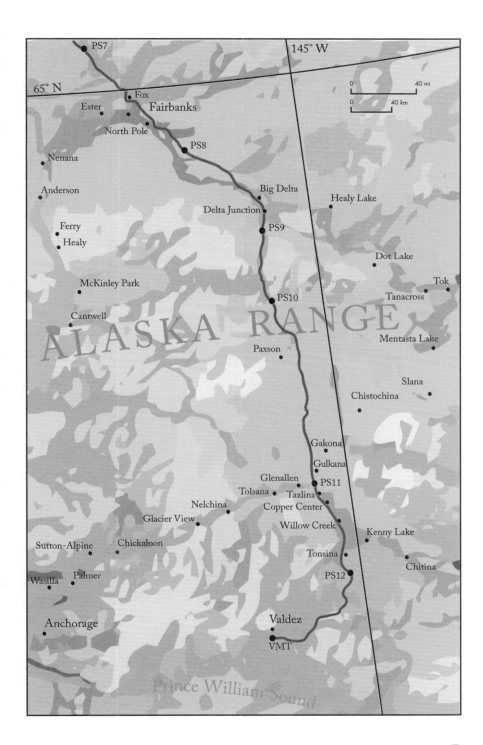

PS7

145° W

65° N

Fox

Ester

Fairbanks

North Pole

PS8

Nenana

Anderson

Big Delta

Healy Lake

Delta Junction

PS9

Ferry

Dot Lake

Healy

Tok

McKinley Park

Tanacross

PS10

Cantwell

ALASKA RANGE

Mentasta Lake

Paxson

Slana

Chistochina

Gakona

Gulkana

Glenallen

PS11

Tolsana

Tazlina

Nelchina

Copper Center

Glacier View

Willow Creek

Kenny Lake

Sutton-Alpine

Chickaloon

Tonsina

Chitina

Wasilla

Palmer

PS12

Anchorage

Valdez

VMT

Prince William Sound

0   40 mi

0   40 km

Introduction

O n April 17, 2013, I attended a luncheon sponsored by the
Sourdough Chapter of the International Right-of-Way
Association. My busy schedule as an environmental consultant had prevented me from regularly attending the monthly meetings, but this time I
made a special effort to be present. The chapter's monthly flyer advertised
Armand Spielman as the luncheon speaker. Mr. Spielman would discuss
his book, *A Project That Reformed Alaska and Its Legislature*, a memoir of
acquiring the right-of-way for the Trans-Alaska Pipeline System (TAPS).

My assistant high school football coach and longtime friend, Daniel
Beardsley, also coaxed me to listen to Armand's talk. "Jay, Bob, and I
used to work for him," said Dan. "He's a walking encyclopedia. You
need to hear his story."

Dan was referring to Jay Sullivan and Bob Ylvisaker. Jay was also an assistant football coach when I played for the Lathrop High School Malemutes
in 1973. He had died only six months earlier and I was still in denial that
this gigantic man was gone. I had worked with Bob on various projects over
the past 20 years and cherished his friendship. Thus, if Mr. Spielman was the
ringleader of these men, I was going to carve out some time to hear his lecture.

When the time came for the luncheon presentation, Bob came forward and introduced Armand Spielman to the crowd. After a short
narrative, Bob extended his hand and said, "And without further ado,
let's give Mr. Spielman a welcome applause."

Amid polite clapping, a well-dressed and distinguished-looking
elderly man slowly made his way to the podium. He grasped the podium

with both hands and smiled as he scrutinized the crowd. Afterwards, he turned to Bob and said, "Not a bad reception for an 89-year-old man, eh?" Then Armand proceeded to mesmerize the audience for thirty minutes recounting sporadic adventures of federal, state, and private land acquisitions. He would have continued for another half an hour if Bob had not intervened and brought the luncheon to a timely close.

"Don't forget to buy Armand's book before you leave," reminded Bob as everyone clapped and stood to leave. I was first in line with a $20 bill in my hand. Armand graciously wrote on the inside cover, "To Michael, w/compliments. Armand Spielman."

I began to leaf through the small blue book on my way to the parking lot. By the time I got to my truck, I was hooked. I knew many of the characters mentioned and was familiar with the pipeline corridor described. Armand's writing style was detailed and factual, but I kept thinking to myself, *There is so much more to this story. People need to know their personalities and the full background of their decisions.* I began to hatch an idea. I could collaborate with Armand to rewrite his book into a full-fledged documentary with vivid descriptions of the men involved.

But how do I broach the idea to Mr. Spielman, I mused as I drove back to work. I decided to call him. A few days later, I asked Bob if he had Armand's telephone number and told him what I was planning. Bob thought it was a great idea and gave me Armand's home number.

I cold-called Armand Spielman. That was a bad idea. Mr. Spielman did not know me from Adam. He remained silent as I awkwardly tried to describe my intentions. Finally, Armand cut me short. "It's copyrighted," he said curtly and terminated our conversation.

OK, I thought as I hung up the telephone. *That didn't go well.* I contemplated my problem for a few minutes before stumbling across the obvious solution that I should have pursued from the beginning. I called Bob back and asked him to intercede. He agreed and the following day I received a telephone call from Armand. He was direct and to the point, "Mr. Travis, Bob Ylvisaker explained your intentions. I would like to meet you and discuss your idea further. Say, lunch next Thursday at 11:45 at the Petroleum Club?"

I could hardly believe the turn of events. "Yes, sir! I'll be there. Thank you." After we said our goodbyes, I promptly called Bob back and thanked him profusely.

I arrived at the Petroleum Club a few minutes early for our lunch meeting. When I inquired at the front desk about my appointment with Armand, the hostess surprised me by replying, "Oh, yes. Mr. Spielman is here waiting for you. Please follow me."

She led me to a plush meeting room with a single small table elegantly set in the middle. There sat Mr. Spielman. He slowly rose and firmly shook my hand. If he remembered me from last week's book sale, he did not show it. We ordered our food and progressed through small talk until our lunch was served. Then, Armand turned to our waitress and dismissed her with a polite, "That will be all." She nodded and left the room closing the door behind her. He turned to me and said, "Now, explain to me what you want to do and why."

I took a deep breath and launched into a discussion of my past relationships with Jay, Dan, and Bob. I told him how much I would like to write their story and I could do that by expanding the work he had already done. I told him that we could coauthor the book. When I was finished, I let the cards fall as they might and let Armand decide if he wanted to collaborate.

Armand took a sip of his wine as he contemplated what I had told him. Then he smiled as he replied, "I thought the world of Jay. We were very close. And I've known Dan and Bob since they were young men. I'd like to see a book written about all of us working on the TAPS line. How do you propose to proceed?"

He's warming to the idea. "I'd first like to develop a story outline based on your book. I want to write our story starting with you joining the project. Then I want the story to unfold chronologically following the outline. I will need to interview you frequently to describe the events. I'll have to also interview Dan and Bob and search for other sources to fill in any gaps." Then I added, "Of course you will have to read each chapter and approve it. I'll incorporate your comments and you'll see how the story develops."

Armand nodded and replied, "That sounds reasonable. How long do you think this will take?"

I sighed as I answered, "Probably a little more than a year. The story will cover your life from 1969 to 1975–the year you left Alyeska. A lot happened in that span. If I have to dive into the library archives, it may take even longer. I want to do this right."

I think Armand wanted to hear my last comment. He stuck out his hand and said, "So, let's do it! Deal?"

"Deal," I replied as I shook his hand. We immediately went to work on the project. Armand called me frequently to bounce ideas around. Once we hammered out the story outline, we assigned tasks to ferret out information and flung ourselves into the project. Writing the story seemed to energize Armand. When we met, his infectious laughter and fascinating stories about TAPS kept me mesmerized, and most importantly, our friendship flourished.

In 2014, Dan, Bob, and another past associate, Warren Krotke, and I celebrated Armand's 90th birthday with him. We met for lunch in a back room of the Cattle Company. I felt like I had been included in some sort of private club. I could tell these men truly loved each other. They had developed a bond forged by working side by side through uncertain times. I soaked in their stories of adventure, hardship, and comedy.

All these men contributed to the story. The result was a rare peek into the inner workings of land acquisitions for a mega-project. Sometimes the tasks they faced seemed daunting, if not impossible, sometimes chaotic. They tried to bring some sense of order to their process, but flamboyant personalities, backroom politics, special-interest groups, strong landowner sentiments, and outright greed destroyed any resemblance of structure.

While Armand and I kept the story as factual as possible, we had to extrapolate probable conversations that occurred between characters. Many of the exchanges were actual quotes from newspaper articles, books, the National Archives and Records, the Loussac Library archives, and interviews. We included a bibliography at the end of the book.

Thanks to these men who were willing to share their stories and the sources mentioned, we believe we captured an interesting piece of history. We hope you enjoy the story.

Sincerely,
Armand C. Spielman and Michael D. Travis

Contents

Chapter 1

The Call

Armand Spielman received the feared telephone call towards the end of the business day–the hour when most dismissals occurred. He stoically told his supervisor, Gordon Davis, that he would report to his office within a few minutes. As he put down the receiver, Armand slowly massaged his handlebar mustache as he looked around his office. The walls were adorned with memorabilia of developing the Swanson River and Soldotna Creek Double Oilfields. Now things were going to change–forever.

Ever since his beloved Richfield Oil Company had completed merging with Atlantic Refining in 1968, his colleagues had been swatted down like flies–victims of streamlining and other management maneuverings. Armand knew this day would come, but it still startled him and stirred some anger in his soul. After all, he had started at an entry-level position in their Los Angeles office in 1955 and worked his way to full-fledged landman. His struggle had required hard work including attending night school to earn his college degree. If it hadn't been for his lovely wife Jacque's raising their three children, Armand was sure he would never have attained his position.

Then the company had needed his skills in Alaska. So in October 1960, Armand and Jacque rented their home, packed up the kids, and flew to Anchorage. The work was good and challenging–acquiring lands to drill and produce oil and gas in remote areas of the Kenai Peninsula, and Armand loved it. Now, nine years later, Armand could see his career crumbling before him. He felt betrayed.

Armand pushed away from his desk, stood up, and glanced out the window. The March 1969 afternoon sun still streamed into his office, proving that the days were quickly lengthening and spring was near. *The kids are probably home from school,* he thought as he strode out the door and headed to the stairwell. *The dinner conversation tonight will be interesting.*

He scarcely noticed the fresh paint smells wafting through the stairwell as he climbed the two floors to the managers' level. The 11-story building on 8th Avenue and G Street was newly constructed and named the ARCO Tower to commemorate the merger. Armand opened the hallway door, squared his shoulders, stuck out his chest, and marched to Gordon's office. He was determined to receive his firing with dignity and grace.

He stopped in the doorway and waited for Gordon to look up from his reading. Sure enough, there was Armand's open personnel file on his supervisor's desk. That clinched it. He needed no more confirmation of what would happen next. It was only a matter of time.

Armand did not know Gordon Davis very well. Gordon came from the Atlantic Refinery side of the merger and managed the ARCO Alaska lands office, which consisted of Armand and three others. Gordon was wearing his reading glasses as his finger traced some important information in Armand's file. A few minutes passed before he was aware of Armand's presence.

Gordon smiled as he took off his glasses and motioned for Armand to come inside. "I'm sorry, Armand. I didn't see you standing there. Please come in and close door behind you." *Textbook firing,* thought Armand as he stiffly complied. Gordon continued, "Please sit down. I need to talk with you for a few minutes. I want to confirm a few points in your personnel file."

"All right," replied Armand as he took a seat, "what points need clarification?"

"Well, it says here that you worked as a land title analyst within the Richfield Los Angeles Pipeline Department. Is that correct?"

Armand nodded as he answered, "That's right, but that was eight years ago." This line of questioning surprised him.

"Um . . ." mused Gordon as he studied Armand. Armand felt uncomfortable under his stare. "Please tell me some of your duties as you remember them."

Armand suddenly realized that he wasn't going to be fired, but he could not fathom Gordon's intentions. Somewhat relieved, but still uncomfortable, Armand began to recite his various responsibilities. "Well, I worked with several land title companies to document ownership of potential right-of-way acquisitions. Then I learned to perform my own research at county recorder offices. But my job also included working with the pipeline engineers to determine their right-of-way requirements. The land requirements not only included operational needs, but temporary grants to stage construction equipment and pipe. If they needed special materials to bed the pipe, I also acquired land for gravel and sand. Then I went to work acquiring the pipeline corridor right-of-way and access permission." The whole time Armand elaborated on his work experience, Gordon rubbed his chin and looked at him as if he had to make a hard decision.

Finally, Gordon terminated the interview. He rose, shook Armand's hand and said, "Armand, I need to discuss your qualifications with the Land Department Vice President, William Albright in Dallas, before we go much further. I would appreciate it if you kept this conversation between us, OK?"

Puzzled, Armand replied, "All right. Maybe someday you will tell me what this is all about?" Gordon nodded, but remained silent. Armand left Gordon's office with his head swirling with questions and hoping he would soon have answers.

"Oh, I don't know, darling," replied Jacque as she placed the dinner dishes into the sink. "Perhaps you are making much out of little." Her

French accent gave her voice a pleasant feminine quality that Armand always enjoyed. He had met and fallen hopelessly in love with her in France during World War II. They married in Manhattan, New York, and Armand brought her to Saint Louis to live with his mother until his commitment to the army was over. He still marveled at his good fortune to marry such a remarkable woman.

"Perhaps," answered Armand as he leaned against the kitchen counter and watched her fill the sink. "I just can't shake the feeling that Gordon has something up his sleeve. In fact, the whole company lately acts like they are hiding some monumental secret."

Jacque appeared to contemplate her husband's observation as she began to wash the dishes. Finally she spoke without looking up, "Could it have anything to do with ARCO last month announcing a new pipeline from Prudhoe Bay to Valdez?"

Her comment piqued his interest. He grabbed a towel and began to dry the dishes as she cleaned them. "You know," replied Armand as he put a dish in the cupboard, "I think you might be right. ARCO will need to move the oil to a port. Only a pipeline can do it efficiently and a pipeline of that length will need lots of right-of-way."

Jacque looked up to Armand with a satisfied smile and then asked, "Why is Gordon so secretive with his own people?"

Armand had to consider his answer before replying. "Well, for one, it's probably not totally his decision. ARCO is sharing the costs with British Petroleum and Humble. They probably want to hold their cards close to their chest until they decide what they need."

"Well, maybe they will realize that they need you, dear."

Armand put down his towel, slid his arm around her waist, and kissed her cheek. "Maybe," he repeated. "We'll just have to wait and see."

The second call from Gordon Davis came on a Friday, two days after the first one. He requested Armand's presence in his office. This time Armand's curiosity quickened his step and Gordon was waiting for him.

"Please sit down," Gordon said as he motioned for Armand to take a chair. "I have an offer for you."

Oh, no! He's going to transfer me, thought Armand. *If they ship me to Saudi Arabia, Jacque will leave me and take the kids to France for sure*. He slumped down in his seat and waited for the axe to fall.

Gordon seemed oblivious to Armand's distraught face and launched into his speech. "Armand, I'm sure you are aware that our Prudhoe Bay State #1 well struck oil last year. It turns out it struck a lot of oil. Last June, the Sag River #1 well confirmed that the reservoir was enormous. The day after the strike, our CEO, Robert Anderson, and a few others from Humble Oil and British Petroleum formed a new organization called the Trans Alaska Pipeline System or TAPS for short. Mr. Anderson announced last month that TAPS will design and construct a pipeline from Prudhoe Bay to Valdez. The headquarters is in Houston, Texas."

"So you are transferring me to Houston," moaned Armand.

"What?" responded Gordon with surprise, "No! Is this why you look like you've been gut-shot? Listen, the companies are cost-sharing a new Anchorage office and we want to staff it internally. Of our four landmen, you're the only one with pipeline experience. So, I'm offering you the assignment. You will be on loan to TAPS until the pipeline is constructed and then you would come back to us. So, what do you think?"

Armand's mind was reeling at the implications. Here was his chance to start on the ground floor of a cutting-edge project. If successful, it would be the crowning pinnacle of his career. He calmed himself before he replied, "Where is the new office and when do they want me?"

"The new office is being set up in the Kaloa Building on C Street here in Anchorage. And they really want you to report tomorrow."

"Tomorrow's Saturday."

Gordon gave Armand a knowing smile and said, "Monday is fine, I'm sure. Will you take it?"

Armand took a deep breath, stuck out his hand, and gave Gordon a solid handshake. "Yeah, I'll take it." A month later, Armand would realize why Gordon was smiling.

Chapter 2

Valdez

The following Monday morning, a neatly dressed Armand entered the TAPS office on 1689 C Street at eight o'clock sharp, carrying only his satchel. The whole office was awash in turmoil. Fifteen men were squashed into office space suitable for eight. Men with loosened neck ties and rolled-up dress shirts carried furniture into tiny rooms and tacked corridor maps to the walls. Others dragged files across the floor, some in cardboard boxes and others in cabinets. A sense of urgency permeated the air.

Armand dodged several charging men and weaved his way into the main room. There he saw a man who obviously was the center of the firestorm holding a telephone to his ear while directing the men where to put the furniture. Armand knew he was in charge by the way the men jumped at his commands. So, Armand approached him cautiously.

"Yeah, yeah, I know, John. You need the survey data as soon as possible. Wait, hold on for a sec," the man ripped the phone from his ear and pointed to two men carrying a desk. "Hey! I told you guys to put that desk in the far room. Got it?" Then he turned his attention to the caller on the line, "Sorry about that. I'll call you when I hear from

Anderson today. Got ya. Bye." He slammed the phone down on the receiver, blindly turned, and almost crashed into Armand.

The man pressed his lips together as he looked Armand up and down. Then he bellowed, "OK, who the hell are you?"

Armand stood straight and stuck his hand out as he replied, "The name's Spielman. Armand Spielman. ARCO assigned me to be your landman."

The man looked lost for a moment before his eyes flickered as he recalled a previous notification. He nodded, accepted Armand's hand, and shook it hard once before releasing it. "Right. Been looking for ya. My name is David Henderson. You can toss your satchel in the last room down the hall. We're short on space right now. You'll have to share it with two other men. We'll have a staff meeting in 30 minutes to introduce you and get you up to speed. Welcome aboard."

"Thank you, Dave," replied Armand, "I'll be ready to go in a few minutes."

Armand's new boss looked sternly at him and said, "The name's David." Before Armand could respond, David spun around and charged off to solve a myriad of other issues.

OK. Armand took a deep breath before making his way down the bustling hall to his new office. The office was scarcely larger than a broom closet. The lone desk filled half of it and three chairs crammed the other half. A black rotary phone rested on the desk. Armand looked at the threadbare room and muttered to himself, "What have I gotten myself into?"

At that precise moment, a hand slapped his back and he heard a voice with a thick British accent say, "Don't look so down in the mouth, chap! Things will only get worse." Armand looked to his left and saw a smiling middle-aged man in a wool tweed blazer. He winked and said, "The name's Goulston. Gordon Goulston. Looks like we are going to be bunk mates, say what?"

Armand had to laugh. "You're right. We would fit better if they installed bunk beds instead of chairs. I'm Armand Spielman, landman."

Gordon shook Armand's hand. "I'm a pipeline engineer from BP, England side. I hate to tell you this chap, but I understand a few more blokes are supposed to show their smiling faces here soon. We'll be like sardines in a can."

Armand and Gordon got acquainted for a few minutes until David's bellowing voice announced the start of the staff meeting. Men carried chairs to the front room and soon a level of semi-order prevailed. David stood in front and addressed the men. "Gentlemen, we'll try to have a staff meeting every Monday morning. Things are happening fast. So these meetings are mandatory. Got it?" Everyone nodded so David continued, "First I want to introduce Armand Spielman from ARCO. He'll be our landman, you know, procuring right-of-way and leases. Helping us get gravel and so forth." Armand nodded to everyone.

"Sorry, gentlemen, for the cramped space. We are working on getting better accommodations, but this will have to do in the meantime and the rumors are true. More people are coming from around the globe." The men emitted a low groan.

David smiled before continuing, "Think we got it bad? TAPS just opened an office in the Polaris Building, an old hotel in Fairbanks. Ben Anderson from Humble Oil is the office manager and they are stuffing it with engineers from Michael Baker Company. The way Ben tells it, there are so many people smashed inside that a man could faint and he would never hit the floor." This comment generated a few chuckles.

"Fairbanks's first priority is to survey and design a haul road off the Elliott Highway north of Livengood to the Yukon River. We will use the haul road to build a bridge across the Yukon and then push the road to Prudhoe Bay. The road access will allow us to build the pipeline.

"TAPS has contracted four companies in Japan to manufacture the 48-inch steel pipe. It should be arriving in Valdez in a few months."

All this news caused Armand's mind to swim. He lifted his hand to speak. David was not accustomed to interruptions and reluctantly acknowledged him. "Yeah, what's on your mind, Armand?"

Armand stood and asked, "I was just wondering. How are we going to move the pipe from the freighters docking in Valdez to the storage area, and where is the storage area? I bet it has to be enormous to store that much pipe." The room went silent. Everyone, including David, seemed to avoid Armand's gaze.

David cleared his throat and answered, "Well, um, I guess we hadn't thought of that."

Armand smiled and said, "Then I know what my first assignment is, don't I?"

During the first week of May 1969, Armand drove to Valdez to secure a pipe storage yard. Winter had not yet released its grip on Thompson Pass. Armand marveled at the 20-foot-high walls of snow that the Highway Department had thrown up along the sides of the Richardson Highway. Only the roof of the two-story maintenance building was visible at the apex of the pass. As Armand dropped down into the Keystone Canyon, the snow gradually dissipated.

Armand had not visited Valdez since the 1964 Good Friday earthquake. Although he had heard that the entire town had relocated about four miles west on the north shore of the Valdez Arm, he was still shocked at the transformation. The original town site consisted of a few abandoned buildings and scattered broken trees and debris. The tsunami had obliterated the once massive docks—only snapped pilings remained.

Armand continued driving the Richardson to the relocated Valdez. In contrast to the old site, the new town was well organized and spacious. Armand could tell that some homes had been relocated, but he also spotted many newly constructed houses scattered throughout the neighborhoods. The new Valdez was a testimony to the resilience and optimism of the Alaskan spirit.

Armand checked his watch and saw it was only four o'clock. He still had time to meet with the Valdez city manager. Tired as he was, Armand drove straight to the Valdez City Hall. Much to his surprise, the manager was waiting for him.

"Small town," the manager said as he shook Armand's hand warmly. "The calls started coming in about someone in a sports coat checking out the old town site. I figured it was you." He steered Armand to a conference table with several large sheets of paper spread over the top. Armand quickly recognized that the papers were surveyed plats of old

Valdez. "After you called me yesterday, I took the liberty of pulling the plats of the old town site. I think it would be perfect for storing pipe. The ground is an old glacier moraine, so it's rock solid. How much do you need?"

Armand had prepared himself by asking the same question of Gordon Goulston. Gordon's eyes sparkled when he replied, "By Jove, I was just contemplating the problem. Do you know what limits the stack height of pipe? It's the bloody hoop stress. Small diameter pipe is strong and you can stack it to the heavens, but our lovely 48-inch pipe can dimple if stacked too high. I calculated the bottom pipe can handle a stack of four high—no more. TAPS is thinking we'll have to store about three hundred and fifteen miles of pipe in Valdez. If one considers stacking the pipes four high, we will need about fifty acres. So double it to account for movement and support facilities. If you can get more, all the better."

Armand looked at the manager and confidently said, "I need to lease a hundred acres with an option to lease a hundred more."

The man blinked before replying, "OK. We can do this." His finger traced several lots on the plats as he continued, "We can replat these parcels into Tracts A and B. Then lease them to you to get your first hundred acres. Then we can lease Tract C to you, too, if you need it. Will this work for you?"

Armand was stunned at the ease of the transaction for such large tracts of land. He shook the manager's hand to cinch the deal. "Yes," he replied, "it will work well. Can you plot the tracts by tomorrow morning? I'll take them back to Anchorage and you mail me the lease agreements when you finish the replat."

"Sure. It won't take me long at all. Stop back by ten o'clock and I'll have them ready."

Armand said goodbye and drove to the brand-new Valdez Motel to get a much-needed rest. Later that night as Armand closed his eyes to sleep, he couldn't help but wonder if the rest of the right-of-way would be as easy to obtain.

Chapter 3

Washington

With the pipe storage yard secured, Armand knew it was time to focus on the project's larger needs–the pipeline right-of-way. The task seemed daunting to Armand and he floundered for two days as he tried to grasp the complexities of the entire system. He interviewed many engineers and discovered they needed two project corridors–one for the pipeline and the other for a haul road. Armand struggled with deciding the best approach to acquire the right-of-way.

David provided the answer. "Armand," he said in his normal brusque manner, "our Washington DC team will be arriving tomorrow. TAPS hired them to help us secure our right-of-way permit from the U. S. Department of the Interior. For the next five days, they will be your only priority. Understand?"

Armand was relieved. This was the support he needed. "You can count on it, Dave, uh, David," he replied. David nodded before plowing through the crowded office to solve another crisis. Armand watched him go and wondered about the type of men on the D.C. team. *Were they really landmen?*

The next day, David introduced three DC men to Armand. Armand's suspicions were right. They were all attorneys. Their leader was a tall, soft-spoken Humble Oil attorney named John Knodell. After spending several hours with John, Armand determined that he was professional and experienced with the inner workings of Washington. John seemed to have a grasp of the enormous task of securing the federal right-of-way.

At the end of their visit, John pulled Armand aside and asked him, "I need you to travel back to Washington with us and help us write a comprehensive pipeline application letter to the Bureau of Land Management. You should plan for a two-week visit. I know this is short notice. Can you do it?"

Armand quickly assessed his family's situation. *The kids will start summer vacation soon. Jacque can manage while I'm gone. Nothing is currently pressing.* "Yes. I can be ready to leave tomorrow, but I'm a little confused. I'm preparing the same letter for the BLM in Anchorage."

John smiled and said, "The right-of-way decision will not be made here in Alaska. It will be made in Washington and with a great deal of fanfare, I might add. We'll show you the ropes when you arrive." Armand suddenly felt like a little fish in a very big pond.

Two major problems were about to profoundly influence Armand— unselected Alaska lands and unclaimed Alaska Native lands. Both were related through the 1959 Alaska Statehood Act. When Congress approved statehood, the Statehood Act authorized Alaska to select 103.5 million acres—more than a quarter of the entire state. By 1969, Alaska had barely started the selection process. This same Act also barred the State from selecting any land historically claimed by Alaska's Eskimos, Athabascans, and Aleuts. Again, Alaska had only poked at the problem till now.

The oil companies brought these problems to a head by requesting more drilling leases from the State. As Alaska offered more lease-bidding opportunities, the Alaska Natives began to voice their displeasure to the federal government that some of these leases were on their historically used lands. U.S. Interior Secretary Stewart Udall responded by freezing all transfers of federal lands to Alaska and putting a hold on potential drilling leases on federal property until the Native land issues were addressed.

The Nixon administration entered the Oval Office in January 1969. As Secretary Udall left his post, he fired one last salvo by extending the land freeze until December 31, 1970. Then, with a twist of irony, President Nixon appointed Alaska's governor Walter Hickel as the new Secretary of the Interior.

Critics stated that Hickel had a history of development at the expense of the environment. They pointed to his 1968 construction of the infamous "Hickel Highway" shortly after he became governor as proof of his recklessness. The Hickel Highway bulldozed a 400-mile winter road from Livengood to Prudhoe Bay. It crossed the frozen Yukon River and punched its way to Bettles, where it followed the John River to the village of Anaktuvuk Pass. There it threaded its way down the north side of the Brooks Range and across the frozen plain to Prudhoe Bay. Eighteen-wheelers drove supplies to support the oil industry. While some lauded the boldness of the project, others were aghast at the lack of environmental oversight. All agreed that the highway gave Walter Hickel an unusually high level of controversy that was uncommon for a US secretary appointment. In response, the US Senate lambasted him during his confirmation hearings. During the confrontations, Hickel assured the Senate that he would not remove Udall's land freeze without consulting Congress first—even though the freeze represented a huge obstacle to TAPS. Hickel emerged unscathed and confirmed.

To the surprise of all, Hickel kept his word. He quickly set up the North Slope Task Force and then renamed it the Task Force on the Environmental Protection of Arctic Alaska to study the effects of oil development. Hickel appointed his undersecretary, Russell Train, as the chairman. In response, the US Senate Interior and Insular Affairs Committee, chaired by Henry "Scoop" Jackson, appointed a competing conservation committee.

The stage was set to receive Armand's right-of-way application. However, Armand could not have anticipated the chain of events it triggered.

Armand arrived at Washington National Airport late in the evening during the last week in May. Bedraggled and jet-lagged from his cross-country odyssey and the five-hour time difference from Alaska, he could barely stand on his feet. With his left arm cradling his briefcase and raincoat, John Knodell put his free hand on Armand's shoulder and steered him towards the baggage claim. Armand numbly complied. "You'll get used to the trip, Armand," John said gently as they walked down the marble hall. "I'm afraid you will have to make several of these trips before we are done."

After grabbing their bags, John whisked them outside and into a cab. Armand was so tired that he scarcely noticed as they drove by the famous Washington landmarks. Finally, they stopped at a hotel. John nodded and said, "Here's home for a while, Armand. Your room is paid. Charge what you need to it. I'll send someone over to pick you up around ten. Get some rest and we'll show you the ropes tomorrow." John stuck out his hand and Armand gingerly shook it. "Good to have you here, Armand. Good night."

At ten o'clock sharp the next morning, the front desk rang and told Armand that a gentleman was waiting for him in the lobby. Armand felt much better although his biological clock told him the time was very early. He walked into the lobby and found a young man in his early twenties dressed in a stylish blazer with tailored slacks and shirt, an impeccable silk tie, and expensive, trendy shoes. Although Armand was neatly dressed in a short-sleeved shirt and sensible tie, he felt a bit outclassed. The young man's enthusiasm melted Armand's misgivings.

"Mr. Spielman?" asked the young man as he shot out his hand and gave Armand a hearty handshake. "My name is Don Parker with Connole and O'Connell. Very pleased to meet you! I've never met an Alaskan before. How do you like DC?"

Armand could not help but laugh and replied, "I have lived in Alaska for only eight years. People there call me a cheechako. I need a few more years to reach the ranks of a sourdough."

Don wasted no time by gesturing to the door and said, "I have no idea what you just said, but I can't wait to discuss it fully. I've got a cab waiting outside. Shall we go?" Armand gestured to Don to lead the way and followed him out to the taxi.

Armand gazed upon the bustling city as the cab negotiated the crowded and curving streets. He saw people briskly walking to important appointments with hands clutching briefcases. Everyone seemed oblivious to the marvelous monuments around them. Even Don seemed unmoved as he talked unceasingly.

"What do you think about this pipeline business? Eight hundred miles from the frozen north to an ice-free port in southern Alaska! I didn't know Alaska even had an ice-free port. An ARCO engineer told me the North Slope is nothing but miles of toondra. What's toondra?"

Armand thought Don was nice, but his prattle was starting to irk him. He smiled and replied, "It's pronounced tundra—wet spongy ground over permafrost."

Don nodded vigorously, "Permafrost. I heard that term constantly during the project orientation meeting last week. What is it?"

Armand quickly realized Don was clueless about the complexities of building a pipeline in Alaska. *This guy is supposed to help me write a right-of-way request?* He unconsciously sighed and said, "It's soil with an average temperature below thirty-two degrees Fahrenheit. Often, the soil contains so much ice that it collapses when it melts."

Don gave Armand a polite nod, obviously not comprehending the explanation or its implications, and conveniently pointed out the window and said, "Oh look. We are here." The cab stopped in front of an old granite block building. Two marble columns marked the grand entrance. Don paid the cab and led Armand into the building.

The law firm of Connole & O'Connell occupied the second floor. Judging by the beautiful carpet and mahogany trim, Armand thought the company must be doing well. A young woman met him, asked to take his coat, and offered coffee—an offer he gratefully accepted. As she returned with the coffee served in a fine china cup and saucer, Don came back with John Knodell and two other men. Armand accepted the coffee with his left hand and instinctively dropped his satchel by his feet to free his right.

"Good morning, Armand," greeted John as he shook his hand. "I trust Don took good care of you. I have two other gentlemen for you to meet." John turned to the older man and said, "Armand, this Quinn O'Connell, principal attorney at Connole and O'Connell."

The corners of Quinn's eyes crinkled as he smiled and heartily greeted Armand with a thick Irish brogue, "The top of the morning to you, Mr. Spielman. I hope your wee trip to our fair city did not tarnish your agreeability with us, did it now?"

Armand liked this short stout man. He looked to be in his late fifties by his graying blond hair and fair skin. "The name is Armand," he answered as he shook his hand. "May I call you Quinn? And I'm doing fine. Thank you for asking."

Quinn almost laughed as he replied, "Armand it is and Quinn it is. I think we will get along dandy."

John was pleased with the exchange and almost forgot to introduce the young man standing next to him. "Oh, Armand, I must introduce this fine young man to you. This is Josh. Quinn assigned Josh and Don to assist you in developing the right-of-way request. They will be your constant companions while you are here."

I'd rather work with Quinn, thought Armand as he shook Josh's hand. "Pleased to meet you, Josh. Do you have any prior right-of-way experience?"

"No sir," replied Josh. "I just graduated from law school this month."

Great.

Not wasting any time, Quinn motioned for them to move into a conference room prepared for their meeting. On top of a 20-foot-long solid oak table lay piles of thick sheets of plotting paper. Each pile was at least a foot high. Armand examined the top sheet of the closest pile and discovered it was a surveyed pipeline and haul road alignment. He randomly grabbed a few other sheets and found that not only the proposed pipeline was represented, but associated facilities such as pump stations and camps were also shown.

Sensing his amazement, John explained, "Fresh from Houston and Fairbanks. These sheets represent our best guess on the pipeline and haul road route. It also displays the facilities required to operate the system. Welcome to command central, Armand. This is where we will develop our right-of-way request."

Armand immediately grasped the significance of the sheets. "So you want us to develop a request letter that references the alignment plots. We are going to need a truck to deliver it."

"Aye, right on both points, laddie," answered Quinn. "I'd pay a king's ransom to see their faces when you pull up with this load, I would."

Armand shook his head in disbelief.

Armand's patience was wearing thin. The two young gentlemen assigned to assist him were more burden than help. Don and Josh possessed no skills to read a plot nor did they intend to learn. Instead, they begged Armand to tell them stories about Alaska. Armand half-heartedly complied, but he knew his company was paying him to get the task done—not to idly pass the day spinning yarns. After five days of single-handedly plodding forward, he was about to tell his young accomplices to get lost.

"Armand," asked Don, "how did the TAPS engineers know where to build the line so quickly?"

"They don't," replied Armand without looking up from his work. "It's their best guess."

"We're filing a right-of-way request on a guess?" Josh asked incredulously.

Josh's usage of the word *we* rankled Armand. "That's right. As the engineers refine the pipeline and road alignment, I will amend the application." Both men nodded in unison as they watched Armand work. Armand felt their eyes on him for a few minutes more until he could not stand it any longer. He put down his notepad and asked, "Don. Please summon Mr. O'Connell."

Don looked puzzled and replied, "Um, sure. What's this about?"

"Just do it." Don nodded and quickly left the room. Josh squirmed uncomfortably under Armand's stare.

A few minutes later, Quinn bounded into the room with Don in close tow. "Armand, my good man, what service may I provide to you, sir." Quinn could always make Armand smile.

Armand motioned to Don and Josh and said, "Quinn. Please dismiss these gentlemen. Because of their . . . 'assistance', I am at the point that I need your review of our work—sort of a quality control." This was news to Don and Josh. They looked at each other in disbelief.

Quinn was wise enough to see through Armand's ruse and gave him a sly wink as he said, "Splendid! It tickles my heart to know these fine men have done such a fine job. Gentlemen, you are dismissed. Please report to your supervisors for reassignment. Good day." Don and Josh were speechless. They slowly turned and walked out of the room. Armand and Quinn watched them go.

"That bad?" asked Quinn.

"Another hour and I would have broken into your Scotch cabinet."

"That bad," stated Quinn. "So, where are we? Despite your accomplices, did you make much progress?"

"Actually," replied Armand, "I finished, but the two of us need to start at the beginning again and review my work to ensure that I did not miss anything. Can you help me?"

Quinn smiled broadly and said, "Absolutely, laddie, but first, let's consume a wee bit of lunch. No sense starting the task on an empty stomach, can we now?"

Quinn chose a small quiet pub that was a comfortable two-block walk from the office. John Knodell surprised Armand by joining them. Armand had a hunch this was not a chance meeting. After they ordered and drinks were brought to the table, John cut to the heart of the matter.

"Armand," John said quietly, "we need to discuss two issues."

Armand took a sip of his hard cider before replying, "All right, John. What's on your mind?"

"Well, the Houston office picked a man to be your in-house legal counsel. His name is Harry Brelsford. He'll be moving to Anchorage sometime next year. In the near future, I want you to visit the Houston office and meet him. You two will be working very closely as the project develops. OK?"

Armand nodded, "Sure. What kind of man is he?"

John smiled as he answered, "He's a bit of a Banty Rooster, but a good, smart man. He pays attention to detail. I think you guys will work things out."

Armand took a gulp of cider. *A little rooster. Great.* "I'll give it a whirl, John. What else do you want to discuss?"

This time John leaned toward Armand before speaking softly, "Armand. Don't take this wrong. Everyone in TAPS is very pleased with your work, but frankly, we think you are spread too thin. This project is about to explode with thousands of land issues that we can't wait for you to solve on your own. Management would like you to recommend a private right-of-way contractor for us to hire. Then we would like you to move into a management role and oversee their work. Harry will assist you when he shows up in Anchorage. Can you help us do this?"

Armand slowly put down his mug and smiled as he looked at John. He was actually relieved. The long hours were not only stressing him, but Jacque and the kids were starting to suffer, too. "That would be fine with me, John," he answered. "I need to pace myself or I'll burn out before the pipeline is built."

Armand continued, "As far as a right-of-way contractor goes, I do have a recommendation. It's Jay Sullivan. He owns Land Field Services. He's your man. I worked with him on the Swanson River oil fields when Jay was a landman with Chevron. He also acquired the right-of-way for the Nikiski pipeline. I understand he has an office in Fairbanks, right across the hall from ours." Armand lifted his mug for another drink.

John nodded and said, "OK. I'll check him out to make sure he's not a pushover."

Armand snorted and spit his cider back into his mug. He wiped his mouth with the back of his hand and said with a laugh, "Don't worry. That's one thing Jay has never been accused of." Years later, John would remember Armand's comment.

Chapter 4

Land Field Services

The shotgun blast ricocheted off the tops of the black spruce behind them and echoed down the Middle Fork Koyukuk River valley. As both of his surveyors hit the ground, Jay Sullivan noted that Arctic John Etalook had purposely aimed high. "Get off my land! I ain't funnin," bellowed John. He chambered another shell and fired it to make his point.

Jay responded in a soothing voice from behind a fallen tree, "Now, John, there's no need to revert to violence. We're just a survey crew. We'll take a few line shots and we'll be out of here in a jiffy. What do you say?"

"Like hell you will!" bellowed John. "You guys just keep comin. Last week some guy flew over and dropped a roll of string to mark a trail across my land. Whose idea was that?"

It was mine, thought Jay. He looked down at his terror-stricken crew and said, "Wait here. I'm going to talk to him."

His surveyor, Doc, lifted his head and whispered, "You're plumb crazy, Jay!"

"Maybe," answered Jay. "Stay put."

Jay raised his voice and stated, "John. I'm coming out. We need to talk." Hearing no response, Jay straightened his six-foot, five-inch frame and stepped out into the opening. He stretched his arms out along his sides and opened his massive hands to show John that he was not armed. At first Jay could not see John in the thick boreal forest.

He took another step forward and froze when he heard John yell, "Stop!" Jay slowly looked down and until he saw a small wizened Eskimo emerge from the brush holding an enormous shotgun. Jay was amazed that he could hold the gun so steady and true. Despite his small size, the man looked very capable.

Jay gave him a disarming smile and said, "The legendary Arctic John Etalook, I presume."

From behind his shotgun, John appraised the gigantic Irishman standing in front of him. Finally he asked, "Who are you and what do you want to talk about?"

"My name is Jay Sullivan, John. Michael Baker Company hired us to complete some survey work. We'll be off your land in less than an hour if you let us."

John kept the shotgun pointed straight at Jay. "You have no right to be here."

Jay slowly shook his head and said, "John, did you ever file your allotment with the Bureau of Indian Affairs?"

The shotgun lowered a bit before coming up again. "Don't have to," replied John, "been here since the '40s."

With compassion in his voice, Jay replied, "John, do yourself a favor. Take Esther with you and go down to the BIA and file your allotment. It beats trying to shoot every man near your property." John lowered the gun and took his finger off the trigger.

"How do you know these things?" asked John.

Jay lowered his hands to his side and said, "Because this is what I do. Now, how about letting us survey through? We'll be off your land in no time."

Jay's chartered flight in the Aurora Air Service Cessna 206 from Wiseman to Fairbanks took about an hour and a half. Jim Pippen, a trusted friend, was at the controls. Jim's wife, Shirley, was Jay's invaluable secretary. Thus, the Pippens were very important in Jay's life.

Jay always flew in the copilot seat for three reasons. His 270-pound frame necessitated that he take the right seat so Jim could balance the weight. His long legs required a seat that he could slide back. Lastly, Jay loved talking with Jim through headphones while they flew. It added to the excitement of flying in the Alaska bush.

"I'm telling ya, Jay," boomed Jim through Jay's headphone, "I've never seen such activity in these parts! You can see the swaths cut through the forests for the pipeline and road. They even punched some landing strips along the way. I've already been into a few of them."

Jay nodded and answered, "Yep. My boys and I have put in our share of those cuts. Some were hard going, too. Have those Michael Baker guys kept you busy?"

"They sure have, Jay. But I'm not complaining. I need to keep this plane flyin' to pay the bills. Speaking of that, thanks for hiring Shirley. Her salary helps keep me in business."

Jay smiled as he turned to Jim and replied, "My pleasure, Jim. If we help each other out, I think we'll come through this pipeline project just fine."

Jim returned the smile as he checked his instruments and said, "You can count on us."

As Jim descended over Fairbanks to land at the East Ramp of the Fairbanks International Airport, Jay scanned the city. He was always amazed at the resiliency of the residents. Fairbanks had suffered a catastrophic flood in August 1967, less than two years before. Now, Jay was hard pressed to see any lingering effects of it. People had rebuilt and removed the debris. The Chena River looked harmless as it flowed idyllically through the city within its banks.

Jay had benefited from the flood. When the water receded, Alaska Title and Guarantee (AT&G) hired Land Field Services to rehabilitate their plats and records. The project was big enough for Jay to justify opening a Fairbanks office. He had chosen his office location with care. TAPS had leased most of the second floor of the Polaris Building–the eleven-story high-rise that was the tallest building in Fairbanks. It was located on First Avenue in the heart of downtown. Jay grabbed one of the remaining rooms believing his survey business would benefit. He rented Suite 209.

To lower lodging costs when Jay traveled from Anchorage, he also rented a house at 319 Fifth Avenue, which was only five blocks from the office. Jay and his employee and longtime friend, John Pate, used the backyard clothesline to hang and dry the AT&G plats. The house was sandwiched between the Laborers Union Hall and a log cabin. It looked small from the street, but had a large apartment downstairs and three bedrooms on the ground floor. In a pinch, Jay could quickly house a crew.

As Jay completed the AT&G work, Michael Baker hired his company to help them survey a pipeline route. The project couldn't have come at a better time. Instead of laying John off, Jay hired two more employees plus a secretary. The Fairbanks office was beginning to bear fruit.

After an uneventful landing, Jay drove to his office with a fresh set of survey notes. His team would organize the notes and then hand them to Ben Anderson across the hall for processing. As Jay entered his office, his secretary, Shirley, greeted him. "Welcome back, boss. Did the miners give you any problems?"

"Naw," replied Jay as he grabbed a handful of mail from his in-box and skimmed the addresses. "Delightful folk. Talk your ear off if you let'em."

"Yeah, right," Shirley replied dubiously as she shook her blonde curls. "I bet."

"Any calls?" asked Jay, not looking up from the mail.

"Just one," replied Shirley with excitement. "It's from a man named John Knodell. He called from Washington DC! He said Armand Spielman recommended he call you. Mr. Knodell reminded me that they're five hours ahead of us. He would like you to call him as early as possible tomorrow."

Jay took the message and hesitated for a moment as he thought out loud, "Armand Spielman. That's a name I haven't heard since the Swanson River days." His mind started spinning about the implications of a man calling from Washington DC.

Curiosity tore at Jay's sleep. He tossed and turned and finally threw off his blanket and yelled out, "To hell with it!" Although his alarm clock showed 3:30 a.m., Jay knew he was awake for good. He got up, showered, downed a cup of warmed-over coffee, and walked outside into the bright sunshine of the sub-arctic summer morning. Neither the singing birds nor the mild temperature betrayed the early hour. Jay walked the five lonely blocks to his office.

After organizing his desk, Jay assumed his relaxed and focused position. He leaned back in his swivel chair, stretched out his legs, and put his massive boots on the table. Then he pulled the rotary telephone next to him and carefully dialed the number Shirley had written down.

The telephone service in Fairbanks had come a long ways since the '67 flood, but it was still inferior by Lower 48 standards. Jay was not certain, but he suspected his office was on a party line that was shared by at least two others. Thus, he told his people to be careful what they said because you never knew who was listening.

Jay waited as Alascom slowly channeled his call through a satellite system to link with the continental United States land-based network. Seasoned Alaskans learned to compensate for the conversational delays generated by the system. The first-timer always spoke over the other party because they interpreted the silence on the other end as an invitation to talk. After a little practice, one could carry on a halting conversation, but the service was expensive. So, idle talk was kept to an absolute minimum.

Jay heard the familiar hissing sound like water running through a tube as the switch gear processed the connection. Then a recorded voice stated, "Thank you for using Alascom." Jay knew this was the final stage of the process and prepared to talk. He heard a distant phone ring twice before a young woman answered, "Thank you for calling the law offices of Connole and O'Connell. How may I help you?"

Jay replied, "My name is Jay Sullivan. I am returning Mr. John Knodell's telephone call. He called me yesterday."

"Yes, Mr. Sullivan. Mr. Knodell informed me that you would be calling and instructed me to interrupt his activities and patch you through immediately. One moment, please."

Really? A bigwig DC lawyer waiting for little old me. I wonder why? He must want something. Within seconds, John Knodell came on line.

"Mr. Sullivan?" greeted John. "It must be four-thirty at your office! When I said early, I didn't mean before dawn."

Jay had to smile before responding, "Mr. Knodell, there is no dawn in June in Fairbanks. How may I help you?"

John caught the subtle jibe. "Yes, of course, land of the midnight sun and all. I forgot. Please allow me to get to the point. I am the lead consul for the Trans Alaska Pipeline System consortium. TAPS for short. We need a contractor to assist us in acquiring the necessary right-of-way. Armand Spielman recommended your firm. Are you willing and able to help us?"

Hello! Lady luck shines again. Jay waited several seconds to ensure the line was clear before answering. The delay also allowed him to calm his voice. "Um. . . yes. I believe we have the capacity to help you. What did you have in mind?"

"Excellent!" responded John. "You will initially report to Armand. You can send your invoices to me. Eventually, a Mr. Harry Brelsford will relocate to Anchorage. He will be the Alaska lead counsel and the ultimate authority and approval of your services. I would like to send you a contract spelling out your responsibilities and compensation. Would you, by chance, have a telecopier? I can send it for your review."

Jay hated new-fangled electronic equipment. He replied, "No, I don't."

Jay detected a whiff of annoyance as John responded, "OK. I can have a courier bring the papers to you within two days. In the meantime, I suggest you procure one." Jay remained silent.

After a few seconds, John continued, "Before we conclude, I must ask you a few questions. Not personally knowing you, I must confirm your credentials before we entrust you with such an important responsibility. I'm sure you understand."

Should be interesting. "OK. Shoot."

Jay heard the rustling of paper before John began, "I see people address you as Jay, but your first name is actually Paxton, correct?"

"Correct. I prefer P.J. or Jay."

John continued, "Served in Korea. Severely wounded. Decorated for valor. Worked in the Swanson River oil and gas fields as a landman for

Chevron. Married. Thirty-six years old. Wife is Nancy. Three daughters. All of this is correct?"

"Yes, it is."

"All right," mused John. "One second please." Jay could hear him shuffle some papers before continuing, "I'm afraid I need to ask you a couple of piercing questions that came up during your background check. Ready?"

No, thought Jay as he felt his ire stir. "I'm still here."

"So, how does one get kicked out of Arizona State University and lose a four-year football scholarship before his very first semester?"

The question hit Jay like a fist across his jaw. Jay sat up straight and thought, *The man did his homework*. He let a full minute pass before he answered, "A prank that backfired during summer training."

"I see," responded John. "Is that how you ended up in Korea?"

"Yes. I lost my deferment and was about to be drafted, so I joined the marines."

"Sounds like you have a flair for the dramatic, Mr. Sullivan. That could be good and bad for our project." Jay did not respond. After an uncomfortable minute, John continued, "So, tell me, was your father a vice president with Chevron when you worked at Swanson?"

John hit a raw nerve that caused Jay's anger to flare. However, Jay was astute enough to realize that John was baiting him. He took a deep breath to calm himself and replied, "That's correct. He was brought over when Standard Oil merged with Chevron. What's your point?"

John didn't hold back, "Did your father pull some strings to get you the job?" Jay almost hung up. Truth was he had been haunted by the same question the entire time he worked at Chevron. No matter how hard he worked, someone always thought he got special treatment. His father was one of the reasons he had left Chevron to start his own business. Jay felt driven to make his own mark in the world.

Again, Jay took a few seconds to settle himself before answering, "To the best of my knowledge, no. My father did not apply his influence to help me. I rose in the ranks based on my own abilities and accomplishments. I left Chevron to pursue other opportunities."

John sounded mollified, "All right. I had to ask. I am sorry that I made you feel uncomfortable. Welcome aboard. You will receive your contract in a couple of days."

After saying their goodbyes, Jay hung up, leaned fully back, and placed his hands behind his head and rubbed his buzz-cut hair. He needed to think. His instincts told him that he was on the cusp of something monumental. He was going to need help and probably more space. His office was really a converted hotel room—too small to accommodate more staff. The room next to him was open. He could lease it, knock out a wall, and combine the two spaces into a larger one. He thought about a hundred other details before hunger overtook him. Jay rousted himself from his reverie, walked the two blocks to the Star of the North Bakery restaurant, and ordered breakfast.

By 8 a.m., Jay was back and ready to go. He gave instructions to Shirley to find the Anchorage TAPS office number. When she returned with it, he called Armand to thank him for the opportunity. The office secretary answered and said, "I'm sorry, Mr. Sullivan, but Mr. Spielman just left to meet with the BLM."

"When will he be back?" asked Jay.

"I don't know, but he left with a pickup-load of documents."

Chapter 5

The Process Begins

U ncertainty had spurred Harry Brelsford to suddenly visit Anchorage in June 1969. He had met Armand Spielman only once and could not attest to his abilities and character. TAPS was about to submit their right-of-way application to the BLM and he couldn't allow such an important task to be trusted to an untested man. Harry was also ignorant about how one actually submitted the application. So, out of necessity, Harry called Armand and told him to hold the submittal until he arrived.

Armand was finalizing the right-of-way application when Harry called. A little miffed at Harry's lack of confidence, Armand delayed presenting the application to the BLM and picked Harry up at the Anchorage International Airport two days later. When Harry, a short man, stepped off the airplane impeccably dressed in a wool blazer, tailored shirt, tie, slacks, and wing-tipped shoes, Armand immediately understood John's comment about him being a banty rooster. However, the two quickly realized they had like minds when it came to acquiring pipeline right-of-way and became fast friends. Armand introduced Harry to David Henderson when they arrived at the office.

"Pleased to meet you, Dave," said Harry as he shook his hand.

"The name's David," replied Henderson as he looked down upon Harry. Then he spun away and strode into a crammed meeting room.

"OK," said Harry as he watched him go.

Armand laughed and smacked Harry across the back. "I did the same thing. Welcome to Anchorage. Come on. I'll show you the BLM application." Armand steered Harry through the crowded hallway to the backroom where Armand shared an office.

Harry looked at the desks sandwiched together and the rolls of survey plots carefully stacked against the wall and exclaimed, "How do you get any work done in here?"

"It's tough," replied Armand as he handed Harry a seven-page letter. "Here's our right-of-way request. I can walk you through it."

Harry took off his jacket and draped it over the back of a chair before sitting down and concentrating on the letter. "Please give me a few minutes, Armand. I need to read it first." Armand nodded and left him alone for a while before returning with two cups of coffee. As he was handing a cup to Harry, Armand noticed Harry's finger stopping at the end of the letter. "Where are these?" asked Harry.

"You mean the attached survey plats? Right here," replied Armand as he pointed to the stack of rolls along the whole length of the back wall.

"Oh my," muttered Harry under his breath. "Why so many?"

Armand smiled and answered, "Because the BLM requires plats scaled to one-inch-equals-a-hundred-feet. At that scale, eight hundred miles of right-of-way generates a lot of rolls."

Harry nodded and asked, "How were you going to get them to the BLM?"

"Rent a truck," replied Armand. "We don't have a company pickup and these rolls certainly won't fit in a car."

Harry sucked in his breath and said, "OK. I'll rent it. Let's plan on delivering the package first thing tomorrow morning." Harry went silent for a moment as he contemplated the enormity of the package and then continued, "You know, Armand, I've never been involved in something so big."

Armand nodded as he too looked upon the plats and replied, "Nobody has, Harry."

Early the next morning, Harry drove the rented pickup to the BLM office at 555 Cordova Street. Armand navigated and suggested a direct route down Sixth Avenue so that they could park in the loading zone directly in front of the building. The rolled survey plats filled the truck bed.

"OK, we're here," said Armand as he pulled a large manila envelope from his satchel. "Let's go in and register our application."

"What about the plats?" asked Harry.

Armand laughed as he replied, "Oh, I imagine that we'll have to carry them in when the time comes. They'll let us know."

Armand and Harry walked through the front double doors. The clerk's office was immediately to the left. Armand approached the window, which was really a half door with a small wooden counter, and caught the attention of the woman working at her desk. She took off her reading glasses and let them dangle on a beaded tether around her neck. "Yes? How may I help you?"

All business, thought Armand. He gave her his most charming smile and said, "We want to file a right-of-way request on behalf of the Trans Alaska Pipeline System."

The clerk gave Armand a frown of uncertainty as she stiffly stood and walked to the window. "May I see your application?" Armand carefully opened the envelope and handed her the letter and a fifty-dollar check. The clerk put on her reading glasses and carefully read the letter while Harry and Armand stood in front of her. After an uncomfortable five minutes, she put down the letter and scrutinized the check. "Very well," she finally said, "everything appears in order. Where are the plats referenced in the letter?"

Armand jerked his thumb to the doors and said, "Right outside. Would you like us to bring them inside?"

The clerk took off her glasses and answered, "Yes, please. You may hand them to me."

Armand turned so she couldn't see his devilish grin as he replied, "Yes, ma'am. Back in a jiffy."

Harry and Armand blocked the front doors open and began carrying the rolls, two at a time, inside and passing them to the clerk through the window. Within thirty seconds, she was overwhelmed and began stacking the rolls along the wall.

"This is highly irregular!" she gasped. "How many more rolls do you have?"

"Oh, we just started," replied Armand. "We have a whole pickup-load." The clerk immediately called upstairs for help. Two men appeared shortly and assisted Harry and Armand with unloading the truck.

When the unloading was completed, Armand calmly walked back to the clerk, who stood appalled as she looked upon her devastated office. "May I trouble you to date-stamp the front page and give me a receipt for the check?" he asked sweetly.

The clerk raked Armand's throat with a cutting glare. Then she calmed herself. "Yes, of course," she replied with a forced steadiness. "One moment, please." She found her stamp on the floor among other knocked-over items and punched the ink onto the first page. Then she fired up the thermocopier and burned Armand a copy. With the remainder of her professional resolve, she wrote out a receipt and gave it to Armand.

Armand politely bowed and said, "Thank you, ma'am. If the Land Office has any questions, please refer them to me."

"You can be sure of it," she replied curtly.

Armand motioned for Harry that they should leave. Once they were in the truck and out of earshot, they looked at each other and broke out laughing.

"I thought she was going to shoot us both!" exclaimed Harry as he wiped tears from his eyes.

"She would've if she'd had a derringer hung around her neck instead of glasses."

"So what happens next?" asked Harry as he started the truck and put it in gear.

Armand thought for a second before replying, "Burt Silcock, the BLM state director, will forward the letter to his boss, Boyd Rasmussen, in Washington DC. I imagine a formal reply will be issued by the

Secretary of Interior. The plats will stay here and will be studied by the District Land Office."

"Hm," mused Harry as he drove. "The Secretary is your old governor, is he not?"

"Yes. Walter Hickel."

"Is that good or bad?"

Armand stroked his mustache as he thought about his answer and then finally replied, "I honestly don't know, Harry."

Unbeknown to Armand and Harry as they drove laughing away from the BLM office, other forces were moving in Washington DC that would define how the proposed TAPS pipeline would be built. On the same day when they filed the right-of-way request, Interior Undersecretary Russell Train submitted a list to John Knodell of seventy-nine questions the Federal government wanted answered before they would approve the pipeline project. The questions covered engineering and environmental aspects of the project. John forwarded the list to the TAPS Houston office for review and developing a response. The list hinted at the detail that the government would eventually demand from TAPS.

Two weeks later, Walter Hickel wrote a letter to Robert Anderson, TAPS president, stating the right-of-way would be granted "as expeditiously as possible" after the government was satisfied that all legal, regulatory, and environmental requirements had been met and "the interests of the Native people have been safeguarded." TAPS would learn that the government would be extremely difficult to satisfy.

Jay entered the buzzing Anchorage TAPS office in late June. The secretary told him where he could find Armand. Stopping at the door, he grinned and greeted Armand in a booming voice, "Armand Spielman, you traded your downtown office for this? I think you took a step or two backward."

Armand and Gordon Goulston looked up from their work and gazed at the gigantic man filling the doorway. Gordon remarked, "He bloody well be your chum, Armand, because if he means to do you harm, you are on your own!"

Armand smiled, stood up, and offered his hand. "Good to see you, Jay. Have problems finding the place?"

Jay's handshake engulfed Armand's hand. "Glad to see you, too, Armand. Naw. No problem. Just followed the pipeline litter to your door. Easy."

Armand introduced Gordon to Jay. "Gordon, this is Jay Sullivan. He's the man I was telling you about who will help us acquire the right-of-way."

Gordon jumped up and shook Jay's hand. "Top of the world to you, Mr. Sullivan. I do say that I'm relieved to hear that you are on our side. I'd hate to face you in a dark alley."

Jay grinned and replied, "Sometimes I hate to meet myself in a dark alley. Pleased to meet you, Gordon. You guys are packed in here like sardines. You would think TAPS would spring for more spacious digs."

"One would think, Mr. Sullivan," answered Gordon. "They'll come around in a day or two."

"Come on, Jay," said Armand as he ushered him back into the hallway. "Let's go somewhere and get a cup of coffee so we can hear ourselves talk. We need to discuss where to prioritize our efforts." Armand led Jay back down the hall when they almost collided with David Henderson.

"Oh, David," greeted Armand, "I have someone I want you to meet. This is Jay Sullivan of Land Field Services. He will be helping us with the right-of-way."

Jay stretched out his hand and said, "Good to meet you, Dave."

David started to say, "The name's –," but one look at the big Irishman stopped him. There was something about his demeanor that suggested he called people what he wanted. "Yeah, likewise," continued David. "Sorry. Gotta go."

"Delightful individual," remarked Jay as they watched him disappear into the cubicles.

Armand patted Jay on the shoulder and said, "Let's get out of here." They drove to a coffee shop nearby where they could talk and discuss their strategy.

After they got situated, Armand put down his cup and laid out Jay's instructions. "Jay, we need you to first address the right-of-way needs of the haul road from Livengood to the Yukon River. Coordinate with Ben Anderson's group in Fairbanks for the route. And for heaven's sake, avoid the Native allotments the best you can."

Jay laughed, "Yeah, that's easier said than done. Funny how new allotments spring up along any route Ben selects, but we'll try. On a related subject, how do you want to amend the BLM application as the engineers refine the pipeline and haul road routes?"

"I've been thinking about that," answered Armand. "We should plan on meeting on a weekly basis to review the changes. Then we'll go over to the BLM Land Office and the Alaska Department of Natural Resources Land Office and modify the plats. This way the governments will always have a current set."

Jay nodded, "Good idea. I will get to see Nancy and the girls more often, too. What is your next priority down here?"

Armand took another sip of coffee as he contemplated his answer. "I've got a feeling that Valdez will be calling my name again real soon. Fluor Engineering is about to release their marine terminal design and we have no land to put it."

In late June, Robert Anderson, ARCO CEO and TAPS president, arrived in Anchorage like a whirlwind. He met with his troops and told them they were working on the greatest project ever attempted by private interests. Then he flew all possible pipeline and haul routes by helicopter to gain a personal appreciation of the land and the challenges it presented. He left undaunted, his employees motivated.

In July, Armand's prediction came true. Several large rolls of pipeline alignment maps arrived at the Anchorage TAPS office. The maps contained the latest pipeline centerline and pump station locations. It also displayed the first conceptual drawings of the Valdez marine terminal.

The proposed terminal was enormous. Fluor Engineering of Irving, California designed the facility to be located across the arm from Valdez. It consisted of support facilities, 18 storage tanks, a power plant, and two supertanker loading berths. The tanks would sit on bedrock 660 feet above sea level to protect them from future tsunamis.

The scope of the terminal amazed Armand, but the fact that Fluor proposed to site the facility on 802 acres of US Forest Service land concerned him. TAPS could not occupy the site or further the design until Armand acquired the land. The next day, Armand copied the terminal boundaries, prepared a right-of-way plat and access request, and hand-delivered it to the Anchorage Forest Service office. Thinking that he might need legal support, Armand sent a copy of the application to John Knodell in Washington DC.

Armand's instincts proved right. A few weeks after Armand applied for the Forest Service use permit, George Atkinson, president of the A&G Construction Company, leased a homestead with an option to buy it from Mrs. Oma Day. The Day homestead covered most of the level land between the Valdez Arm and the Forest Service holdings. This location was the most logical area where the oil pipeline would cross to the new marine terminal and to build the future tanker berths.

Armand thought leasing the homestead was too coincidental to have happened by chance. Obviously, someone at the Forest Service had leaked the fact that TAPS had filed a permit application for the marine terminal site. Mr. Atkinson validated Armand's suspicions when he filed a lawsuit against the Forest Service to prevent them from issuing the special use permit to TAPS.

Meanwhile, Land Field Services had their hands full at Livengood. Before TAPS, Livengood was a quiet gold-mining district located about 70 miles northwest of Fairbanks off the Elliott Highway. At Livengood, the highway bent to the west and headed to Manley Hot Springs. TAPS planned to construct the haul road at this bend to the south bank of the Yukon River, creating a four-way intersection. Since gold miners were entrepreneurs at heart, they quickly recognized a business opportunity in the making–a new high-volume highway intersection. Every time Ben Anderson's group surveyed the intersection location,

Native allotment stakes mysteriously appeared at the corners. Ben and Jay moved the location four times before finally giving up.

The Fairbanks TAPS office completed the Livengood-to-Yukon-River survey by the first of August. Jay and Armand wasted no time in submitting the right-of-way application to the BLM. Walter Hickel notified the Senate and House interior committees that his office approved the application and issued the right-of-way to TAPS. TAPS immediately hired the Burgess-Houston Construction Company to build the highway segment. Bruce Campbell was the Burgess-Houston project manager.

While the first road construction started, the Trans Alaska Pipeline System reorganized. Humble Oil kept their 25 percent stake, but ARCO and BP elected to reduce their shares from 37.5 percent to 27.5 percent apiece. Five companies then bought into the remaining 20 percent. They were Mobil (8.5%), Phillips (3.25%), Union Oil (3.25%), Amerada Hess (3%), and Home Oil Company of Canada (2%).

During the end of August, the US Interior Department released their draft technical and environmental stipulations that would eventually accompany the TAPS right-of-way permit. In September, the Interior Department held two days of hearings in Fairbanks to discuss the stipulations. Extremists from both sides attended. From the preservationists, David Brower, the leader of FOE (Friends of Earth) and previous Sierra Club president, was the most vocal. He exclaimed that the stipulations had loopholes large enough to sail a ship through them.

Pro-developers presented the other view that we had studied the problem enough and it was time to build. Alaska's freshman senator, Mike Gravel, argued that the Alaska Native standard of living would rise from the improved economy. He also voiced the Fairbanks residents' opinion that Alaskans were fully capable of protecting their environment without outsiders interfering.

On September 12, the Valdez Copper Basin News published its first newspaper edition. Valdez had been without a newspaper since the 1964 earthquake. Even though the Valdez-Copper Basin was a weekly publication, Valdez residents welcomed it with open arms. Its first front page announced that the Japanese freighter, *Alaska Maru*, was arriving on the thirteenth with the first delivery of 48-inch pipe for

TAPS. Valdez had been expecting the pipe arrival since the TAPS dunnage for stacking pipe had arrived the previous week on another ship.

Valdez residents decided the pipe arrival deserved a celebration. The second page of the newspaper displayed the following events:

- Open: All visitors register at the Centennial Building at the corner of Meals Avenue and Chenega Street.
- 9:00 a.m. till noon: *Alaska Maru* tour.
- 1:00 p.m. to 4:00 p.m.: No planned activities. Fishing boats available for charter.
- 4:00 p.m. to 6:00 p.m.: Open house at the bar of your choice. No-host cocktail hour.
- 7:00 p.m. to 10:00 p.m.: Dinner and presentation of guests at the Growden-Harrison Elementary School on Lowe Street.
- 10:00 p.m. until ?????: Dance at Growden-Harrison Elementary School.
- Noon until midnight: Continuous movies at the Eagles Hall. No host.

The longshoremen would unload the pipe from the City Dock—the same dock that the state ferry, *Tustumena*, used. With freighters arriving twice a week and each taking several days to unload, city officials quickly realized that their small dock could not accommodate both uses. They tried to schedule the arrival of the ferry on one of the few vacant days, but the *Tustumena* could not cover the vast distances from Seward, Whittier, and Cordova in time to maintain the schedule. Thus, the *Tustumena* frequently canceled its Valdez stops, which angered the residents.

On October 1, Armand was pleasantly surprised to find the US Forest Service land use permit on his desk for the Valdez marine terminal. The Forest Service had taken less than four months to process his application. Armand examined the permit and was surprised to discover that the Forest Service's Alaska Division Office had handled it. He had thought the Alaska Office would have forwarded the application to their Washington DC office. *Probably saved me a lot of time processing it locally.*

Armand sent copies of the permit to John Knodell and Harry Brelsford before pursuing the real purpose of acquiring the Forest Service use permit, requesting the State of Alaska to select this land on behalf of the TAPS from the federal government. Armand immediately drafted a letter to his friend, Joe Keenan, director of the ADNR Land Office. The letter requested the Alaska land selection officer to file a land selection application with the Secretary of the Interior for the 802-acre parcel. The letter referenced an attached copy of the Forest Service permit.

Armand envisioned the following process to acquire the marine terminal land. After receiving and studying the ADNR land selection request, a designee of the Secretary of Interior would send a letter back to the ADNR tentatively approving the land selection. The approval would hold the land for Alaska until the final transfer occurred. This process would take years before DOI issued a land patent to the State. The patent would give Alaska full rights to the land including all subsurface resources and authority to lease or sell any portion. Armand's ultimate goal was to purchase the tract from ADNR after DOI issued the patent.

A week after sending the ADNR letter, John Knodell called Armand. John had reviewed a copy of the letter and had also received a call from the Houston engineering office. The marine engineers were designing five docks to load supertankers. The bathymetry indicated the docks must extend at least 3,000 feet from the shore to provide enough depth for the tankers to maneuver. John wanted Armand to amend his letter to include all islands and rocks above mean high tide. Armand called Joe Keenan and described John's request.

"I can understand their reasoning," replied Joe. "The engineers probably want to anchor their docks to something solid. We can amend the application, Armand, but I need you to write me a letter spelling it out. Then we can send an amendment to the DOI. However, there is something else that I need to call your attention to."

"Oh, what's that?"

"The tidelands. You will need to lease the submerged lands from ADNR before building on them. I recommend TAPS lease the entire ocean frontage along your proposed marine terminal site. This way, if the design changes, you have your bases covered."

Armand scratched his head for a moment as he thought. "OK," he finally said, "I think that's good advice. I'll send you a letter shortly amending our land selection request and then I will send you a tideland lease application. Thank you, Joe, for bringing this to my attention."

"Not a problem, Armand," replied Joe. "Just doing my job."

Burgess-Houston upgraded the winter trail to the Yukon River in late October 1969, as it continued to build the haul road between Livengood and the river. TAPS then prepared to assemble their workforce to build the haul road to Prudhoe Bay. Although government opinion was still divided on the sufficiency of the right-of-way permit, Walter Hickel and Russell Train made it known that they believed enough analysis had been done to authorize the road. In response, TAPS awarded a contract to Tundra Contractors, Inc. to build an ice road across the Yukon River that could support heavy equipment. Tundra Contractors was the first Alaska Native-owned company to work on the project.

Everyone believed the entire project was only weeks away from government authorization. Armand and Jay scrambled to file an updated right-of-way application with the BLM on December 29 for the pipeline and haul road centerlines. TAPS was pulling out all the stops to hasten the project. During all the activity, nobody paid much attention to the fact that President Nixon was about to sign the National Environmental Policy Act (NEPA) into law. Within a few months, they would.

Chapter 6

Law as a Weapon

O n January 1, 1970, President Richard Nixon signed NEPA into law. NEPA was America's first all-inclusive environmental policy that affected all levels of federal government. Federal agencies invoked NEPA when they planned to designate funds or implement a major federal action or decision. Before designating the funding or decision, the act mandated the responsible federal agency to perform an environmental analysis. Depending on the significance of the action, an agency would complete one of following three documents:

1. Categorical Exclusion – This small document covered mundane and common actions such as maintenance and planning activities.
2. Environmental Assessment – Agencies performed this focused analysis on projects deemed not to have significant impacts.
3. Environmental Impact Statement (EIS) – An EIS is an intensive study performed by a multidisciplinary team. It requires rigorous public involvement and detailed recommendations with mandatory mitigation measures to offset the anticipated impacts.

NEPA also created the Council of Environmental Quality to ensure federal agencies complied with the act. The council possessed great power over every branch of government. It also submitted an annual report to the President concerning the nation's quality of the environment.

Writers of NEPA envisioned it to be a tool for the common layman to become involved in federal decisions and to have a say in federal spending and permitting. What the NEPA creators and TAPS officials never anticipated was that special-interest groups could grind the process to a halt by questioning the thoroughness of the environmental document. With no test cases, the new law was ripe for court-ordered injunctions while the legal system sorted out the congressional intent and requirements.

TAPS paid no attention to the passing of NEPA. With the ice bridge completed across the Yukon River, TAPS awarded contracts to Associated-Green, River Construction Corporation, H.C. Price, Arctic Contractors, and Burgess-Houston Construction to drag their equipment and supplies north along the Hickel Highway and other winter trails. TAPS directed the contractors to build 12 camps north of the Yukon River and stage their construction equipment in anticipation of the Department of the Interior's granting the right-of-way in the near future. Since TAPS did not have any permits to build the haul road and pipeline, the organization was taking a huge gamble. However, with the favorable messages coming out of Washington DC, TAPS had every reason to believe federal approval was imminent.

Walter Hickel determined that he could grant the pipeline and haul road right-of-way under the Minerals Leasing Act of 1920. This act allowed the Secretary of the Interior to allocate right-of-way to support the development of natural resources. However, there was one major restriction. The Act restricted the right-of-way width to 50 feet, 25 feet on each side of the centerline. Neither the pipeline nor the road could comply within these narrow confines, but that did not deter Hickel. He was confident that allowances for additional corridor widths could be made, so he announced to the nation that his department was ready to permit the entire pipeline and haul road right-of-way.

During the first week in January, Harry Brelsford called Armand and directed him to order preliminary title searches for all private lands that might be crossed by the proposed pipeline and haul road routes. "That's a lot of title research," responded Armand coyly. "Do you mind who I use?"

"No," answered Harry, "Who do you recommend?"

Armand promptly replied, "Alaska Title and Guarantee. They're big enough to handle the order."

"That's great, Armand. Please get the title searches ordered ASAP."

Armand chuckled as he answered, "Well Harry, I already did that several months ago. I met with Hal Lydell, AT&G manager, and showed him our alignment sheets. He is pulling the private parcels from the sheets and performing the preliminary title searches right now. I expect to see some of his work shortly."

Harry was impressed. He hesitated before continuing, "Ah, Armand, don't take this wrong, but how good of a land title analyst are you?"

"I can hold my own," answered Armand, "but I sure would appreciate some help and I know just the man for the job. His name is Herman Schmidt and he works for the BP land department here in Anchorage. He used to be the vice president of Title Insurance and Trust Company in Los Angeles. I always used him when I worked for Richfield Oil down there. He's a good man and knows his stuff. We probably can't get him, though. BP likes him."

During the silence that followed, Armand heard Harry scribbling on paper. Finally, Harry replied, "OK. I'll handle it. Thanks, Armand. Goodbye." Armand hung up and wondered if he had just dragged Herman into an unwanted adventure.

The following week, Armand walked into his office one morning and heard a familiar voice say, "Hello, Armand." He looked up and saw Herman Schmidt sitting in his chair drumming his fingers on his desk. "I understand you are responsible for this."

Gordon Goulston exclaimed, "I say, old chap, I didn't realize you wielded such ruthless power! Imagine, yanking a man out of his comfy office into this raging pit at the mere snap of your fingers. I truly underestimated you, Armand."

Armand was stunned that Harry had orchestrated the move so quickly. "Ah, Herman, I can explain . . . "

Herman broke out laughing and said, "Don't worry about it, Armand. BP cut me a sweet deal. I'll be working for you every other day. It'll be a good change of pace." He rose and shook Armand's hand.

Armand was relieved that Herman was being such a good sport about his part-time reassignment. "It's good to have you, Herman. And not a moment too soon, I might add. We just got the first title reports from AT&G that will require your expert review."

Herman nodded and replied, "Sounds good. I'm ready to roll. First, direct me to the coffeepot. Then I'll shovel out a spot to work in this hovel. You guys really need to expand your office space."

Armand laughed and said, "Tell me about it, Herman. Coffee is this way."

In the deep foggy recesses of Armand's mind, a phone was ringing. *Am I dreaming?* As he climbed out of the deep well of sleep, the telephone kept ringing. Jacque moaned as she turned over next to him and buried her head into her pillow. Armand blinked himself awake and groped for the phone on the nightstand. His hand found it and knocked the receiver off its cradle. It bounced on the carpeted floor. A voice trickled out of the receiver, "Hello? Hello? Armand? Is that you? Are you there?"

Armand used the sounds to find the phone, grab the cord, and dragged the receiver to his ear. "Um, hello?" he croaked, "Who is it?"

"Armand! This is David Henderson. Wake up. I've got a mission for you. Come on now. On the double!"

Armand's eyes focused on the nightstand alarm clock. It read 6:30 a.m. Since it was the first week of February, the morning was still pitch-black. *What on earth?* Armand took a deep clearing breath and answered, "Yeah, Dave, er, David. What do you need?"

David was all business as he laid out his orders. "Look Armand, Alaska Secretary of State Robert Ward, and Commissioner of the Highways Department Robert Beardsley need to review the haul road alignment sheets today. Hickel is about to issue the right-of-way permit for the road and he just asked for the State of Alaska concurrence. This is big, Armand! I need you to hand-carry the alignment sheets to them and explain the route. I've got a set of sheets and a plane ticket waiting for you at the office."

Armand felt his anger rise, "Do you realize it's Sunday?"

"Yeah and there's only one flight to Juneau today. It leaves in two hours and you better be on it!" The phone went dead.

Jacque groaned, "Who was it, honey?"

"An idiot!" growled Armand as he slammed the phone down. "I'm going to Juneau and I've got less than two hours to catch the flight." Jacque watched her husband stagger to his feet and shuffle to the bathroom. In a few minutes, Armand was washed, shaved, and dressed. He bent over his wife, kissed her goodbye, and said, "I should be back tonight. I'll call you if something comes up."

As Armand started his ice-cold car, he calculated the time it would take to pick up the alignment sheets and get to the Anchorage International Airport. *It'll be close.* He shoved his reluctant car into gear and drove down the snowy dark street. Armand negotiated the slippery streets as quickly as possible. Minutes seemed to tick by at an accelerated speed. He flew into the office parking lot and glanced at this wrist watch. *Thirty minutes before departure. I'll never make it unless . . .*

Armand turned off his car and ran for the office door. The alignment sheets and ticket were on the receptionist's desk. Armand noted their presence and ran straight for David Henderson's office. David was there. "Hand me the company car keys," demanded Armand.

"What?" replied a surprised David, "What do you need them for?"

"Do you want me to make that plane or not? Give them to me!" David blinked for a second before reaching into his desk, retrieving the keys, and placing them into Armand's outstretched hand.

Armand snatched them and pointed at David saying, "Don't ever do this to me again." Before David could respond, Armand ran down the hall, retrieved the sheets and ticket, and bolted outside. He threw the sheets into the backseat and fired up the car. Then he sped out of the parking lot to the airport.

He skidded to a stop outside the terminal in front of the Western Airlines ticket booth five minutes before his plane was to leave. *I've got no time to park!* He jumped out and grabbed the sheets. He left the car running as he sprinted into the terminal and flagged down the ticket agent. She processed his ticket and called the gate to hold the flight as Armand awkwardly ran as fast as he could cradling the alignment rolls. He did not catch his breath until the alignment sheets were safely tucked into the overhead compartment and his seat belt was fastened.

"Stupid David," muttered Armand as he put his head back and the jet fired up its engines. "At least it's not my car idling out front."

The flight to Juneau was uneventful, which was a tremendous relief to Armand. He had heard the horror stories of weather preventing the jet from landing and being stranded in Petersburg or Ketchikan. A taxi took him to the Secretary of State's office in the capitol building. Robert Ward and Robert Beardsley were waiting for him.

"Armand Spielman, I presume," Robert Ward warmly greeted him. "I hope your unexpected trip wasn't too upsetting. I'm Robert Ward and this is Robert Beardsley, the Commissioner of Highways. You can call him Bob."

Armand gave each man a weary hand shake and said, "Pleased to meet you. I didn't think I would make it and I may have lost our company car in the process."

Robert cocked his head and asked, "How so?"

"I left it idling out front of the Western Airlines ticket booth. I didn't have time to park before the plane left."

Robert looked at Bob and asked, "Can you handle this?"

Bob laughed and said, "Yeah, just a minute. I'll be right back. I'll call the airport manager and his men will take care of it."

As Bob left, Robert turned his attention to Armand and the alignment sheets. "Armand, we have a room with a conference table where we can lay out these sheets. Let's go there and you can get set up. Then you can walk us through the haul road route when Bob gets back. OK?"

"Sure, lead the way."

Robert led Armand to an opulent conference room adjoining the governor's office. A long hardwood table sat in the middle of the plush carpet and the walls were ordained with oil paintings of Alaskan landscapes. "Governor Miller uses this room for staff meetings. It'll work fine for us," said Robert as he turned on the chandelier lights. Armand unrolled the sheets and spread them in order showing the haul road from the Yukon River to Prudhoe Bay.

Bob entered the room smiling and announced, "No problem, Armand. Your car was still running when they found it. A maintenance worker drove it to the parking lot and threw the keys under the seat. You can pick it up when you return."

The news was a relief to Armand. After his anger subsided, he had fretted about the prospect of explaining to David how the company car got stolen. "Thank you, Bob. I appreciate you handling my predicament. Now, let me walk you through our proposed alignment. We'll start at the Yukon River Bridge . . ."

"Bridge?" repeated Bob. "Thank God! We heard rumors of a tunnel. We, the State, definitely want a bridge."

"Well TAPS needed to look at all options including a tunnel. The bridge won out. In fact, you'll be able to hang a second pipe on this one."

"A second pipe?" asked Robert.

"Yes," replied Armand, "a gas line."

Robert and Bob exchanged glances before Robert nodded to Armand, "Please continue."

Armand put his finger on the alignment sheet just north of the Yukon crossing and began to move it north as he spoke. "We will follow the Hickel Highway route north with a few deviations to lessen the grade. We then depart from the Hickel route at Prospect Creek and move towards the Dietrich River valley."

"Why's that?" asked Bob. "I thought the John River and Anaktuvuk Pass were the easiest way to the North Slope? No steep passes and gradual grades on both sides?"

"It is," answered Armand, "but there are two good reasons for choosing the Dietrich valley. First, following the Dietrich River up to the Chandalar Shelf and Atigun Pass is the most direct route, which means a shorter pipeline. Second, residents of Anaktuvuk Pass were not happy about us laying a pipeline and punching a road through their hunting grounds. The Pass is a choke point for caribou migration. We will miss most of the migrating caribou if we use Atigun Pass."

"But I've flown over the Shelf and Atigun Pass," replied Bob. "They were steep, sharp formations. TAPS will have their work cut out for them to blast a road and pipeline into the side of those slopes. The whole area is prone to avalanches, too. Are you sure this is the best route?"

Armand nodded and said, "No doubt this route has its challenges, but overall TAPS believes this is the best course." Robert urged Armand on with a nod. "OK. From Atigun Pass we will follow the Atigun River north to Galbraith Lake then continue north past Toolik and Slope Mountain. We eventually meet up with the Hickel Highway at Sagwon. From here, we follow the Sagavanirktok (Sag) River north to about 10 miles south of Prudhoe Bay. There we will turn northwest for 12 miles to the proposed site of Pump Station 1 next to the Putuligayuk (Put) River."

Bob asked, "Besides the Yukon, how many other major river crossings will you have?"

Armand replied, "Well, we need to cross the South Fork and Middle Fork Koyukuk Rivers south of the Brooks Range and the Atigun River as it veers east down the Atigun Canyon. Of course, we will have hundreds of smaller bridges and culverts along the way that will have to be built."

Robert and Bob peppered Armand with questions until the late afternoon. Bob looked at his watch and proclaimed, "I don't know how to tell you this, Armand, but you missed your flight back."

Armand was dismayed. He had forgotten that Juneau was one hour ahead of Anchorage. Robert laughed and said, "Don't worry. We'll take care of you in style. We greatly appreciate your time on such short notice. So, how would you like to be Governor Miller's guest tonight?"

Armand blinked and asked, "What do you mean?"

Robert started rolling up the alignment sheets and answered, "We'll put you up in the Governor's Mansion and then in the morning drive you to the airport. How's that sound?"

"That sounds great," replied Armand. Then under his breath he muttered, "Jacque will never believe this."

———————————

Robert Ward escorted Armand to the Governor's Mansion, which was only two blocks away from the capitol building. Although it was still afternoon, the sun had long ago set–a combination of Alaska winter and the steep lofty mountains surrounding Juneau. The street lights illuminated the narrow sidewalk as they walked with a light mist falling. Armand was thankful that he had left the alignment sheets with Bob. He would have had a tough time keeping them dry.

The Governor's Mansion was well lit. Even in the darkness, Armand could tell the house was immaculate. It was crisply painted white with green trim. The walkway leading to the front door was shoveled clear of snow and swept. Robert led Armand to the door and rang the doorbell. As they waited, Armand could hear laughter coming from inside.

A doorman opened the door and recognized Robert. "Mr. Ward, please come in. The Governor is entertaining a few legislators tonight."

Robert smiled and said, "Thank you, Don. The Governor is always a gracious host. Tonight, we have an honored guest who will spend the night. Allow me the honor to introduce Mr. Armand Spielman. Mr. Spielman works for the Trans Alaska Pipeline System."

Don smiled and said, "Pleased to meet you, Mr. Spielman."

"The pleasure is mine," replied Armand. "Sorry for dropping in unannounced."

Don gave Robert a knowing smile and said, "That's quite all right, Mr. Spielman. I can assure you that this happens frequently. We can easily accommodate you. This way, please." Don led them to the living room where four men with drinks in their hands were obviously enjoying each other's company. They looked up as Armand and Robert entered.

Someone yelled, "Robert, my good man! Pull up a chair and have a drink with us."

Robert grinned and said, "Can't tonight, boys. I promised the wife that I would be good and come home at a decent hour. Keith, I brought you a guest for tonight. Let me introduce Armand Spielman to you. He's from TAPS and he came here on short notice today to walk us through the proposed haul road corridor."

A tall, well-groomed man with black hair stood up and walked over to Armand. "Pleased to meet you," he said as he stuck out his hand. "I'm Keith Miller."

Armand instantly recognized him as Alaska's governor from television programs and newspaper articles. "The pleasure is mine, Governor."

"Please, Keith is fine. No need to be formal. Please sit down. We'll love to talk with you about the pipeline project. What's your poison?"

Armand replied uncertainly, "Uh . . . scotch and water?" Don nodded and disappeared.

Robert squeezed Armand's shoulder and said, "I think you're set. I'll have a driver pick you up at eight tomorrow morning. Good night."

"Thanks, Robert. I enjoyed meeting you."

Robert waved as he left. "Likewise, Armand. I'm sure our paths will cross again."

As Armand watched him go, he turned his attention back to Keith Miller. Armand knew the Alaska legislature had appointed Keith as the governor after Walter Hickel accepted the Secretary of Interior post with the Nixon administration. Armand was amazed how these men were the exact opposite of each other. Walter was older, short, and stout with graying hair. Keith was about 45 years old, tall, and trim.

"So, Armand," began Keith, "what do you think the chances are that Hickel will issue the right-of-way to build the haul road and pipeline?"

Don entered the room with a tumbler full of brown liquid and handed it to Armand. "Here you go, sir. Gentlemen, dinner will be served within the hour." He excused himself and exited the room.

Armand felt slightly embarrassed because he was not accustomed to being served drinks and having all eyes upon him. "Uh . . . I think the chances are good. However, he's got some potholes to negotiate around."

"Like what?" asked one of the men.

"Well," continued Armand, "like Alaska has not selected all lands due to them when granted statehood. Also, Alaska and the federal government have not fully granted the Natives their land rights. So, any pipeline or road right-of-way grant is open to challenges from private and Native parties."

Keith took a long sip of his drink before replying. "My Department of Natural Resources has been looking into these problems and alerted me to a possible solution."

Armand took swig of his drink and nearly gagged. It was a strong one. He exhaled and asked, "Really? What are you planning?"

Keith swirled his drink, smiled, and said, "I'd rather not elaborate at this time. I'll pull the rabbit out of the hat, so to speak, if I have to."

I can hardly wait, thought Armand as he gingerly sipped his drink.

Dinner was enjoyable and filling. The men carried their dishes into the kitchen and continued drinking there. Armand had enough and needed to go to bed. He said goodnight to the men and Don took him upstairs to his bedroom. Unfortunately, it was located directly above the kitchen and the raucous laughter wafted through the floor.

Before Armand dismissed Don, he asked him if there was a telephone he could use to call home. Don pointed to a phone on a table and told him he could use it. As Armand dialed, the merriment beneath rose to a new crescendo.

Jacque answered on the second ring. "Hello." Someone laughed like a hyena under Armand.

"Hi, Honey. It's me. You'll never guess where I'm at."

Jacque replied tersely, "Armand? Where are you? Are you in a bar?"

"No!" he answered as he plugged his free ear with his finger. "I'm upstairs in the Governor's Mansion. Governor Miller is entertaining some guests below me."

"Well, it sounds like they're having a great time."

"They are," replied Armand. "Hopefully, they'll taper off soon so I can get some sleep. I should be home by late tomorrow morning. I love you."

"I love you, too, Armand. Goodnight."

———————————————

Armand had an uneventful trip back to Anchorage. True to Bob Beardsley's word, he found the company car parked in the parking lot with the keys hidden under the seat. Armand felt a sense of accomplishment as he drove back to the office. His meeting had gone well. The governor was on board with the haul route. All signs pointed to approval of the project.

Armand pulled into the office lot and turned off the car. He got out and playfully tossed the keys in the air a few times as he casually walked into the office. Opening the door, he was greeted with a beehive of activity. Telephones were ringing off the hook. People looked frantic as they answered calls from Houston and DC. David Henderson was shouting orders and screaming into phones.

The activity puzzled Armand as his attempts to stop people for an explanation were brushed off or ignored. He finally wormed his way back to his office where he cornered Gordon and asked him what was happening.

"By Jove," exclaimed Gordon, "don't tell me you haven't heard? The Natives are suing TAPS!"

Between February and April, 1970, TAPS took a salvo of legal punches that brought them to their knees. On February 4, 1970, the Native villages of Bettles and Allakaket sued TAPS in Alaska Superior Court for breach of contract. They said TAPS had promised them jobs and TAPS had hired non-Native firms to haul equipment north. The villagers alleged that these companies would not hire Natives. TAPS denied any promises or agreements for Native hire.

Walter Hickel announced his Department was ready to issue the pipeline and haul road right-of-way through the Mineral Leasing Act. He said they were still waiting for TAPS to fully answer the list of technical questions that Russell Train had sent to them last June. The Department of the Interior would shape those answers into permit stipulations.

On March 9, five villages and 10 Athabascan Natives filed suit against TAPS in Alaska Superior Court, and in Washington DC Federal District Court. The plaintiffs were Native Villages of Allakaket, Bettles, Minto, Rampart, and Stevens Village. The Athabascans were William Pitka Sr., Charles Evans, Andy Simon Jr., William Williams, Pollack Simon, Arthur Wipliam Sr., Clarence Charlie, Charlie Titus Sr., and Wipson Titus.

The Native villages and Athabascans requested Alaska Superior Court Judge Eben Lewis to grant them $20 million in damages and $20 million in punitive damages from TAPS. According to the Natives' complaint, TAPS representatives had approached the Tanana Chiefs Conference (TCC) and given assurances of preferential employment opportunities in exchange for a waiver of their tribal constitution and bylaws that required federal approval before granting land to an outside party. On July 27, 1969, the TCC executive committee developed a resolution granting a waiver with the condition that Natives would receive employment opportunities and the other Native regional associations would receive contracts to assist in constructing and servicing the pipeline. The TCC resolution stated the waiver was on behalf of the five suing villages. The TCC Native name, Dena' Nena' Henash (DNH), approved the resolution.

TCC had quickly created the DNH Development Corporation to capitalize on the upcoming employment and contracting opportunities. However, according to TCC, TAPS did not offer any contracts to DNH to haul equipment north or assist in setting up construction camps. Even more insulting, TCC alleged that none of the TAPS contractors wanted to hire DNH for any work. Thus, the villages revoked their waiver and sought damages for breach of contract. Judge Lewis stated that he would research TCC claims and offer a recommendation on how to proceed by late April.

During the following weeks, TCC and TAPS traded barbs. During one of these exchanges, TAPS lawyer Paul Robison confirmed that TAPS had participated in some waiver discussions with TCC, but nothing was put in writing. If there was a contract, it was verbal and Mr. Robison believed it was null and void.

The Native suit filed in federal district court did not seek damages, but requested the court stop Walter Hickel from granting right-of-way across Native lands. Judge George Hart was assigned the case and began to collect information.

On March 26, the Wilderness Society, FOE, and Environmental Defense Fund filed suit in DC federal district court against the Secretary of the Interior to cease and desist implementing the Mineral Leasing Act of 1920 to grant the pipeline and haul road right-of-ways. The conservationists charged that the Secretary was violating the Act by attempting to grant excessive right-of-way width. The Mineral Leasing Act restricted projects to a 50-foot-wide right-of-way, 25 feet on each side of centerline. The pipeline and road required at least 200 feet–100 feet on each side of the surveyed centerline.

On April 1, District Court Judge George Hart issued a temporary injunction preventing Walter Hickel from issuing a pipeline right-of-way across 19.8 miles of land claimed by Stevens Village. Stevens Village was a small settlement of fewer than 80 people located on the north bank of the Yukon River, a few miles upstream of the proposed bridge crossing. Judge Hart disavowed the other claims because their traditional lands were not near the project. He stated that the federal government must solve the Alaska Native land issues before he would lift the injunction.

Governor Keith Miller wasted no time responding to Judge Hart's injunction. On April 3, Governor Miller sent a telegram to Walter Hickel stating that he was invoking the Act of July 26, 1866 (also known as the Lode Act). The Lode Act allowed a state to designate right-of-way for constructing roads across federally-owned lands in the public domain. Miller declared, "I am authorizing the Trans Alaska Pipeline System to proceed with construction of the permanent road to secondary standards from the Yukon River to the Prudhoe Bay." The members of TAPS thanked the governor for his decision, but withheld further comment until they studied the ramifications of this action.

On behalf of the Native villages of Bettles, Allakaket, and Stevens, the Alaska Legal Services Corporation filed a third suit in federal district court in Anchorage, Alaska on April 5. The suit requested an injunction against Governor Miller's and Commissioner Beardsley's granting right-of-way on federal property across traditionally used Native lands for the haul road. Alaska Legal Services argued that the Lode Act did not give the Governor authority to grant right-of-way through Native lands.

Then on April 6, the Wilderness Society, FOE, and Environmental Defense Fund threw their knockout punch. They amended their March lawsuit to charge that the Department of the Interior had not implemented NEPA. They stated that DOI should perform an EIS before issuing the haul road and pipeline right-of-way because issuing the permit would constitute a major federal action.

Judge George Hart analyzed the environmental groups' assertions and agreed. On April 13, 1970, Judge Hart issued a second injunction halting the haul road. This time the ruling was rooted in solid ground–not the vague assumptions on what constituted Native land. The TAPS project was stopped in its tracks.

Several men tried to resurrect the project. On April 15, Governor Miller ignored the Alaska Legal Services lawsuit and announced Alaska would hire TAPS subcontractors to build the haul road and then TAPS would reimburse the State within five years at an annual interest rate of 7.5 percent. The US Department of the Interior and US Attorney General John Mitchell immediately began to research if Alaska truly had the legal standing to grant the right-of-way. Their preliminary analysis showed that it did. However, Alaska could only grant the road right-of-way. The Lode Act would not grant a pipeline corridor. TAPS quickly realized that without a guaranteed pipeline, they ran the risk of not getting a return on their haul road investment. Thus, they began to quietly dampen Governor Miller's enthusiasm.

State Representative Don Young from Fort Yukon organized a legislative hearing in Juneau on April 17, seeking evidence that the Alaska Legal Services had misrepresented Stevens Village in their April lawsuit. Representative Young produced an affidavit signed by members of the Stevens Village Council stating they opposed the injunction. Young said he suspected misrepresentation when Council President Charles Evans sent him a letter expressing his wish that the suit would be thrown out of court. Armed with this knowledge, Young requested the state attorney general investigate the claim.

Assistant Attorney General Robert Price testified at the hearing. He said he visited the village and obtained an affidavit that the villagers wrote and signed. The affidavit documented that the village wanted no part of the injunction and they did not realize what Alaska Legal Services was seeking. Price stated that the villagers simply thought they were joining the TCC action to force TAPS to provide jobs to Natives.

John Hedlund of the Alaska Legal Services Corporation spoke at the hearing. He produced a document signed by the DNH Development Corporation authorizing his organization to take any actions necessary to obtain construction contracts from TAPS. Alaska Legal Services believed filing an injunction against the State to prevent a future haul road from crossing Steven Village's land was the most prudent method to force TAPS to relinquish contracts to DNH.

The hearing ended in a stalemate. Subcommittee chairman Tom Fink of Anchorage summarized the hearing by stating, "Apparently, we're going to get conflicting affidavits. How are we going to resolve this? Are these people changing their minds or what?"

During the last week in April, John Knodell and Quinn O'Connell surprised Armand with a telephone call. Although Armand liked both men, he knew a joint call meant they needed something and his voice betrayed his suspicions. "Gentlemen, to what do I owe the pleasure of this call?"

"Hello, Armand," replied John.

"Top of the morning to you, Armand," greeted Quinn. "We've got a wee problem to discuss. Can we beggar a moment or two of your precious time, laddie?"

"I'm all ears," replied Armand as he took out a notepad and prepared to write notes.

John spoke softly, "Armand, we need to show some good faith in Native hiring. We were wondering if you possibly had some tasks that we could hire some villagers to perform."

Armand took a deep breath before answering. "Uh, John, was there any truth to the rumor that you had Paul Robison promise contracts to the Tanana Chiefs Conference in exchange for permission to cross Native lands?"

Deep silence prevailed. Then Quinn replied weakly, "Armand, would you think badly of us if we said yes?"

I knew it, swore Armand under his breath. "So now you want me to come up with something for them to do." Armand gave them a statement, not a question.

John continued, "It's a little more complicated than that. We think it would be bad form to hire residents of Stevens Village, Bettles, or Allakaket. Our intent would be too obvious. You will need to look at other TCC villages."

Armand groaned and shook his head. "John, I'm going to need a few days to get my mind wrapped around this. I am also going to call Jay Sullivan. He's got a way for figuring out things in a pinch. Let me bounce a few ideas off him and I'll get back to you."

John replied, "Good idea, Armand. Sorry for dropping this task on you. We'll be anxious to see what you and the unflappable Mr. Sullivan conjure up."

"The same," seconded Quinn. "Next time, we'll try to keep you in the loop, as they say, laddie. I hope there are no misgivings on your part."

Armand wanted to vent his displeasure, but held his tongue. He calmed his voice and replied, "I will call you in a few days to discuss some ideas. Goodbye, gentlemen." His mind was spinning with conflicting thoughts as he hung up. He was angry about how educated and knowledgeable men could have acted so recklessly. Now, he was tasked with cleaning up their mess. How was he going to solve this problem with John's constraints?

Armand sat in quiet contemplation for a few minutes before picking up the telephone and calling his trusted friend Jay. As Armand waited for the call to process through the network, he thought about the bond forged between them. They met at least once a week and talked daily on the phone. The close coordination allowed them to synchronize the right-of-way plat updates at the BLM and ADNR land offices. They worked well together and Armand trusted Jay completely.

Shirley picked up on the second ring. "Land Field Services, how may I help you?"

"Shirley. This is Armand. Is that big lug of a boss of yours around? I need his help."

Shirley gave Armand a soft laugh and replied, "Armand. It is so good to hear from you. What has it been, at least twelve hours since we last talked? We really must chat more often. Yes, Jay's here. I'll get him. One moment, please." Armand liked the bantering.

Jay came on within a few moments. "Good morning, Armand. How goes it in Anchorage land?"

"Well, to be honest, Jay, not too good at the moment. I just got a call from Knodell and O'Connell. They gave us an impossible assignment."

"Now you've piqued my interest," answered Jay. "Please proceed." Armand summarized the phone call and laid out the employment request. As Armand explained the situation, Jay performed his deep-concentration ritual of closing his eyes and rubbing his balding head. When Armand finished, Jay kept silent for a few seconds, thinking. Then a flash of inspiration caused him to sit up straight. "Armand, I've got an idea. A few days ago, I had a man from the village of Beaver come into my office inquiring about work. He had virtually no work experience or training, but he said he was willing to do anything. He also said that there were several men just like him back home. We could set up a survey training program and use them on my survey crews. What do you think?"

This is what Armand liked about Jay–his ability to conjure solid and innovative solutions to the most vexing problems. "Sounds like a plan to me. Make the necessary inquiries and I'll coordinate with Knodell and O'Connell. Goodbye, Jay, and thank you. You did it again."

Jay produced a low laugh and said, "Well, we are not out of the woods yet, but it's a start. I'll let you know what I find out. Goodbye, Armand."

When Jay hung up, he yelled for John Pate to come. John was an ex-marine like himself and an ex-Chevron employee. Jay had worked with him on the Swanson River and Soldotna Creek oil fields. He was a confident and forthright man who Jay relied on to carry out tough assignments. "John, I've got a hard one for you and if we are successful, it will solve our surveying problem."

John nodded and said, "By problem, you mean to prevent Ocean Tech from phasing us out of surveying?" Ocean Tech was trying to consolidate all TAPS surveying as a cost-control measure. Jay and John could see the handwriting on the wall and their dwindling survey work proved it.

"Yep, that problem," answered Jay, "and TAPS is going to be very thankful for our services, too. Here's what we have to do. . ."

On May 7, Joe LaRocca, the *Fairbanks Daily News Miner* reporter, interviewed Armand and Jay at the Land Field Services office. Ten men from Beaver sat stoically behind folding tables and cradled cups of coffee. Joe smiled at them. He could tell they were extremely uncomfortable being displayed like zoo animals. Joe turned his attention back to the curiously interesting men in front of him. The smaller, older man, Armand, was clearly in charge. Joe estimated his age to be in the late 40s. The younger man, Jay, towered over the two of them. He radiated a brash confidence. Joe pegged him to be in his late 30s.

Joe readied his notepad and asked, "Mr. P.J. Sullivan, what exactly does Land Field Services do?"

Jay leaned forward and said with a seriously straight face, "We are an Anchorage cadastral surveying firm."

"I see," replied Joe as he scribbled on his pad, "and what will you train these men to do?"

Jay responded in a precise manner. "These men will be working as apprentice surveyors under a job-training program designed to qualify them for advanced positions. I will assign them to survey parties which are presently tying in mining claims to the survey of the proposed haul road right-of-way."

Joe remained silent as he wrote his notes. Then he looked up and addressed Armand. "As TAPS representative, what, sir, are your impressions of the program?"

Knodell and O'Connell had prepared Armand for this interview. Drawing from their coaching, he answered, "From all indications so far, we will soon have competent chainmen and rodmen, and, hopefully, even some instrument men from the group. This is my first experience with this type of practical training program for Alaska Natives, but I'm sure it won't be my last. From what I am seeing, I have high hopes for the program to continue successfully as we move southward along the proposed route."

Joe looked up from his pad and asked Armand a penetrating question. "Is this training program the result of the recent Native lawsuits against the pipeline project?"

Management had especially grilled Armand on how to answer this question. Armand cleared his throat and replied, "It has always been TAPS policy to require contractor hire of Alaskans, particularly residents of areas where work is in progress, whenever possible. The successful example set by the men of Beaver promises to make it possible to expand those possibilities to the fullest extent."

Joe glanced at Armand and then at Jay. Neither man cracked a smile at the canned statement Armand had just uttered. Joe decided to end the interview and keep everything upbeat. He thanked the Beaver residents and wished them well as he left.

Jay waited until the door was shut and he could no longer hear Joe's footsteps heading for the stairwell before letting out a whoop and slapping Armand across the back. "Armand, old friend, I'm submitting your name for an Oscar! Excellent performance!" Then he addressed his future students, "Gentlemen, you are dismissed. Thank you for being such good sports. We start tomorrow at eight sharp. Understand. If you are not here, you don't get paid. See you."

Armand and Jay shook hands with the men as they filed out. As they watched them go, Jay said to Armand, "I've also got an idea about DNH. How about letting them do the hydroseeding from Livengood to the Yukon? The entire stretch is in terrible need of erosion control."

Armand arched his eyebrow and replied, "Hydroseeding? Jay, where do you get these ideas?"

Jay smiled and said, "Always looking for opportunities, dear friend. You could put Knodell to work twisting some arms over at Burgess-Houston to swing a contract to DNH. They'd love it! Burgess and DNH could train men from all the Native villages. It would be high profile."

Armand rubbed his chin as he thought about it. "You know, Jay, it just might work. I'll talk to John and Quinn. Another great idea. Thank you."

Jay slapped Armand across his back and said, "That's what I'm here for, Armand. Now, let's go to the Travelers Inn and celebrate. We must toast our new training program."

"Sounds good, Jay," responded Armand. "By the way, do you think our program will help lift the lawsuits?"

Jay shook his head as he grabbed his coat and said, "Naw. There are other issues that will tie up the courts like Native lands and that pesky EIS. However, our new program will give us one big benefit."

"Oh," asked Armand, "what's that?"

"It will allow us to get caught up. We now have a chance of settling all the mining claim disputes before DOI grants the right-of-way permit." Jay ushered Armand out the door before continuing, "In other words, we won't get shot."

Chapter 7

Time to Catch our Breath

June 1970 was a month of decisions–all major and precedent-setting. During the first week of the month, TAPS announced that they would shift the northern end of the haul road alignment 10 miles to the east from the Put River to the new State Deadhorse Airport along the Sag River. This refinement had three distinct advantages. The shift shortened the route by three miles. It allowed easy access to gravel sources within the Sag River. The route would be supported by a full-service airport.

On June 16, 1970, the TAPS Houston office sent a telegram to its five construction contractors revoking their letters of intent. To keep the heavy equipment staged at the camps and to prevent the companies from declaring bankruptcy, TAPS purchased some of the equipment, provided financial compensation for work performed, and contracted the companies to provide caretakers for the camps. TAPS planned to use the camps to support their engineering and environmental studies and surveying work.

During mid-June, President Nixon tapped Russell Train to be the first chairman of the Council of Environmental Quality. This appointment was extremely awkward for DOI Secretary Walter Hickel. Now his right-hand man was for all purposes his regulator. Secretary Hickel muttered one day that Train was given "authority without responsibility." With the DOI developing the EIS, TAPS worried what would happen if Train disagreed with the findings and wondered what agency would prevail. The injection of Train's office into the right-of-way procurement added new legal and bureaucratic elements never encountered by natural resource developers.

Towards the end of June, TAPS directed Burgess-Houston to contract DNH Development Corporation to revegetate the haul road north of Livengood. During construction, Burgess-Houston had cut through unstable, ice-rich slopes that melted and slumped. The resulting erosion moved tons of silt into adjacent creeks and wetlands. The cut slopes needed vegetation to anchor the soil and prevent it from eroding.

Hydroseeding was the most efficient method for revegetating the 56-mile section between Livengood and the Yukon River. Fertilizer and seed was mixed in a tank and sprayed along the slopes. Some training was required to ensure the proper mixture was evenly distributed. DNH rose to the occasion by chartering an airplane to fly to Allakaket, Bettles, Rampart, Stevens Village, and Minto and recruit men for the project. Then Burgess-Houston sponsored a weeklong training program to teach the men about the principles of hydroseeding before starting the actual work.

The hydroseeding project was a complete success. The slopes grew thick carpets of grass and the erosion subsided. TAPS officials filmed the work and final results and frequently showed the documentary as proof of TAPS working closely with Alaska Natives.

On June 30, TAPS officially notified Governor Miller that they would not participate in his haul road project. TAPS believed that if they reimbursed the State for building the road under the Lode Act, DOI could not guarantee that they would issue the right-of-way for the pipeline. Thus, TAPS might not realize a return on their enormous investment. They believed the risk was too high to invest in Miller's scheme.

Keith Miller felt embarrassed and betrayed. He had notified the State legislature on June 18 to convene in a special session to ratify an agreement between TAPS and Alaska to build the haul road. He issued the call after he had "received reasonable assurances from TAPS that a plan for constructing the highway could be worked out." Now after the TAPS reversal, Miller was forced to address the State in a radio broadcast on July 2 and rescind his request. The legal maneuvering had now completely stopped the pipeline and haul road projects in their tracks.

On August 14, 1970, the TAPS consortium incorporated and formed the Alyeska Pipeline Service Company to construct and operate the Trans-Alaska pipeline. The following companies owned Alyeska: SOHIO (BP) 28.08 percent; ARCO 28.08 percent; Humble 25.52 percent; Mobil 8.68 percent; Union Oil 3.32 percent; Phillips Petroleum 3.32 percent; and Amerada Hess 3 percent. The consortium consolidated the engineering in Houston, Texas and situated their corporate headquarters in Bellevue, Washington. Alyeska appointed Edward Patton as president. David Henderson continued to manage the Alaska office.

The name Alyeska was an archaic spelling of the Aleut word meaning "Great Land." The name "Alaska" was derived from this word. The main purpose for forming Alyeska was to increase management efficiency. Up to this time, the consortium had voted on all major decisions. This procedure was time-consuming and awkward. Now, the newly formed company had the authority to pursue the design, construction, and ultimately the operation of the pipeline system. The consortium had full faith that Edward Patton could steer the project on a straight course for completion.

A triangle of Lower 48 offices supported the Fairbanks and Anchorage Alyeska staff. These were the Bellevue, Houston, and Washington DC locations. Alyeska had strategically located their headquarters in Bellevue because it was located halfway between Alaska and Houston and Washington DC. Bellevue also had ample office space and land to expand within the crowded Seattle area. Managers could then shuttle to the appropriate office within one day without having to fly the entire length. The Houston-to-Fairbanks leg sometimes took two grueling days.

The consortium transferred their best employees to the Houston office. Here, engineers, scientists, and technicians gathered to design the pipeline system and support the US Department of the Interior attempt's to develop the EIS. Although the newspapers stated the project was stalled, the Alyeska offices buzzed with activity.

Harry Brelsford and John Knodell paid the Anchorage office a quick visit during the first week in September. Harry wanted to explore the office before permanently moving to Anchorage in October. Both men were appalled at the crowded conditions. Employees were stumbling over each other and the noise level was deafening.

The visit reached a crescendo when David Henderson called a full staff meeting in the tiny sole conference room to allow John and Harry to address them. The men had to stand crunched together to fit. The ones in the back could not see Harry standing in front. Finally out of desperation, David pointed at Armand and shouted, "Armand! You must find us a larger office. *Pronto*! Understand?" The men would have clapped, but they couldn't move their arms. Instead, they murmured in agreement.

The next morning, Armand began his search. He started in the downtown area, but he could not find anything that would accommodate Alyeska's expanding needs. So, Armand started expanding his search radius to the Anchorage outskirts. Here he stumbled upon a new building on the corner of Bragaw Street and Reka Drive. Doctor Homay owned the building and it housed his medical office. However, he occupied only a small portion of it.

Armand liked what he saw. The building was well situated on a three-acre parcel with plenty of parking space. He parked, entered the building, and found the receptionist. Armand addressed her, "Good afternoon, Miss. I would like to talk to someone about leasing the open office space."

The young woman smiled and replied, "Good afternoon, sir. Dr. Homay instructed me to direct all inquiries to his wife, but she is not here at the moment."

"OK, is it possible to arrange a meeting?"

The receptionist took out an appointment book and said, "Yes it is. How about ten a.m. tomorrow? Does that work for you?"

Armand smiled and said, "Yes it does. Please reserve that time for me. My name is Armand Spielman."

The woman wrote down Armand's name in the book. "OK," she said, "Mrs. Homay will meet you tomorrow."

The next day, Armand returned with David so he could pass judgment on the office space before Armand proceeded with the negotiations. They met Mrs. Homay and she showed the men the available space. As David stood rubbing his chin as he inspected the building, Mrs. Homay asked him, "What kind of business are you in?"

David looked stoically at her and said, "We are in charge of building the oil pipeline across Alaska. So, our needs will increase dramatically over the next few years. I doubt that we would fit in your office space very long."

"Really? How interesting," replied Mrs. Homay. "Did you know the ground floor is designed to expand horizontally and vertically? Not only can we build an addition, but we can add two floors to accommodate your expanding needs. I'm sure we could work something out."

David arched his right eyebrow. Armand could tell he was very interested. In his abrupt manner, he asked, "How much?"

"Rent?" replied Mrs. Homay, "Fifteen cents per square foot."

David gave her a sharp nod, stuck out his hand, and said, "OK. Please draw up a lease agreement for this vacant space with an option to construct a second floor. Deal?"

Mrs. Homay smiled, gently clasped his hand, and replied, "Deal." They shook on it.

"Please contact Mr. Spielman when you have completed the lease agreement. He will pick it up and review it." Armand gave her his card.

"Will do, Mr. Henderson," replied Mrs. Homay as she read Armand's card. "The agreement should be ready in a few days."

True to her word, she called Armand at the end of the week and told him the agreement was ready. Armand picked it up and David signed it. Armand got it recorded and returned a copy of the lease to Mrs. Homay.

Armand immediately secured a contractor to renovate the vacant portion of the building into offices. By the last of October, Alyeska Pipeline Service Company moved into their new, roomy accommodations. For decades to come, Alyeska's address would be 1835 South Bragaw Street.

Harry Brelsford called Armand at the end of September to discuss the right-of-way acquisition process in general terms. Harry's intent was to gain a broad understanding of the challenges that lay ahead. "Armand, where are most of the private parcels located?" asked Harry.

Armand answered, "The pipeline will cross the bulk of the private lands in the Fairbanks area. Although we will try to skirt the populous areas, we can't avoid the homesteads and mining claims. As we punch north through the Fox area, we will cross many mining claims, too. We also will run into them in the Middle Fork Koyukuk River valley. And don't forget the private lands around the Valdez Arm as the pipeline approaches the marine terminal."

Harry seemed to consider this information for a moment before commenting, "So, it appears Mr. Sullivan's group is well positioned to help us with these parcels."

"They are," responded Armand, "and I've got them focused on gathering ownership information and contacting owners about our intent to purchase right-of-way."

"That's good, Armand. So, this leads me to my next question. How do you keep track of changes in land ownership on federal and Alaska lands?"

"That's easy," replied Armand. "Every month, Jay and I meet in Anchorage and take a roll of alignment sheets to the BLM Land Office. We compare the federal plats with our surveyed plats. If we find any discrepancies, we mark them on our sheets with a yellow highlighter. Then we repeat the process at the State Lands Office. Afterwards, I prepare a letter to the head draftsman in Houston that details the changes. The draftsman then corrects our plats and sends me a new set."

Harry was impressed. Armand's method was simple and effective. "Good show, Armand. Now, I have only one last immediate concern–Valdez. Have you ever actually walked the marine terminal site?"

Armand thought for a moment before answering. "No, I haven't. Are you concerned about stumbling across marked mining claims?"

"Bingo!" replied Harry. "You hit the nail on the head. Since mining is allowed in National Forests, I want to make sure we've checked that parcel out. Please take Herman with you and spend some time down there walking the site. Take lots of notes and write down anything you see that is not a tree or a rock."

"All right, Harry. You do realize we're talking about a thousand acres of thick brush, forest, and mountainous terrain? This is going to take us a few days and Herman and I are not spring chickens anymore."

Harry replied firmly, "I have full confidence that you two will comb the property thoroughly. Let me know what you find. By the way, Armand, I have another concern about the marine terminal."

By the way Harry's voice changed to a flat tone, Armand knew something serious was up. "What's that?"

"You know that George Atkinson filed suit in federal court to prevent the Forest Service from transferring the land to the State, correct?"

"That's right, Harry," replied Armand. "Any landsman worth his salt can see the suit is trying to force us to buy land at an inflated price. Are you concerned that we will not prevail?"

"No, Armand, my concern is Atkinson's legal counsel. I think he has someone very astute and ruthless behind him. Did you know he just filed for a US Army Corps of Engineers permit to build a small dock off Jackson Point? That dock will directly conflict with our terminal. Someone is playing with us."

Armand went silent with the implications of Harry's revelation. Harry continued, "Anyway, Armand, it's imperative that you go down to Valdez and have a look around. Be careful and report to me what you see."

As Armand put the phone down in its cradle, he glanced at the adjacent desk and saw Herman smiling at him. "I heard my name and 'no spring chicken' in the same context," he said.

Armand nodded and replied, "Herman, how would you like to go on a hike? You know, get out of the office and get some fresh air."

"Armand, what are you roping me into this time?"

Armand just smiled back and said, "We're going to Valdez."

The following Monday, Armand and Herman drove to Valdez and arrived in the late afternoon. The weather was unusually beautiful. Herman had never been to Valdez, so Armand took some time to show him around and explained the history of the area. First, he drove through the pipeline storage yard. Pipe stacked four high covered acres of the site.

"And more is coming," said Armand. "It will take them another two years to ship the pipe from Japan." Armand pointed at the surrounding area and continued, "This whole area was once the town of Valdez until the 1964 earthquake wiped it out. The residents moved the town farther up the arm to protect it from future tsunamis. Now, let's drive out to where the marine terminal will be and then go to town."

They drove about five miles along the newly constructed gravel Dayville Road until it ended at Allison Creek. Silver salmon were spawning in the sloughs and creeks next to the road. An occasional brown bear dined on caught salmon by the streams. Armand and Herman sat in their car staring across the creek at the thickly vegetated hills before them. "Well, there it is," said Armand.

Not taking his eyes off the forbidding forest, Herman answered, "What have I ever done to you, Armand? I thought we were friends."

"We are," replied Armand as he shifted into reverse to turn around, "and we are going to have a grand adventure tomorrow. Let's check into the motel and get some dinner. You'll feel better about things in the morning."

As they were registering with the Valdez Motel, the owner asked, "Who do you fellas work for?"

Typical small-town talk, thought Armand as he finished signing the registry. "We work for TAPS. We'll be inspecting the future terminal site tomorrow."

"Really?" replied the owner. "The site across the bay? Last week, we had two guys from the State visit it, too. They said they were appraisers. Are you appraisers?"

Armand found this information extremely interesting. "No, but we deal with them. You're sure they were from the State?"

"Yep," answered the owner as he flipped the registry page back. "See here. They listed their address as Department of Natural Resources, Lands Department."

Armand looked at Herman and said, "Looks like the State is setting a price tag for the terminal site. We'll have to find out what it is."

That evening over dinner, Armand recounted to Herman the history he had gleaned from the BLM files about the Dayville Road and the land that someday would become the marine terminal. "The army built the road around the Valdez Arm in the late 1890s and constructed a military outpost called Fort Liscum. When the US Government surplused the Fort in 1918, the Department of the Interior reacquired the public domain property. Walter Day from Valdez filed a 160-acre homestead claim on the old Fort Liscum parade grounds. He called the homestead "Dayville" and renovated an old military building to live in. Thus, Valdez renamed the Fort Liscum Road the Dayville Road.

"Mr. Day passed away a few years ago, but his wife Oma still lives in Valdez and their son Walter H. and daughter-in-law Gloria run the local newspaper–the <u>Valdez Copper Basin News</u>. I understand Mrs. Day leased the homestead to Mr. George Atkinson, president of A&G Construction Company, with an option to buy it.

"When I found the Day homestead on the township plats, I noticed that the Day family had another claim within our planned marine terminal site. The claim was for a federal trade and manufacturing site. I made a special note of its location. So tomorrow, we'll need to inspect this area closely."

"Great," said Herman between mouthfuls of food. "Did the BLM files say anything about herds of bears roaming the site?"

"No," replied Armand as he dove into his steak, "but rest assured they're there."

Armand and Herman got an early start the next morning. They parked at the Allison Creek pullout, put on their rubber boots, and prepared to bushwhack through the forest. Armand stopped Herman and said, "Ah, Herman, there's something I need to tell you."

Herman looked at Armand with a little fear in his eyes and asked, "Like what, Armand?"

"Our survey crews encountered a few bears when they were marking the site boundaries. Some guys got chased around a bit. We need to be on the lookout. OK?"

Herman put his hands on his hips and said, "Please tell me that you brought a gun?"

Armand shook his head. "No, I didn't. We're going to have to keep our eyes peeled. Let's go." Armand started to pick his way across the creek.

Herman watched him go before muttering, "That's just great." Then like a condemned man, he trudged after Armand.

They felt their way through the thick brush for several hundred yards until they stumbled upon a path. The passageway looked like someone had widened an existing bear trail. Surmising that this was the surveyors' entrance, they followed it to the outer boundary line. The boundary was well marked with flagging and cut trees and brush. They decided to follow the line up the mountainside and inspect the higher elevations first.

When they arrived at the site corner marker, they found vast bushes of ripe salmonberries. "Little wonder that there are bears around here," said Herman as he munched the sweet fruit. "So, what exactly are we looking for?"

Armand plucked a fat salmonberry from a bush and said, "We are looking for signs of human activity such as cabins, holes in the ground from someone digging, and corner post markers for a mining claim. Actually, anything that's not natural."

"So, we shouldn't record that," said Herman as he pointed below. About a hundred yards downhill, the brush and trees were moving as something big ambled through them. They had little doubt what it was.

"No, I think we should avoid that big furry thing. Stay close." They spent the morning combing the mountainside and found no evidence of past human occupation. However, they did periodically stumble upon evidence that bears ruled the area. Steaming dung piles and sounds of something big pushing through the brush reminded them they were not alone. Finally, Armand suggested they drop down to the ocean and investigate the federal trade and manufacturing claim. Signs of relief were visible across Herman's face.

They headed downhill to a little bay called Swan Port. The bay was formed by a narrow spit extending into Valdez Arm and then curving almost back to the shoreline. A clump of spruce trees grew at the end of the spit by the bay entrance. The bay formed a natural fish trap and swarms of silver salmon milled in the clear waters. Armand took a deep breath and said, "Beautiful spot, eh Herman? This is the area of the trade and manufacturing claim. Let's make our way to the end of the spit and see what's there."

The spit provided easy walking and they soon entered the spruce trees at the end. Here, they found an old sawmill under a rough shelter supported by log posts. It looked like it had been abandoned for years. "OK. Here's the reason for the claim. They were cutting lumber here for sale and use back at the Day homestead."

After they recorded their findings, Armand said, "Well, Herman, I think we accomplished everything we set out to do. Let's call it a day." Herman sighed with relief. They found their way back to the car without incident and no bear encounters. Herman was exhausted from their trek. So they spent the night in Valdez and drove back to Anchorage the next day.

On September 28, 1970, Jay called Armand in a panic. "Armand, one of my survey crews screwed up. They attempted to survey across a mining claim by the Delta River without gaining permission first. The owner threw them off the property."

Armand asked the obvious question, "Can we route the pipeline around it?"

"No," answered Jay, "the Richardson Highway is too close and the mountains and river push us across the claim. We need this right-of-way."

"So, how can I help, Jay?"

"Could you please take Keith Christenson and pay the owner, Dr. Stolting, a visit? You know, smooth some feathers?" Jay sounded desperate. Keith worked for Jay in his Fairbanks office as a lawyer specializing in land law.

Jay must have really ticked off Dr. Stolting, otherwise he would have visited the owner himself. "OK, Jay. When can you send Keith down?"

"How about tomorrow?" asked Jay. Tomorrow was Saturday.

Armand hesitated before replying, "That doesn't leave me much time to prepare, Jay."

"I know, but I truly believe we've got to nip this in the bud before Dr. Stolting lays down the hammer and forces us to seek legal action. You really need to talk to him tomorrow. Keith can bring you up to speed on the land status and history of the claims as you drive up. The camp doesn't have a telephone, so you guys will arrive unannounced. I'm sure he'll let you in when he finds out who you are."

Armand took a deep breath. His gut told him this had all the earmarks of a total catastrophe. He could envision the future <u>Anchorage Times</u> article about a miner shooting two Alyeska employees for trespassing. Still, this was Jay Sullivan asking for help. Armand could not turn his back on him. "All right, Jay. I'll do it. Send Keith down early tomorrow morning and we'll drive up."

Jay breathed a sigh of relief and said, "Thank you, Armand. I owe you."

"No, you don't owe me, Jay," replied Armand, "but I want you to be more careful next time, understand?"

"Understand, Armand."

Armand met Keith at the Anchorage International Airport early Saturday morning. Keith was a small man who always spoke softly and intelligently. He wore a light coat, a dress shirt, slacks, and loafers–not exactly clothing suited for rural Alaska. "Good morning, Keith," greeted Armand as he shook Keith's hand, "Ready for a long drive?"

Keith looked dubious as he replied, "I guess I'm as ready as I can be."

"Then let's go. You can fill me in as we drive north." They piled into Armand's car and headed north on the Glenn Highway. The 250-mile trip took them to Glennallen and then farther north on the Richardson Highway. The autumn leaves were almost gone from the trees and the land was braced for the full fist of winter. The mountains were already shrouded in snow.

Keith looked out the window at the stunning landscapes as he summarized what he knew about the Mount Si Project. "Dr. Thomas Stolting has a series of unpatented mining claims along the Richardson Highway just below where Phelan Creek enters the Delta River. His camp is at milepost 212.5 on the east side of the road. He has guards posted at the camp entrance 24 hours a day."

"Well," continued Keith, "our survey crew was shooting the pipeline centerline along the Delta River when one of Stolting's guards halted them. The guard escorted our party chief into their compound. There, Stolting gave him a tongue lashing in a heavy German accent and told him to stay off his property."

Great, thought Armand as he drove in silence. *We're going to get browbeat by a German dictator.*

They arrived at Mount Si in the late afternoon and drove up a small dirt road to the gate. An armed guard immediately met them. Armand quickly explained the purpose of their visit and requested an audience with Dr. Stolting. As they were parking, Armand leaned over to Keith and said, "Let me do the talking. If things get hot, then you jump in. OK?"

Keith looked at Armand with trepidation and quipped, "When things get hot? They might shoot us if things get hot!"

Armand patted Keith's shoulder as he replied, "Just play it by ear. Let's go."

The guard marched Armand and Keith into the compound and into an office where they saw a small man with a goatee leaning back in his chair drumming the fingers of his right hand on his desk. The guard sat down next to them, folded his arms across his chest, leaned back, and gave them a knowing smile that said, *You're in for it now*! Silence prevailed except for the constant finger drumming.

Armand interpreted the awkward pause as his cue to present his case. "Dr. Stolting, my name is Armand Spielman and this is my associate Keith Christenson. We represent the Alyeska land office. We're here to sincerely apologize for our survey crew not attaining your permission to survey across your claims. On Monday morning, I will write you a letter formalizing our apology and restating that our survey crews will always inform you of their intentions before they enter your claims."

Armand's apology generated an unanticipated reaction from Stolting. Within a heartbeat, his face went from frowning to rage. With clenched teeth, his drumming fingers rolled into a fist which he lifted high in the air and slammed down on his desk as he yelled, "*Nein*! You will not cross my property! *Begreffen?*"

Terror shot across Keith's face as his eyes snapped wide and his mouth fell open. He almost tumbled backwards as Stolting's voice roared over them. Armand glanced at Keith and realized he was on his own. *So, much for jumping in when things get hot, Keith.* Armand turned to face Stolting. He was not going to let this tyrant bully him. He calmed himself and replied, "Sir, do you own your claims?"

Stolting's head snapped back at the question before he recovered and pointed his finger at Armand and shouted, "That's none of your business!"

"Sir, my business is to know who owns what. You have unpatented mining claims. They're just pieces of paper giving you permission to mine. I have written permission from the state and federal governments authorizing my company to survey across public domain lands, which your claims are. Now, shall I report back to the BLM and ADNR that you are not upholding the stipulations of your claims or will you cooperate with our survey request?"

Silence again prevailed. As the seconds ticked from a distant clock, Stolting's face gradually softened and lost its anger. Finally he replied, "Your letter would be a wonderful way to begin. I look forward to receiving it."

Armand took his acknowledgement as a tactful sign that it was time to leave. He patted Keith's leg and said, "Very good, Dr. Stolting. It was a pleasure meeting you. You will receive my letter next week. Let's go, Keith." Without a handshake or another word said, Armand and Keith stood and waited for the guard who appeared lost about what to do next. Stolting nodded his approval to the guard to escort the men back to their car.

They spent the night at the Paxson Lodge and drove back to Anchorage on Sunday. True to Armand's word, he wrote and mailed the letter to Stolting on Monday, hoping the letter would smooth future communications with the Mount Si Project.

———————————

When Harry Brelsford moved to Anchorage in late September, Alyeska was in the throes of moving to their new spacious Bragaw office space. Therefore, the Koloa Building was in disarray and little work was actually being done. To avoid the chaos, Harry suggested to Armand, "Let's take a trip to Fairbanks. I haven't met the unflappable Jay Sullivan and his crew, yet. It will be a great excuse to get out of here until the dust settles. How about it, Armand?"

Armand smiled and replied, "It'll be my pleasure. I will make the arrangements."

They arrived at the Fairbanks International Airport on a frosty October morning. When Jay stepped forward to heartily greet them, Harry took a step back and gawked at his size. Jay seemed oblivious to Harry's surprised face and engulfed his hand with a mighty shake. Armand took control of the situation and smacked Jay across the shoulder as he said, "Good to see ya, Jay! You're looking fit."

"Same to ya, Armand," replied Jay with a huge grin across his face. "Good to have you guys up here. I'll load you into our truck and take you downtown to the office. We'll bring you up to speed on what we are working on. Then I was thinking we should walk across the hall and pay the Alyeska office a visit. How does that sound?"

Harry recovered from his shock and said, "That sounds grand, Jay. I would like to get a feel of what's happening around here."

"And you shall," replied Jay as he ushered them to the baggage carousel. After retrieving their luggage, Jay led them to the parking lot out front. There, Harry first witnessed the Fairbanks custom of idling your vehicle while waiting inside the terminal. The whole lot was filled with idling cars with small exhaust plumes wafting straight up. Jay threw their bags in the back of the pickup and told them to get in. The men crowded together in the cab with Harry squished in the middle.

Jay drove the narrow two-lane Airport Road to the intersection of University and Airport Way. Here, the road became a straight four-lane divided throughway that took them past the newly constructed theme park called Alaskaland. A mile farther, Jay took a left on Cushman Street and drove to the heart of the city. He turned right on First Avenue, which followed the Chena River and parked in front of the Polaris Building.

Jay guided them to the second floor Land Field Services Office, Suite 209. Shirley Pippen greeted them when they entered. "Armand!" she cooed as she rose to hug him, "It's so good to see you again."

Armand smiled as he returned the embrace and replied, "Good to see you, Shirley. I'm so glad your uncouth boss didn't drive you away. This place would be drab without you."

Armand turned to Harry and said, "Shirley, this is Harry Brelsford. He will be supervising Jay and me as we slug through the right-of-way acquisition. Harry, this is Shirley Pippen. Nothing happens in this office without her scrutiny."

Harry reached out his hand to Shirley. She hesitated for a moment as she gazed upon his meticulous dress, including his silk tie and fancy dress shoes. She blushed when she realized that she was gawking, took Harry's hand, and said, "I'm sorry for staring, Mr. Brelsford. I am not used to seeing a well-dressed man in these parts. Welcome to our office."

Harry was unruffled. He smiled and said, "That's quite alright, Mrs. Pippen. Please call me Harry. I'm sure we'll be talking frequently on the phone as the project develops."

"Harry," said Jay, "I want you to meet the other scoundrels in this group. Here is John Pate. John worked with me at Chevron." The big, stocky ex-marine stepped up to Harry and shook his hand.

Must these men be so big? thought Harry as he shook John's massive hand. Then Jay introduced Keith Christenson, who was Harry's size. Harry breathed a sigh of relief.

As Harry and Armand took off their coats and got comfortable, Shirley brought them cups of coffee, which they gratefully accepted. Jay then gave them an overview of their efforts.

"Harry," began Jay as he placed his finger on a large map that he had rolled out on a table, "we are surveying the private parcels that may be crossed by the pipeline and haul road routes. Ocean Tech is surveying the route as it crosses public domain lands."

"Any conflicts with Ocean Tech?" asked Harry.

Jay hesitated before speaking, "Not really. We have some spats about who's surveying unpatented mining claims, but nothing serious. Land Field Services focuses on private holdings, homesteads, and mining claims. We try to stay out of each other's hair."

Harry nodded and asked, "How do you organize your information on each parcel?"

Jay smiled and ushered them to the filing cabinets. He opened a drawer and showed them the folder tabs. Each tab had an area description such as "Valdez" or "Wiseman" and a federal or state parcel identification number. The files were further delineated by amendment numbers. Harry and Armand recognized that his system was simple but effective, and Alyeska could incorporate his files into any system they might develop.

"How many survey crews do you have, Jay?" asked Harry.

"We have three crews—one north of Prospect, one in the Fairbanks area, and the other south of Delta Junction. They should be wrapping their season up within a few days."

They spent the morning reviewing Jay's operation and then Jay took them to the Alyeska office. Armand introduced Harry to Ben Anderson. Ben brought Harry current with the haul road design and material needs. This was the first time Harry heard that millions of cubic yards of gravel would be needed to build the road across vast stretches of permafrost. This would require large material procurements from state and federal agencies.

"You know, Ben," mused Harry as he looked at the haul road alignment, "I would like to see the first section of the road. Any chance of someone driving me up?"

"Sure," replied Ben. "I'll do it. Let's plan on leaving at seven a.m. tomorrow. I can get you up to the bridge site and back in a day. Sound good?"

Harry nodded, "That sounds marvelous! I'll be here at seven. See you then."

Jay drove Harry and Armand to the Travelers Inn to check into their rooms. The Travelers Inn was Fairbanks's newest hotel located on Nobel Street, only a few blocks from the office. Walter Hickel had started the hotel construction in 1969 with plans to eventually include a fine dining restaurant and lounge. He even touted a name for the future expansion–the Bear and Seal.

Jay dropped them off at the hotel with the understanding that they would meet up at the Land Field Services office at six. Jay would then escort them to the new Petroleum Club for dinner. The Club was located on the top floor of the Polaris Building.

Harry and Armand decided to walk the five blocks to Jay's office. Night had descended on Fairbanks by the time they started their trek into town. The air was cold and clear with the stars shining exceptionally brightly against the blue-black sky. Harry gazed up at the heavens and suddenly stopped. His face filled with amazement as he pointed and asked Armand, "What's that?"

Armand looked up and saw a spectacular display of swirling lights dancing across the sky. "That, Harry, is the northern lights. We get them in Anchorage too, but not as clear as here. Beautiful, aren't they?"

Harry stood transfixed as he said quietly, "I've heard of them, but never seen them before. Stunning." Armand patted him on the shoulder to urge him forward and led him down the street to Jay's office.

———————————

Early the next morning, Harry and Armand left on separate assignments. Ben Anderson took Harry to inspect the Haul Road and Armand walked downtown to Second Avenue to visit an old business acquaintance about leasing a northern pipe-storage yard. Armand stopped at the Fairbanks Office Supply and asked the girl who waited on him if Mr. Cliff Burglin was in.

"That's my dad," she replied. "He's having coffee with Mr. Stepovich at the Star of the North Bakery next door. You could go see him or wait here if you like."

"I'd hate to disturb him," answered Armand. "I'll wait a little while." She nodded and went on with her business.

A few minutes later, Cliff and Mike Stepovich entered the store. Cliff took a step back when he saw Armand before giving him a hearty handshake. "Armand, you old scoundrel, what are you up to? No good, no doubt."

Armand laughed as he replied, "Good to see you too, Cliff. Alyeska needs to lease the Bentley Trust land that we discussed on the phone a couple of months ago for a pipe storage yard. I was hoping we could go out and see it before we commit." Then Armand turned to Mike and greeted him, "Mike, it's been a long time. How are Matilda and the family?"

Mike Stepovich had been the last territorial governor before Alaska became a state. He had been Cliff's business partner when the two purchased federal oil and gas leases in 1964. Armand eventually bought those leases from them on behalf of Richfield Oil Company. Armand marveled what a small state Alaska was when it came to knowing important people. Because their wives were very active in the Catholic Church, Jacque had met and socialized with Mike's wife, Matilda. They became close friends. Mike smiled and said, "Matilda is doing fine. The kids are growing like weeds."

"That's great, Mike. Please give Matilda my regards and tell her Jacque says hello, too." Then Armand turned to Cliff and said, "Are you up for a trip?"

"Sure," replied Cliff, "but Mike here is going to be involved in any lease language."

Armand elbowed Mike in the ribs and said, "Kind of thought so. Tough to keep a lawyer out of anything."

Mike threw up his hands and said, "Hey, somebody has to watch out for the Trust! Cliff here will give away the farm if I don't look over his shoulder every moment. Promise me, Cliff, you won't sign anything until I have had a chance to read it, huh?"

Cliff grabbed his coat and hat as he shook his head and said, "Armand, let's get out of here before Stepovich says I'm not fit to drive." Armand shook Mike's hand goodbye and they piled into Cliff's pickup and drove north on the Steese Highway.

The Bentley Family Charitable Trust Land was the site of the Bentley Dairy from 1922 through the 1940s. The family's holdings stretched from the Chena River to the foothills north of Fairbanks. Bobby Miller, in partnership with the Bentley family, established the Miller-Bentley Equipment

Company in 1953, the same year the Steese Highway was rerouted around the property in conjunction with the opening of the Wendell Street Bridge. Miller operated a junkyard on the site for over two decades.

In 1969, Miller, along with his nephew Cliff Burglin, established the Bentley Family Charitable Trust, as there were no surviving members of the Bentley family and their land had not been sold. The Trust took income from the family properties and distributed it to charities, particularly libraries, stretching from Fairbanks to northern California.

As they came to the foot of Birch Hill, Cliff turned off the road onto a dirt trail leading west. The leaves had completely fallen from the trees, which allowed Armand to inspect the land as they slowly drove down the single-lane path. "How much land were you thinking you might need?" asked Cliff.

"At least a hundred acres," replied Armand as he recounted his Valdez experience. "Maybe more."

"Well, as you can see, Armand, this land is as flat as it gets. You have good access off the Steese Highway leading north to the Haul Road and one more big plus that I haven't mentioned."

Armand turned to him and asked, "Oh? What's that?"

Cliff smiled as he negotiated the truck over a fallen black spruce tree and said, "You can build a rail spur directly into the lot. We are only one mile from the Alaska Railroad switchyard. Then Alyeska could transport building materials, pipe coating and bending equipment, and pipe by rail. That could definitely speed things up, uh?"

Armand's mind was spinning at the implications. "Yes, it could, but I'm going to need to send a couple of pipeline engineers up here to double-check things before we talk terms. I can get them here within a week if that's fine with you."

"Sure. What's their names?"

Armand smiled and said, "The gentlemen's names are Sweetheart Morgan and Bugger Parrish. I'll have them call you before they come up. Be kind to them, Cliff."

"That's just great," said Cliff as he turned the truck around in a tight clearing and headed back. "Two engineers who sound like gangsters. What could go wrong with that?"

By the end of October, Morgan and Parrish had inspected the Bentley property and found it suitable for pipe storage. They also flagged a potential rail spur route. With the positive review, Mike Stepovich and Cliff Burglin prepared a lease agreement and sent it to Armand. Armand and Harry reviewed it and after some minor tweaks approved it. Mike sent a copy of the final lease to the Fairbanks Recorders Office. By the first of December, 1970, Alyeska began clearing 120 acres of the Bentley property for the future pipe storage area.

Surveyors also shot a line for the new rail spur. Land Field Services began right-of-way negotiations with private landowners, the City of Fairbanks, and the Alaska Railroad Corporation to accommodate the future rail extension. The goal was to construct the spur the following summer.

Harry was very pleased with the right-of-way progress. With two major pipeline storage areas procured, they could concentrate on settling the hundreds of potential private right-of-way disputes that lay long the proposed pipeline and haul road routes. "Armand," said Harry on one December day, "these lawsuits are a blessing in disguise. They're giving us time to catch our breath and get a handle on the private and mining properties. I want you to direct Land Field Services to start touring the alignment and looking for possible conflicts. I don't want any surprises to spring up at the last minute when we finally get the permits to construct."

Armand nodded and replied, "All right. You realize that's hundreds of miles of walking. It's going to take a while."

"Yes," answered Harry. "So we better start now."

November, 1970 was pivotal for the Alaska political scene. On November 2, William (Bill) Egan beat Keith Miller in the gubernatorial race. Egan was well known in Alaska politics. He was Alaska's first state governor, elected in 1959. He served until 1966, when Walter Hickel beat him. Bill had the uncanny gift of remembering names, places, and families. He could meet a man in Juneau for the first time and two years later smoothly greet him on the streets of Anchorage, recounting his full name, his wife's and children's names, and his occupation. In small-town Alaska, this was a huge asset and Miller's support waned because of it.

Egan also rallied against Miller's ineffectual attempt to push the haul road forward. Egan called Miller's efforts foolhardy and vowed a new look at the vexing oil pipeline problem. Warranted or not, Miller could not withstand the folksy and gregarious Egan. Even Miller's relatively new Alaska residency (less than 10 years) was held against him. Egan simply ran over Miller in the election.

On November 25, President Richard Nixon fired Walter Hickel. After the Ohio National Guard shooting of college students during an anti-Vietnam War demonstration at Kent State, Hickel wrote Nixon a letter criticizing the administration's stance on the war. The letter became public and Hickel was not shy on defending it. In October, CBS 60 Minutes interviewed Hickel and asked him if he would resign under the mounting pressure. Hickel stared straight into the camera and said he would step down only "with an arrow in my heart, not a bullet in my back". Nixon jammed a spear into him.

Armand, Harry, and Jay now faced 1971 with a new Secretary of the Interior, Rogers C.B. Morton, and unresolved Native land, pipeline, and haul road issues.

Harry and Armand were looking forward to a quiet Christmas season. Alyeska had completed the move into the Bragaw building and finished the renovations. The colder weather was starting to restrict activities in the north. They could now concentrate on organizing their files and getting ready for next year's push. Thus, when Harry's telephone rang early Wednesday morning on December 15, neither man expected a crisis.

At first, Harry did not recognize the high-pitched, anxiety-ridden voice until he identified himself. "Harry? This is John Knodell! We've got a problem. I mean a big problem! I need Armand to run down to Valdez and solve it, pronto!"

"Whoa," replied Harry as he sank into his chair. John's angst unnerved him. Harry had never heard him so upset. "What has happened? You need to bring me up to speed."

"Yes, yes, of course," answered John. He took a deep breath to calm himself and proceeded with more restraint. "I just got a telephone call from the Valdez mayor. He was really upset and he speaks for the town. The local Laborers Union set up picket lines at the entrances to our pipeline storage yards. The Laborers Union is upset about that Native-owned company, North Gulf Natives, we hired to help Bannister Pipelines remove the shipping bands from the stacks of pipe. Bannister is union and North Gulf is not.

"Well, Al Renk and Sons is our trucking company to move the pipe from the Valdez dock to the yards. They also truck the pipe up the Richardson to Fairbanks. Renk and Sons employ Teamsters truckers and the truckers refuse to cross the picket line. I guess it's a show of union solidarity. So, with no way to move pipe, the longshoremen unloaded the pipe from the ship and stacked it in town along the streets, in parking lots, and on the Valdez dock. The mayor said people are in an uproar about it! Entire streets are now blocked and people doubt that the ferry can dock."

Harry was overwhelmed. He could think to only ask a very obvious question, "So, what do you want Armand to do?"

"I want him to spread some money around and quiet the people! And I want him to get that pipe moved into our yards!"

Pretty tall order, thought Harry. "OK, John. I'm going to put you on hold and get Armand. I just saw him in the hallway. Then I'll put you on the speaker box and you can explain it to him, alright?"

"OK, but hurry!" John sounded exasperated.

Harry found Armand and told him to stand next to him as he activated the telephone speaker box. "John? We're here. Now explain to Armand what you want done."

John wasted no time getting down to business, "Armand, do you have plenty of money in your draft account? If not, Harry can authorize a sizeable increase."

The question rattled Armand. "Why, yes I do. What's up?"

"Good," continued John, "because you are going to need it. The Valdez truckers went on strike. As luck would have it, the largest freighter ever to dock at Valdez to unload pipe arrived–the <u>Halo</u>. With nowhere to go, the longshoremen dumped the pipe throughout the town—all ten miles of it! People are mad as wet hens because their driveways, roads, and parking lots are filled with our pipe. I need you to go down there as fast as you can and make this right."

Armand stroked his mustache as he glanced at Harry. Harry kept silent and nodded. Armand cleared his throat and said, "I see and how do you expect me to make things right?"

John roared, "Spread some money around, Armand! Pay people for their inconvenience, and while you're at it, see what you can do to solve the strike."

Armand shook his head and thought, *I'm just a landman—not a miracle worker.* "OK, John. I'll drive down early tomorrow morning and see what I can do."

"Tomorrow, hell!" shouted John. "I want you to fly down today. If you can't find a commercial flight, then charter a plane. I want you down there this afternoon! Understand?"

Armand remembered a similar edict from David Henderson to travel to Juneau at a minute's notice. The memory rankled him. Armand steeled himself and replied, "I'll give it a shot, John. I'll let you know how I make out."

John's voice belied his irritation that Armand did not jump at his command. "Do that! Contact me ASAP when you have the situation contained."

"Will do," answered Armand. "Goodbye, John." Harry clicked the box dead.

They stood staring at the speaker box for a few moments before Harry said, "I'm sorry, Armand. John blindsided me, too. Can I help you in any way?"

Armand shook his head and said, "Besides shooting Knodell, nothing. I'll call the airlines and find out what's available. Then I'll see what I can do." Armand started walking out of the office and then stopped and turned to Harry and asked, "Why is it that people call us when something bizarre happens?"

Harry smiled and answered, "Because people trust us. They trust our judgment. They know we're honest. That's what landmen do. Now, go get'em." Armand nodded and disappeared down the hall.

As luck would have it, Polar Airlines had a noon flight to Valdez. Armand jumped aboard armed with a light travel bag and his draft book. He landed at one o'clock and rented a car. Since the airport access road met the Richardson Highway close to the Alyeska pipe yards, Armand decided to stop at the Alyeska field office first before traveling into town.

As he walked in, Armand could hear the field manager, Bill Michaelson, screaming into the phone, "I don't give a damn about your Christmas vacations! You guys choose to strike. And what's more, you knew you had a no-strike clause in your contract and you did it anyhow! Either you kick their tails into their trucks now, or you're finished! Understand? Do it now!" Bill slammed the telephone down, looked up, recognized Armand, and said, "I was wondering when someone from the Anchorage office was going to show up. How are you doing, Armand?"

Armand shook Bill's hand and replied, "I don't rightly know, Bill. I was told to come down here and make it right with the property owners who have pipe on their property. What happened?"

Bill shook his head and said, "A bunch of childish nonsense if you ask me. I think I finally got a handle on it, though. You know that Chugach Native-owned company we hired a month ago, North Gulf Natives, Inc.? Well they showed up here last week ready to work. We helped them set up a man camp and they started out just fine. Meanwhile, the Bannister employees got their panties in a bunch over the fact North Gulf was non-union. So they started picketing entrances to the pipe yards. When I questioned them about it, Bannister said it was an 'unofficial' picket, but that didn't matter to the Teamsters. They parked their trucks and refused to haul pipe. Well, the longshoremen can't stop. That Japanese freighter can't be plugging the dock forever. So they started laying down pipe in town wherever they could."

"Is the strike over?"

"I think so. Like a bunch of kids, I had to separate the entrances to their work areas. We'll be erecting signs today–Bannister pipe goes here and North Gulf goes over there. I hired Loomis Protection Services from Anchorage to secure the entrances and clear the pickets. Loomis should be showing up this afternoon. You heard what I said to the Teamsters. They should be moving shortly."

Armand was relieved. Half of his problem was over. "Good job, Bill. I'll go into town and see what I can do to soothe feelings."

Bill looked at Armand with sincere gratitude and said, "Thank you for coming down, Armand. I appreciate your help keeping the locals happy. I have a tough time striking a balance around here."

"My pleasure," replied Armand. "I think I will stop by the city manager's office first. Dale Cutler is a friend of mine."

Bill shook Armand's hand goodbye and said, "Please thank Dale for me, will ya? He gave the OK to stack the pipe in the streets. I don't know what we would have done without his cooperation."

Armand cocked his head and said, "I didn't know that. I'll tell him. Goodbye and good luck."

Armand got back into his car and drove the ten miles into town. He went straight to the City office and found Dale Cutler waiting for him. "Hey, Armand," said Dale as he greeted him, "I was wondering when you would show up."

Armand smiled as he shook Dale's hand and asked, "Now, how did you know I was coming?"

Dale laughed and said, "The rental car agent called me and gave me a heads up–small-town warning system."

Armand shook his head. He remembered the previous year when the same thing happened when he came to meet with Dale's predecessor to lease city property for the pipe storage yards. Nothing was secret in Valdez. "Well, Dale, I understand we've got pipe strewn around Valdez. Alyeska would like to compensate owners for tying up their property. We would like to start with the City and compensate your office for helping us solve this problem."

Dale nodded and said, "That's very noble of Alyeska. What did you have in mind?"

Armand stroked his mustache in thought for a moment before replying, "I was thinking about a thousand dollars. Would that do it?"

Dale smiled and answered, "That is a very generous offer. A thousand would do it."

"Great," answered Armand! He pulled out his draft book, wrote out a thousand-dollar check to the City of Valdez, and handed it to Dale.

Dale glanced at it, put out his hand for Armand to shake it, and said, "Thank you for thinking of us."

"Not a problem, Dale. Happy to do it. Now, can you direct me to the property owners who were affected by the pipe stacking?"

"That's easy," answered Dale, "only one owner got pipe stacked on their land–the Valdez Dock Company. John Kelsey was gracious enough to allow the pipe to be stacked on his land and he's got a mountain of it!"

Dale's reply stunned Armand. "Just one property owner? I was led to believe that the whole town was suffering."

Dale shook his head and answered, "Don't get me wrong, Armand. The town residents are upset about driving around stacks of pipe, but they'll get over it quick enough. However, only one private property has pipe on it. Looks like you heard an exaggeration."

Armand shook his head in disbelief as he imagined how the story got blown out of proportion–Valdez to Washington DC to Anchorage. "It sure looks like it. I know Mr. Kelsey. I think I'll pay him a visit today and thank him."

Dale replied, "Sounds good. I suppose you will be spending the night here in our fair community."

Armand nodded, "Yeah. It's too late to catch a flight back."

"Well, if I think of anybody else you should see, I'll find you."

Armand grinned and said, "You don't know where I'll be staying. How will you find me?"

Dale gave Armand a knowing smile and replied, "I'll know where you are. Thank you for stopping by."

The town's watching me, thought Armand as he got into his car. He drove over to the Valdez Dock Company which was located next to the city dock. The company had warehouses and support facilities to store goods, fishing supplies, and perform boat repairs. It also had a boat yard now filled with pipe. Armand walked into the office and asked to see Mr. Kelsey. The attendant informed Armand that Kelsey was at a meeting and would be back in an hour.

"That's fine," replied Armand. "I'll check into the motel next door and try to come back later." Armand barely got situated in his motel room when his telephone rang. Kelsey was waiting for him in the lobby. Armand grabbed his draft book and ran out the door.

John Kelsey was a distinguished-looking man–always professionally dressed and well groomed. He was one of the town leaders who had helped rebuild the city after the earthquake. Locals knew him for his generosity, hard work, and his ability to see the whole picture–not just the problem at hand. He smiled when he saw Armand, extended his hand, and said, "Good to see you again, Armand. I heard you were looking for me."

Armand shook his hand and replied, "I was and I am humbled that you came to me first. John, I'm authorized to compensate property owners for the inconvenience they suffered from our temporary pipe storage. Alyeska appreciates the use of your boat yard and I would like to cut you a check for a thousand dollars for your troubles."

John smiled and slowly shook his head as he said, "No, Armand. That's not necessary. We are so thankful that Alyeska chose Valdez as the site for the marine terminal. Already, the project has been an economical boon to our community. If I have to be inconvenienced for a few days, so be it."

Armand smiled. He knew John Kelsey would refuse the payment. He was truly an exceptional man. Armand opened his draft book, wrote out a thousand-dollar check to the Valdez Dock Company, tore it off the pad, and handed it to John. "Mr. Kelsey, if you have any sympathy at all for me, please accept this check. In all honesty, my supervisor will give me hell if you don't. Please, sir."

John hesitated for a moment before reluctantly taking the check from Armand's hand. "Thank you. However, this is truly unwarranted."

"No, it's fair," countered Armand. "What's more, if for some reason the pipe is not moved off your property in the next few days, please call me." Armand handed John his card.

The day ended with the landman solving the problems of the day and promoting goodwill for the company. Unfortunately, not every day would end like this.

Chapter 8

Staking Claims

Nineteen seventy-one became the year of the paper trail. The Department of the Interior completed their Draft Environmental Impact Statement (DEIS) early in the year. This was the first NEPA analysis ever done in the United States, so there was no guidance or court cases to direct the investigation. Sailing into uncharted waters, the DOI decided to give every alternative for transporting oil to markets equal weight. Thus, the anticipated pipeline impacts were compared to ice-breaking supertankers, gargantuan dirigibles and cargo aircraft, nuclear-powered submarine tankers, and an Arctic railroad.

NEPA clearly stated that the public must have a chance to review the DEIS and comment on it. However, NEPA failed to mention how to do this. DOI responded by advertising and holding public hearings in Fairbanks, Anchorage, and Juneau. In addition, DOI held hearings in several metropolitan areas in the Lower 48 including Washington DC. Meetings in Fairbanks, Anchorage, and Washington were especially contentious. Shouting matches flared in Fairbanks between developers and conservationists, each accusing the other of deception. Neither side was happy with the DEIS. The developers thought it was too theoretical and a waste of time. The conservationists chanted that the DEIS was a whitewash of the true project impacts and more alternatives needed to be analyzed.

The DOI allotted the Anchorage hearing two full days. It spilled over to five days to accommodate the swelling ranks of people wanting to testify. Some people commandeered the podium and security had to pry the microphone from their hands and drag them away as they shouted their last thoughts.

The Washington DC hearing was the most controversial. Pro and con forces were highly organized for the event. John Knodell and Quinn O'Connell gave carefully prepared statements among catcalls and snorts from the crowd. The Sierra Club and FOE ranted against the DEIS. Then they announced that their teams would perform their own EIS.

The DOI summarized all comments received during the hearing process and written comments sent to them during the public involvement period. The transcripts and letters swelled the DEIS from 256 to over 12,000 pages.

The NEPA process overshadowed another federal effort that had major ramifications for Alyeska–the settlement of Alaska Native claims. The newly appointed Alyeska President, Ed Patton, correctly stated during an Anchorage Chamber of Commerce luncheon that the pipeline design, developing EIS, and permitting meant nothing until the Alaska Native land issues were resolved. Without it, the federal government could not issue land patents to Alaska or grant right-of-way for the project.

The Organic Act of 1884 provided legal standing for Alaskan Natives to claim land. It stated, "Indians or other persons in said district shall not be disturbed in the possession of any lands actually in their use or occupation or now claimed by them, but the terms under which such persons may acquire title to such lands is reserved for future legislation by Congress."

Alaska Natives organized under the Alaska Federation of Natives and the Arctic Slope Native Association (ASNA). Both of these groups claimed rights to over 300 million acres, including the entire North Slope. Because of their legal standing and ferocity, Interior Secretary Udall enacted the federal freeze on granting Alaska land patents until a settlement could be reached. During the next twelve months, Native, federal, state, and oil interests would viciously clash before the passage of a land claims settlement act.

During January 1971, Armand was checking his field notes when he stumbled upon his entry about the State appraisers visiting the future Valdez terminal site. He was curious about the appraised value and it tore at him, but Armand knew this information was confidential. He thought about it for a few minutes and decided to call an old friend who worked in the ADNR Appraisal Office. Al Olson answered on the second ring.

"Al, this is Armand Spielman. How's life treating you?"

"Just fine," replied Al who sounded genuinely pleased that Armand had called him. "How is life in the pipeline business? I haven't talked to you for over a year, now."

After exchanging some pleasantries, Armand got to the point. "Say, Al, the reason that I'm calling you is to see if you guys had finalized the appraisal of the Valdez Terminal tract. I'm trying to manage the expectations of my Washington DC office and prevent sticker shock. I was wondering if you had an idea how much you were going to ask for it."

Al went silent for a moment before answering. "Ah, Armand, you know that information is confidential until we're ready to go public with it."

Armand suddenly felt guilty for asking, but still he pressed the matter. "That's right, but that won't happen for at least six months, maybe longer. I was hoping to get a feel of what you guys were thinking before that. I need to grease the skids in Washington so there's no pushback."

"To tell you the truth, Armand, the valuation will be decided in Governor Egan's Office. I have no say in it." This surprised Armand. "Really? Why's that?"

"Because this project is very high profile and the Governor wants to milk every drop of it."

I bet he does. "OK, Al. Thanks for the information. I'll have Harry make a few calls."

"No problem, Armand. Good luck!"

Two days later, Harry came back with the answer. "A little under ten million."

Armand wrote this value in his notebook as he said, "I think that is a very reasonable price. I'll call John Knodell and convince him, too."

Armand called John immediately. It was past six in the evening in Washington, but John was still there. "Hello, Armand," greeted John. "How are things in Alaska? Cold and dark?"

"A little of both," replied Armand. "Say, the governor's office gave us a whiff of their valuation of the Valdez Terminal tract. The State is thinking they want ten million dollars for it."

"Really?" Armand could hear John's interest pique. "Do you think this is a fair value?"

"Very fair," answered Armand. "I was anticipating twenty."

"OK. I think Quinn and I will pay DOI a visit soon and see if we can get an exception to the Udall land freeze. The quicker the Feds grant a patent to the State, the quicker we can buy it. Thank you for the information, Armand. I'll keep you informed about our progress." They said their goodbyes and Armand hung up wondering what he had just set in motion.

The Houston engineers recognized early in the design process that construction was going to be a logistical nightmare. Efficiently moving pipe to the construction site was going to require three pipeline storage yards, one at each end of the project and one in the middle. They had storage yards in Valdez and Fairbanks. Now they needed one in Prudhoe Bay. BP had transferred Gordon Goulston to Houston so he could work closely with the pipeline design. Gordon called Armand and informed him about their needs for a Prudhoe pipe yard.

"I say, old chap, are you ready for your next challenge?" asked Gordon.

"As long as it is not my Waterloo," replied Armand. He liked jousting with Gordon.

"Good show, Armand. The boys here determined that we need a pipe yard in Prudhoe. Are you game for that?"

"OK," mused Armand. "How big and where?"

Gordon answered, "If we could have our full cake, we would take 150 acres next to the Beaufort Sea. This way we could build a causeway and dock to unload barges and store the pipe close by. Sound doable, old chap?"

"It does. Let me make a few calls and see what I can do. I'll keep you informed."

"Tally ho, Armand."

When Armand hung up, his mind started wheeling about how best to approach the Prudhoe Bay yard problem. He then decided to visit an old acquaintance at ADNR named Dale Tubbs. Dale was Joe Kennan's deputy director of the Land Division.

Dale was anxiously waiting for Armand when he arrived at the ADNR office. Armand had sounded serious on the telephone when he told him that he wanted to discuss something very important. "Armand," greeted Dale as he heartily shook his hand, "what's got you so spun up this morning? Don't tell me Alyeska wants to build the pipeline tomorrow?"

Armand smiled as he shook his head and said, "We're a long ways from that. But to build the line, we are going to need another pipe-storage yard. So, with hat in hand, I'm here to discuss a possible site with you at Prudhoe Bay."

"Sounds intriguing. Let's go over to the plats and see what we have." Dale motioned for Armand to follow him to the plat room where ADNR stored their land files. The room had a large conference table and counters suitable for spreading survey plats and reading them.

Dale pulled a large reference book from the counter and opened it. The book summarized plats and leases throughout Alaska through a series of miniature maps and tables. Dale's finger traced the entries for Prudhoe Bay. After a couple of minutes, he shook his head and said, "Armand, I'm afraid the entire area is covered with oil and gas leases."

Armand scratched his chin and said, "Well, can't we insert a use into a lease? As long as we don't interfere with their ability to extract oil and gas, we should have legal access to the surface."

Dale lifted an eyebrow and asked, "You mean encumber an existing lease? I guess that's possible. Where and how much land do you need?"

Armand put his finger on a land section that bordered the southeastern shore of Prudhoe Bay. "How about a quarter of this map section? That'll give us 160 acres and access to water."

Dale checked the reference table and said, "That would be the ARCO-Humble Oil and Gas Lease. I think that's doable, especially since the use is for storing pipe to transport oil removed from Prudhoe oil leases. I'll send you the lease agreement tomorrow morning, OK?"

Armand doubted that anywhere else in the world could he negotiate a pipe yard lease so quickly. He smiled and shook Dale's hand as he replied, "That will work just fine. Thank you, Dale." Within a few days, Alyeska had their critical staging areas secured with pipeline storage yards in Valdez, Fairbanks, and Prudhoe Bay.

In March, Armand began receiving unsolicited telephone calls about "Dayville land near Valdez." He noticed that the calls came every two weeks, each time from a different caller. He would ask, "Where exactly is this land?" and the callers would answer in vague terms, but they were willing to sell it for around a million dollars if he acted within two weeks or else the offer would be revoked. Armand usually hung up on the sellers and wrote them off as crackpots.

The calls continued for six weeks until one late afternoon a man Armand knew and trusted called and made Armand a similar offer. "Locke Jacobs!" exclaimed Armand, "How did you get tied up in this mess?" Locke was a longtime oil lease broker in Alaska. Armand had first met him in Los Angeles in 1958 when he approached Richfield Oil to drill wells on his lease holdings along the Swanson River on the Kenai Peninsula. He made a fortune when Richfield Oil drilled the successful discovery well that defined the Swanson River Oil Fields. Richfield did not have the money to develop the fields, so they partnered with Chevron to help finance the development. Chevron had sent Jay Sullivan to Alaska to acquire pipeline routes from the Swanson River field to the new Nikiski refinery.

"Oh, I don't know, Armand," replied Locke. "This guy dangled a land option in front of me like a giant lure and, being the big dope that I am, I struck at it. This is the deal. I bought an option to sell the property for $20,000. The terms are that I have to sell it within two weeks."

OK, thought Armand, *this explains the phone calls twice a month.* "Where is the land, Locke?"

"My option is next to the Dayville Homestead by Allison Creek. The guys that I am dealing with want to sell you the homestead and the five-acre trade and manufacturing claim on Swan Port."

"How much do you want for your option?" asked Armand.

"Look, Armand, I only want my $20,000 investment back, but the other guys want a good deal more. Would you be willing to meet with us and see what we've got?"

If anyone else would have asked to meet, Armand would have declined, but out of respect for Locke and pure curiosity, he agreed. "All right, Locke, I'll meet with you. But first, I need to get authority from our Houston office to pursue it. I'll call you back in a couple of days. OK?"

"Sounds good. Thank you." They said their goodbyes and hung up. Armand looked at his watch and realized the Houston office was closed. Houston was four hours ahead of Anchorage. He decided to call them early the next morning.

Armand arrived at his office at six a.m. the next day. He made some coffee, sat down, and dialed his old friend Gordon Goulston in Houston. Gordon answered with his typical upbeat demeanor, "Jolly good morning to you, old chap! I say, what brings you to the world so early? I wasn't expecting any Anchorage folk chirping up for another hour or two."

Armand enjoyed talking to Gordon. "Good morning to you, Gordon. I'm calling because we have an opportunity to purchase the Walter Day Homestead. It's next to Allison Creek across from Valdez. I was wondering if you have any use for it."

"By Jove, we were just talking about it! That homestead would be the perfect place for a construction camp to build the marine terminal. I say we go for it!"

"All right. Can you fax me the authority to pursue it?"

Gordon sounded a little crestfallen when he replied, "I'm afraid that's slightly above my pay grade, old chap. However, I'll see to it right away. Don't despair."

"OK, Gordon. I'll be waiting."

The fax arrived later that afternoon authorizing Armand to proceed with land negotiations. Armand immediately called Locke and told him to exercise his option. "We're interested," he told Locke.

"That's great, Armand," exclaimed Locke, "however, I was just made aware that another person wants to sell his adjoining property, too. I would also like to invite him and his lawyer to the meeting. Is that OK with you?"

Armand thought, *this is getting more complicated than I like.* "All right, I guess it wouldn't hurt to listen to what they have got to say. What's the lawyer's name?"

Locke laughed and said, "King Fish Arnold."

Armand snorted and replied, "Sounds like one of your Unalakleet friends."

"Actually," answered Locke, "he's a bit of a wheeler-dealer, but a good guy. He got his nickname after representing the Cook Inlet Fishermen Association. It kind of stuck. His real name is Bill Arnold. He will be representing George Atkinson, president of A&G Construction Company, and Mrs. Oma Day. George owns the adjoining land."

"OK. I'll have our lawyer, Paul Robison, with me, too. Shall we meet within two days?"

"That will work fine. How about 10 a.m. on Thursday at Bill's office in the Lathrop Building on Fifth Avenue?"

"OK, Locke. We'll see you then." When Armand hung up, he had a feeling Locke had just roped him into something that was far from straightforward.

Before the Thursday meeting, Armand decided he'd better inform Harry Brelsford about the upcoming Dayville negotiations. Harry quietly listened to his explanation. When he was done, Harry remained quiet for a moment as he stared at Armand. Then he said, "Armand, let me get this straight. You think it is in Alyeska's best interest to participate in a $20,000 land scam perpetuated by a lawyer named King Fish Arnold? Also, isn't Mr. Atkinson the one who filed a suit against the Forest Service to revoke our land use permit and filed an application with the Army Corps of Engineers to build a dock right where we want to build ours? Honestly, Armand, I thought better of you."

Armand flushed with embarrassment. He shook his head and said, "It does sound bad when you put it that way, doesn't it? But seriously, if we could gain possession of the homestead and surrounding property, Houston will stage the marine terminal construction from there. I think it's worth our time to hear what they have to say."

Harry drummed his fingers on his desk for a moment as he contemplated the situation. He heard alarm bells going off in his head. Finally he said, "OK, let's call Paul Robison and see if he knows Arnold."

Harry dialed Paul's number and put the telephone receiver on a speaker box. Paul picked up on the second ring. He could tell that he was on a speaker by the cavernous sound. "Paul," greeted Harry, "this is Harry and Armand. May we have a moment of your time?"

"Good morning, gentlemen," answered Paul. "Sure, what's on your minds?"

Harry continued, "Paul, have you ever heard of a guy named Bill King Fish Arnold?"

Paul let out a laugh and said, "Yes, I have. He's quite a character, but actually a nice guy and a competent lawyer. I hate to ask, but why?"

"So, it wouldn't surprise you that he is associated with men trying to make a fast buck off land options?"

"Not at all," answered Paul. "Now you really have my interest. What's up?"

"Well, Armand got sucked up into a Valdez land scam with Arnold and Locke Jacobs. They want to meet in two days to discuss the property and terms. We'd like to have you there."

Paul's voice was thick with anticipation, "I wouldn't miss it for the world. When and where?"

Armand answered, "Ten o'clock, Thursday, at Arnold's office."

"I'll be there," replied Paul. "In the meantime, I suggest we all do a little homework before the meeting and see if we can figure out what land they're talking about."

"I agree," said Harry. "It's the old Dayville homestead and I think Arnold is the genius behind the Atkinson's lawsuit and dock permit application. We'll see you there, Paul. Thank you."

When Harry pressed the disconnect button on the speaker box, he turned to Armand and said, "Armand, you got your work cut out for you. I want you to pull the BLM case files and see who owns what, OK?"

"Got it," replied Armand as he walked towards the door. He was already regretting that he had agreed to meet with Locke.

The morning meeting began in Mr. Arnold's Anchorage downtown office at ten sharp. Bill Arnold chaired the meeting from the head of a moderately large conference table. Sitting around the table were Armand, Harry, Paul, Locke, and George Atkinson. The atmosphere was festive as introductions were made.

Bill was a large, well-dressed man in his late 70s. His balding head and broad shoulders gave him a wise grandfather look. He had a clean-shaven face with savvy eyes that saw everything and revealed nothing. Armand thought his nickname was appropriate because he looked like a huge king salmon sitting at the head of the table.

After a few minutes of cordial discussions, Bill brought the meeting into focus. "Gentlemen, we are here to discuss the sale of two different land holdings associated with the Dayville Homestead. Mr. Jacobs has an option to buy a 30-acre parcel adjacent to the homestead. Mr. Atkinson has a lease and an option to buy 229 acres of land that consists of the homestead, the old Fort Liscum military site, and the trade and manufacturing claim at Swan Port."

"Does anyone have a map of these parcels?" interjected Paul.

Bill shook his head and said, "Not at present. My intent was to determine if Alyeska was interested enough to proceed with negotiations."

"We're interested, Bill," said Paul with a hint of irritation. "We're here, aren't we? You should have been ready with plats and legal descriptions." King Fish Arnold only shrugged.

Armand took the floor. "Gentlemen, I have researched the land status of the Day family homestead and it's true that Mr. Atkinson has leased the property. However, there are several surveys in this area, some with gaps. Are you sure that some of this land is not in the public domain?"

George Atkinson looked over to Bill and nodded at him to address Armand. "Mr. Spielman," said Mr. Arnold, looking down upon Armand as if he were lecturing a wayward student, "you are mistaken. If you had searched more thoroughly, you would have discovered that Mr. Edwin Thorne had two mineral claims in this area. When he abandoned his claims, Walter Day came to me to help him secure the land to adjoin his homestead. I pleaded with the BLM to survey the claims, which they finally did, and Mr. Day purchased it."

"We need maps," groaned Paul.

Harry sliced right to a gnawing question, "Mr. Arnold, did you file Mr. Atkinson's lawsuit against the Forest Service?"

King Fish Arnold studied Harry with a deadpan face for a few moments before replying, "I assisted Mr. Atkinson with the proper instruments to protect his interests."

"Uh, I bet," answered Harry, "and I suppose you assisted Mr. Atkinson with his dock permit application, too?" King Fish remained quiet. Harry went on the offensive. "OK, so here's the deal. Not only will you bring plats and full legal descriptions to our next meeting, but I want to see a draft court pleading to retract your suit and application. Understand? Failing to do so, we will cease our negotiations and when we receive our permit to construct, we will petition the State of Alaska to proceed with condemnation."

Harry had just upped the ante and King Fish knew it. Finally, Bill Arnold asked, "When would you like to meet?"

"As soon as possible. How about in one week? We could meet here, same day and time," answered Harry.

Bill nodded, "That will work fine."

"Good!" replied Harry. "Paul, do you have anything to add?"

"No," answered Paul, "I think you concisely summarized the situation."

"How about you, Armand?"

Armand shook his head and said, "Nothing more except that I will be in Fairbanks at the federal gravel sale next week. I'm really not needed here anymore."

Harry rose and stuck out his hand to King Fish Arnold and said, "OK, Mr. Arnold, we'll meet next week and discuss this situation further. Thank you for your time." Bill stiffly shook his hand and wished him a good day. As Armand grasped his hand and said goodbye, he felt their paths would someday cross again.

Once outside, Harry emitted a long sigh and said, "That William King Fish Arnold is a piece of work."

Paul smiled and said, "Yes he is—the quintessential poker player. I bet Atkinson promised him a percentage of the sale price."

"I agree," said Harry as they approached their parked car. "So, I say we fight fire with fire."

"What do you mean?" asked Armand.

Harry opened the passenger door, looked at Armand and Paul, and said, "When we walk into Mr. Arnold's conference room next week, we'll have Mr. Jay Sullivan at our side. Then we will see how King Fish Arnold likes looking up at his opponent instead of gazing down through his nose at us."

Armand suddenly wished he could be there.

───────────────

The following week, when Armand was negotiating a multi-million-dollar gravel sale with the BLM in Fairbanks, the Alyeska landmen entered Bill Arnold's office. Mr. Arnold solemnly greeted each man at the door and shook his hand. Jay entered last and King Fish Arnold gawked at the size of the man before him. For a split second, Arnold lost his professor-like composure and glanced over at Harry with a look of *What the hell?* This was precisely the effect Harry wanted.

Jay immediately went on the offensive. He smiled as he looked down upon Bill and said, "Mr. William Arnold, I presume. Nice to finally meet the man behind the Valdez scams and swindles."

Bill sputtered in protest, "That is outrageous. Nothing of the sort. We are completely aboveboard . . ."

Jay cut him off. "Well then, Mr. Arnold, if that is true, this meeting will be very short. Shall we sit down and see what you have?" Without waiting for an answer, Jay took a seat at the table between Mr. Atkinson and King Fish Arnold.

The exchange and Jay's presence clearly flustered Bill. He tried to open the meeting with a short diatribe about his client's hard work and integrity, but with a wave of his massive hand, Jay brought the meeting to a head. "Bill, we are not here to evaluate Mr. Atkinson. We agreed to meet on three issues. They are: one–review your proof that your client controls the properties of interest; two–drafts of your intent to rescind your lawsuit and dock permit application; and three–your sale price. Shall we begin?"

"This is highly irregular," protested King Fish Arnold.

"No, it is not," replied Jay, looking straight at him. "You can start by showing us the BLM surveys."

"Let's roll out the plats," said Atkinson. He clearly wanted to get down to business. Arnold reluctantly complied and spread three plats on the table. Jay pounced on them and immediately began to analyze the notes.

The negotiations lasted two hours until a sale price and terms were hammered out. Alyeska agreed to purchase the Walter Day Homestead, associated parcels, and the trade and manufacturing lease for two million dollars. The money would be divided between George Atkinson and Locke Jacobs according to their own prior arrangement. However, Harry, Paul, and Jay were not satisfied with Arnold's assurances that he would revoke the lawsuit and dock permit application. Therefore, they insisted on establishing an escrow account at the First National Bank of Anchorage. The bank would hold the two million dollars in escrow until Arnold withdrew the lawsuit and permit application.

Harry also insisted on one final stipulation—both parties would keep the sale price confidential. He knew if the sale price went public, every scam artist in Alaska would be scheming ways to lock up potential right-of-way lands. Unfortunately, Harry's premonition proved to be very accurate.

Although acceptable terms were finally hammered out, the King Fish Arnold land episode had rattled Harry. The pipeline project was not designed yet and already the scammers were coming out of the closet. Harry knew that more swindlers would ambush them as the project progressed and the only way to minimize problems was to get a handle on possible conflicts. This meant walking the entire route to discover private holdings. Vast portions of the proposed right-of-way crossed public-domain lands. The surveyors marked the route as efficiently as they could, taking survey shots as long as four miles to minimize vegetation clearing and traversing difficult terrain. Thus, the surveyors would miss signs of prior use such as mining claim stakes, surveyed corner posts, and cabins within the route.

Harry was very concerned about these omissions generating another Valdez situation. He called Armand into his office one day in early July and asked him for a status report of Land Field Services inspecting the route. "Armand," began Harry, "what's Land Field's progress of walking the alignment? It's been over eight months since I requested they start. How's that going?"

Armand felt embarrassment creep into his face when he realized that he had not followed up on Harry's instructions. He looked at Harry and said, "Truthfully, I don't know. I got caught up in everything else and forgot to ask. Sorry, Harry, I'll call Jay today."

Harry understood. They had been overwhelmed with other priorities. "It's all right," he said, "but I want a renewed effort on the reconnaissance, OK? I don't want another Valdez fiasco."

"Understood," answered Armand. "I'll call now." No man likes being called on the carpet by his boss and Armand was no exception. As he marched back to his office, he was determined to motivate Jay to execute Harry's directive. He dialed Jay's office and Shirley answered on the second ring.

"Armand," she cooed, "it's so good to hear from you!"

Shirley's voice calmed Armand and completely disarmed him. He felt his humor return as he answered, "Not too bad, Shirley. I was wondering if you could wake Jay up from behind his desk and put him on the phone."

Shirley sighed and said, "I'll see what I can do, but I'm not promising anything." She put Armand on hold. Jay came on seconds later.

"Good morning, Armand," boomed Jay over the phone. "How's Anchor town treating you?"

"Not bad, Jay. Say, Harry asked me this morning how the route inspection was going. He wants to know how far your team has walked the proposed right-of-way. So, where are you?"

Jay went silent for a moment. Truth was that Jay had tried, but he did not have any young men with right-of-way experience to walk the alignment. Jay and John Pate were old war veterans with battle wounds that prevented long-distance hikes. In addition, their cigarette smoking had greatly reduced their endurance. Jay doubted Keith Christenson possessed the physical stamina to perform the work, either. So any inspections done were restricted to the close proximity of a road, which resulted in sporadic checks.

Jay coughed and said, "I'm afraid we're lacking in that department, Armand. We've inspected some short spans, but not the whole line."

Armand was direct and to the point, "Jay, Harry wants to prevent another Valdez situation. Thus, he wants your team to walk the line now. Understand?"

Jay rubbed his buzz-cut head and nodded as he spoke into the phone, "I understand, Armand. We'll get on it."

"Thanks, Jay. Let me know how things are progressing."

When they had hung up, Jay continued to rub his head as he closed his eyes and thought about the problem for a few minutes. Suddenly, a face materialized in his mind. "Bobby!" he shouted as he sprang up and began to walk out of the office.

Shirley called after him, "Where are you going, boss?"

"I'm going to the Traveler's Inn for a drink," bellowed Jay as he opened the door.

"But it's only ten in the morning!" Shirley waited for a reply, but Jay was already down the hall.

By early afternoon, Jay was drunk. He had persuaded the young bartender to surreptitiously serve him drinks before the bar opened at one o'clock. He sat at the bar nursing his whisky on the rocks and smoking the last of his cigarettes. Jay swirled his glass again and looked around the room. He liked to drink at the Kobuk Room in the Traveler's Inn. The bar was newly renovated, clean, and usually quiet–except for the construction in the adjacent room. However, the renovation was nearly complete and the interior decorators were putting their final touches to the Bear and Seal Lounge. Jay thought it looked fancy.

He turned his attention to the young man behind the bar. His name was Bob Ylvisaker and Jay had known him since 1968. Bob was the Kobuk bartender then–working from 6 p.m. to 2 a.m. Jay naturally got to know him well. Since Bob was young and had his days free, Jay had got him a part-time job with Alaska Title and Guarantee reconstructing flood-damaged property files to earn some extra cash. The work was repetitive and mindless, but Bob picked up the basics of land descriptions and legal documents.

Jay had taken a shine to Bob and invited him to his Anchorage home for Thanksgiving. Bob continued to return to the Sullivan household and never missed their yearly Thanksgiving feast. Jay called him Bobby as a term of endearment and a little jibe.

Bob was in his early 30s. He was clean-cut, dressed professionally, and appeared to be under great stress. Jay watched him open boxes of glassware, inspect the contents, and write notes on a clipboard. "Busy day, Bobby?" asked Jay.

Bob barely looked up as he replied, "Yeah. Old man Hickel wants his new lounge opened next week. We aren't even close to being ready."

Jay popped an ice cube in his mouth and sucked on it. "So, you are the lucky man in charge of it?"

Jay's comment produced a wicked grin across Bob's face as he sarcastically replied, "Yeah, lucky me."

Jay looked at Bob thoughtfully and said, "So how does a young man like you get tagged with such an important responsibility?" Bob put down his clipboard, walked over to Jay, and pulled up a stool from behind the bar. Jay could tell he had a story to tell.

Bob's smile gave him a boyish charm. He shook his head and said, "To tell you the truth, I got the job because I was the last man standing. Everyone else had quit from the hectic schedule. I went from bartender, to bar manager, to food and beverage manager. So, here I am. Simple as that."

Jay took sip of whiskey and said, "You know, bartending isn't the only thing you've done in your past, Bobby."

Bob nodded and replied, "You're right. I worked at the title agency for a couple of months, but that was four years ago. I've been a bartender ever since."

As Jay put out his last cigarette, Bob asked, "How's your drink holding up?"

"My drink's fine, but we need to talk."

Bob shook his head and replied, "I better get going. The hotel manager over there is giving me the evil eye." Jay looked over his shoulder and saw an impeccably dressed man scowling at Bob.

Jay snorted, turned to Bob and said, "Just a minute, Bob. I'm prepared to offer you employment that I guarantee will be mutually beneficial. Are you interested?"

Bob stopped dead in his tracks. He glanced at the manager and then back to Jay before asking, "Doing what?"

"Land work with my firm."

Bob nodded and replied, "OK, but we can't talk here."

"All right," answered Jay as he stood up, "let's go to the bathroom. They allow you to go to the head once in a while, right?"

"Every once in a while."

Jay laboriously pushed himself away from the bar and said, "OK. I'm headed there now." He staggered towards the bathroom with a wavering but determined gait. Bob watched him go for a moment before shrugging and following him. When Bob entered the bathroom, Jay was already positioned at a urinal and preparing to relieve himself. Bob took the urinal next to him.

There is an unspoken creed among men not to speak to each other while using the urinal. If anything is said at all, it is to be uttered in brief monosyllable words or consist of reciting a crude joke written on the wall. Nothing else is acceptable. However, Jay never conformed to traditions. He quickly laid out his terms to Bob.

"OK. Here's the deal," said Jay as he urinated loudly. "We've got a large contract with Alyeska Pipeline Service Company and I need help. I can promise you at least two maybe three years of work. I'll pay you one and half times your current salary. You can start tomorrow. What do you say?"

Bob was overwhelmed–by the job offer and by the unorthodox setting. Here he was urinating next to a large man who obviously had too much to drink and had to make a snap decision about a job offer. Bob had heard strange things happened in Alaska, and this was a prime example, but he knew Jay and trusted him. So, Bob went for it. "What the hell? I'll take it. But we'll wash our hands first before we shake on it."

"Outstanding!" announced Jay as he finished up. The old Sullivan charm had done it again.

On April 27, 1971, the Cordova District Fisheries Union (CDFU) filed an injunction in the Washington DC federal court against Rogers C. B. Morton, Secretary of the Interior, and Clifford Hardin, Secretary of Agriculture. The injunction had two parts. The first request was that the court would invalidate the US Forest Service special use permit for the Valdez Marine Terminal. The second request was that Mr. Morton would not be permitted to issue the right-of-way for the TAPS pipeline. Judge Hart once again presided over the court proceedings.

The CDFU claimed that the Forest Service violated their regulations when they issued the special permit to TAPS for the 802 acres in Valdez. According to CDFU, the Forest Service could only issue a permit for a maximum of only 80 acres. Thus, the special permit was invalid.

The CDFU also charged that the DOI did not consider the impacts to Prince William Sound fishing grounds from supertankers shuttling oil from Valdez to the world markets in the EIS. The CDFU was especially concerned about the proposed Valdez marine terminal impacts to the Valdez Arm. CDFU believed the terminal would poison the waters from tanker operations, spills from transferring the oil, and discharging the tanker ballast water. Therefore, CDFU believed that DOI was in violation of NEPA.

In response to the CDFU lawsuit, the Environmental Protection Agency, National Oceanic and Atmospheric Administration, and the Sea Grant Foundation funded biological and oceanographic studies of the Valdez Arm in June 1971. The University of Alaska's research ship, *Acona*, began mapping the bathymetry and collecting baseline biological and chemical data of the benthic and pelagic environments. Special attention was given to anticipated effects from the discharge of tanker ballast water.

Empty supertankers entering Prince William Sound would have their cargo tanks partially filled with seawater. This allowed the tankers to sail lower in the water, which increased stability. Regulatory agencies and conservation groups such as the CDFU were concerned that discharge would contain poisonous concentrations of hydrocarbons and possible invasive species that could harm the surrounding environment. Alyeska committed to building a water treatment plant to decontaminate the ballast discharges before releasing it into the Valdez Arm.

By the end of June, all three pipeline storage yards were in full operation mode, cleaning and coating pipe. The company in charge of the operation, Surfcote, Inc., had mobilized state-of-the-art equipment that cleaned the pipe, etched it with a zinc-based rust inhibitor, and sprayed the entire pipe with an epoxy coating. Surfcote employed hundreds of men statewide to treat the 800 miles of pipe. This made a significant contribution to the economies of Fairbanks and Valdez.

All pipe required for the TAPS project had been delivered to their respective storage yards. The following lists pipe lengths stored at each site:

- Valdez – 343 miles
- Fairbanks – 289 miles
- Prudhoe Bay – 168 miles

Alyeska released more engineering details of the Yukon River Bridge. It would now span 2,280 feet and require massive abutments to withstand the ice scour when the river ice dramatically broke up every spring.

Alyeska also released volume estimates of non-frost-susceptible gravel required to build the pipeline work pad and haul road–56.5 million cubic yards. Some thought this estimate was seriously low and believed it should be twice that amount. Non-frost-susceptible gravel was a critical resource for building across permafrost. The term non-frost-susceptible meant the gravel would not expand (heave) when frozen. To prevent heave, the gravel had to have less than 10 percent fines such as silt. Silt content greater than 10 percent caused water to wick into the strata and expand when frozen. Thus, Alyeska needed good sources of acceptable gravel or prepare to process it to create the required material. Since it was far cheaper to mine acceptable material, Alyeska embarked on an aggressive drilling program to find it.

From June 20 through 25, 1971, Secretary of the Interior Rogers C. B. Morton and his wife Ann visited Alaska for the first time since President Nixon had tapped him to replace Walter Hickel. Unlike Hickel, Morton was a large man (six-feet, seven inches) with a methodical and reserved demeanor. He told the press that he wanted to tour Alaska and understand the national and state issues that dominated the newspapers. Morton carefully avoided questions about his support for the pipeline and restated that his department was committed to assisting Russell Train in completing an EIS that could withstand public scrutiny.

Rogers Morton had no trouble finding Alaskans who were willing to share their views. Everywhere he and Ann went, people were waiting to pounce on them and demand an audience. They greeted his airplane in Valdez, Anchorage, Fairbanks, and Prudhoe Bay. Concerned citizens waited for them at their hotel lobbies or simply grabbed them in the streets. The Mortons were congenial and accepted most speaking offers and even toured the Valdez pipeline storage yard and witnessed the pipeline coating. However, some still believed they were not given an opportunity to voice their concerns, especially the conservationists and Native land claim supporters. Morton specifically addressed the Cordova District Fisheries Union lawsuit by declaring that the DOI would investigate all feasible alternatives to shipping oil to the west coast.

Secretary Morton also used his Alaska visit to announce that he had selected Burt Silcock as his new national director of BLM. This meant Burt had to relocate to Washington DC. Morton appointed Curtis McVee as the acting state BLM director. McVee had served as a deputy to Silcock. Although McVee was well versed in Alaskan issues, Harry Brelsford was sorry to see Burt leave. Harry had a good relationship with Burt and did not know McVee very well.

The US Department of the Interior continued to churn out the final EIS for the Trans Alaska Pipeline System. In July 1971, Alyeska provided the DOI with a full project description for the EIS. The description included the first detailed engineering design. The design planned to elevate about 136 miles of the line. However, Alyeska was still evaluating whether to elevate an additional 240 miles of the pipeline. The company had found sporadic areas of unstable permafrost along the interior route. To minimize surprises, Alyeska began a massive drilling program to collect soil samples every third of a mile along the centerline.

Engineers now realized that the elevated pipeline sections would require an active refrigeration system to stabilize the thaw-unstable permafrost areas. They began to experiment with nonmoving heat pumps called thermopiles. Thermopiles utilized gas (usually ammonia) to pull heat from the ground during the winter and radiate the heat into the air through metal fins. Eventually, a frost bulb would form, anchoring the piles into the ground.

The DOI documented the engineering and environmental studies in the EIS, which now encompassed six volumes plus 26 appendices. This work in progress filled two long library shelves in the DOI library—and it was still growing.

While DOI project approval awaited the completion of the Final EIS and the resolution of Native land claims, the State of Alaska began to slide into financial trouble. The 1969 Prudhoe Bay lease sale had generated about $900 million for Alaska coffers and the government responded by doubling their state budget to more than $300 million for the fiscal year 1970–1971. Then Governor Egan approved a significantly higher budget for the 1971–1972 fiscal year.

Suddenly, Alaska realized they had spent their windfall. The legislature responded by raising the production royalty tax from 4 percent to 12 percent, but the raise would have no effect until oil flowed through the not-yet-built pipeline. Panic swept through the legislative halls as politicians realized Alaska was going broke. This meant the legislators were faced with the politically unsavory choice of cutting the state budget and canceling promised capital improvement projects. The pipeline delay simply had to end. The legislators turned to Governor Egan and demanded that he find a solution.

———————————

Bob Ylvisaker was winded from scaling the short, steep hill, but he was not as devastated as John Pate. The burly ex-marine sat down on a boulder and wheezed, "Hold up a sec, will ya? Stop trying to outrun me!"

Outrun you? thought Bob. He barely crept up the hill. John was clearly out of shape and suffering the effects of decades of smoking and drinking. "Take as long as you want, John. You're the guide."

"Yeah? Well don't forget it," barked John. Bob knew John was masking his embarrassment with bravado. Basically, John treated him well and was a patient and knowledgeable instructor. He showed Bob how to read the alignment surveys, understand stationing on survey stakes, and identify property markers. They were following the pipeline alignment paralleling the Delta River and the Richardson Highway.

Bob sat down next to John and gazed upon the landscape before them. They were in the foothills of the north slope of the Alaska Range. The mountains spread out as far as they could see to the west with snow-covered peaks. Lush summer foliage blanketed the valleys below them. Soft bird calls floated in the light breeze and they could faintly hear the Delta River roar in the distance.

After a few tranquil minutes, John recovered and continued his instruction. He pointed up the brush line and asked, "Do you see that survey stake over there? Go to it and tell me what it says."

Bob got up and walked over to the survey stake. It was a wooden lathe with top sprayed fluorescent orange and a set of numbers written along the side. Bob read the numbers back to John. "It says 125+28 CL."

John nodded as he pulled a cigarette pack from his front pocket and tapped out one. He lit it and pulled a couple of satisfying drags before answering, "OK. The last stake said 120+00. So, where are we in relation to it?"

Bob replied, "We are 528 feet north of it on the centerline."

"Right," said John as he smoked his cigarette. "Which means we are a tenth of mile farther up the line. Sometimes you will see an OL or and OR written on the stake instead of a CL. That means offset left or offset right. When surveyors can't shoot a line because of a hill or a rock, they will offset from the centerline."

Bob nodded as John continued, "So if you find a metal tab marking a mining claim, you must note its location in reference to the closest survey stake."

"I will do that."

John finished his cigarette and looked thoughtfully at Bob for a moment before replying, "I'm sure you will. Well, we've cleared this section of the line. How about being a jewel and go back and get the car? I'll make it to the highway and you can pick me up."

Bob had anticipated this request. He smiled and said, "Sure. Take it easy walking out. I'll meet up with you later."

In September 1971, Burt Silcock officially named Curtis McVee as the state BLM director. McVee had been acting in the position since Silcock had transferred to Washington DC in June. Harry Brelsford readily accepted the appointment. He found Curtis easy to work with and very knowledgeable about the TAPS project. However, Harry had more important issues on his mind than to contemplate the importance of the selection. He had a premonition of something bad brewing in Valdez. As predicted, King Fish Arnold had not yet produced the necessary documents to transfer the Dayville property to Alyeska. Nor had he rescinded Atkinson's lawsuit and dock permit. Since Arnold had failed to provide this documentation in a timely fashion, Harry feared he would also leak the purchase price. Two million dollars was a lot of money–enough to start a stampede to Valdez to lock up other lands that Alyeska would need to build the pipeline.

Harry stared at his office wall as he drummed his fingers on his desk. *Clearly, there is something we could do to head this off. But what?* He contemplated the problem some more before picking up the telephone and calling Armand.

"Yes, Harry," answered Armand.

"Armand, please come to my office. We need to put on our thinking caps and come up with a plan to reserve our potential right-of-way out of Valdez."

"Sounds interesting," replied Armand. "I'll be right up."

Armand arrived a few minutes later and they immediately began discussing options. Then Armand suggested they give Jay a call and bring him into the conversation. "Good idea," said Harry as he dragged his speaker phone into the middle of his desk.

Harry dialed Jay's number and then set the receiver on the cradle on top of the speaker box. They could hear the static as the phone line cleared to Fairbanks. A computerized female voice announced, "Alascom", before ringing the Land Field Services office. Shirley picked up on the second ring.

"Land Field Services. How may I help you?"

Harry announced, "Shirley! This is Armand and Harry. Can you pry Jay loose for us, please."

Shirley smoothly replied, "Armand and Harry. What a treat to have two handsome men call me today! I'll see if I can roust Jay. Please hold." Shirley left two very smug men waiting on the telephone. Jay came on shortly.

"Good morning gentlemen. What do I owe the pleasure of this call?"

"Jay," replied Harry, "I'm trying to head trouble off at the pass. What can we do now to stake our claim on future right-of-way across public domain lands? I fear a land-grab when our purchase price of the Atkinson parcels leaks out. And mark my words, it will leak out."

"Interesting choice of words," answered Jay. "Maybe that's the answer."

"What's the answer?" asked Armand. "I'm not following you."

Jay went silent for a moment before replying with a laugh in his voice, "We stake claims–gold claims." Stunned, Harry and Armand went silent. "Hello? Anyone there?" asked Jay. "What do you guys think?"

"Jay," answered Harry, "Alyeska can't file gold claims. The Alaska Department of Natural Resources would know it's a sham the minute our applications hit their desk."

"True," countered Jay, "but if Land Field Services surveyed, staked, and filed the State claims in my name, ADNR would have to honor them. If the government chose to challenge the validity of the claims, we would still lock up the land for at least two years."

"How large would each claim be?" asked Armand.

"Well, that depends on the topography around the pipeline center-line. Each claim must be mineable. That is, we must be able to remove the gold from where we allegedly discovered it."

"Isn't that fraud?" asked Harry.

"Fraud is such an ugly word," responded Jay. "Encumber is a better term. Miners tie up federal lands all the time on bogus claims. When the ADNR asks for proof of our discoveries, we will fold our hand. But by that time, the State should have granted our right-of-way permit."

Harry and Armand went silent again contemplating Jay's plan. Finally Harry said, "Why is it, Jay, that your schemes always have a certain irrefutable logic to them? Armand, can you see any pitfalls to this plot?"

Armand scratched his chin and said, "I really can't, Harry. As long as Alyeska's name stays out of it, I think it will buy us enough time to get the State right-of-way permit. Of course, ADNR isn't dumb. When they see the claims strung up the centerline, they're going to know what's up."

Jay injected, "I might be able to bestow the old Sullivan charm on the Valdez and Glennallen recorder's offices. You know, ask them to play along for a while and let us go through the motions."

Again Harry went quiet as he brooded over the plan. He knew that his approval was required to proceed. To do nothing was to invite other land scams and possible court battles. Filing the claims would buy them some time, but could backfire with public embarrassment–it wouldn't be the first time. Finally Harry shouted, "To heck with it! We're going gold mining. Do it, Jay."

"Outstanding!" exclaimed Jay. "I'll pull Doc and John from the Koyukuk area to start surveying the claims. Bob Ylvisaker will help them and John Pate will supervise them."

"Good luck, Jay," said Harry as he pushed the button on the speaker box to break the connection. He sat staring at the silent box for a moment before saying, "Armand. What have I done?"

Armand stood up, clasped Harry's shoulder, and said, "You took a risk and gave us a chance to succeed. Don't worry. Jay will pull it off."

Harry looked up to Armand and replied, "But what if he doesn't?"

Bob Ylvisaker arose from his soft warm bed with extreme difficulty to smash the ringing alarm clock. He threw off his covers, staggered to the window, and pulled the curtain aside. He could see the low-lying clouds hanging over the Arm–another typical late September morning in Valdez. *At least it's not blowing*, he thought as he let the curtain swing back. He was sore from a month of hacking brush, pounding stakes, and setting monuments for Land Field Service's mining claims. He looked wistfully at his bed before trudging to the shower. Bob knew that John Pate was only minutes from pounding on his door and yelling, "It's burning daylight!" It was time to get going.

The Land Field Services crew was staying at the Wyatt House. It was a modern facility built next to the ocean. Bill and Cleo Wyatt owned and operated the motel. The crew ate breakfast in the motel restaurant and Cleo packed them sack lunches to take to their work site. The Wyatts were an affable couple who took a sincere interest in people. During their month's stay, the crew and the Wyatts developed a close friendship. Cleo was especially concerned about John's coarse handling of Bob. She did not understand that voicing her thoughts only intensified John's jibes.

Bob met the rest of the crew in the restaurant. Cleo immediately came over to him and said, "How about a couple of eggs, hon?"

John snorted behind his coffee cup, "Just like Mom. I bet she tucks you in bed at night, eh Bob?"

Bob ignored John, gave Cleo a smile, and replied, "Yes. Thank you. That would be great."

Bill came to Bob's rescue and sat down with the men with his own cup of coffee. "Bob, Cleo and I were wondering how to pronounce your last name. Is it Livisucker?"

Bob had heard this question many times before growing up. He shook his head. "No. It's Ylvisaker."

"Uvisoker?"

"No. Il-vis-sak-er. Ylvisaker."

"Il-vi-sok. . . Oh, forget it!" declared Bill. "From now on, you're Bob Silver Salmon." The men howled around the table.

"Hey, Silver Salmon!" yelled Doc. "Pass me the pepper, will ya?"

John chimed in, "Silver Salmon! Remember. No spawning on the job."

Bill realized that he had started something irrevocable and immediately regretted it—especially when he saw Cleo scowling at him from the kitchen. The nickname stuck and, hereafter, Bob Ylvisaker would be known as Bob Silver Salmon or simply Silver.

During the months of September and October 1971, Land Field Services set 148 mining claims from Valdez to Glennallen straddling the proposed TAPS centerline. They claimed the public domain land between Valdez and Tosina Lodge, a distance of 36 miles. From there, they set other claims sprinkled north along the pipeline route to Glennallen. The crew took their survey and property notes back to their Fairbanks office and began sketching diagrams of each claim. The maps showed where each alleged gold discovery occurred, the access to each claim, the claim boundaries, and where each property corner was located.

During November, Governor Egan floated his idea for an all-Alaskan-financed oil pipeline. He proposed to sell government bonds to generate 1.5 to 2 billion dollars. A state-financed project of this magnitude had never been attempted in the United States. Egan said his proposal was on solid ground and he had the research to prove it. He touted other spinoff benefits such as power plants in the Interior fueled by the line. The Alaska legislature highly approved of the idea and applauded Egan for his leadership. Egan immediately developed a task force to pursue the development of an Alaska-owned pipeline.

Within a week of the announcement, oil executives quietly paid Egan a visit and explained to him that due to unforeseen and complicated construction requirements, such as elevating the pipeline over permafrost, the project cost had soared to 4 billion dollars. This cost was far beyond Egan's financing scheme. Whether Alaska liked it or not, they would have to wait for private investment.

Always the classic politician, Egan conceived an idea to gracefully back out of his plan to finance the pipeline. On November 29, 1971, a highly confidential report by the economic consulting firm Harbridge Homes, Inc., was mysteriously leaked to the Anchorage Times. Governor Miller had commissioned Harbridge to develop the report for his pipeline commission, who were considering a plan suspiciously similar to Egan's. The report assumed the pipeline would cost 1.5 to 2 billion dollars and the project was favorable for state investment at that price. However, the report stated that if the project costs exceeded 2 billion dollars, the state could not generate the necessary capital to build and operate the pipeline and the revenue generated would not support the bond remuneration as they matured. Egan declared that the pipeline was now priced beyond the government's capability to finance it and let the Harbridge report speak for itself.

The Alaska Native Claims Act passed both houses on December 14, 1971. President Nixon signed it into law on December 18. A product of lawyers from competing interests, the act was extremely complicated. People joked that law would support hundreds of lawyers for generations as they sorted out the intricacies of the act. Unfortunately, they were right.

John Knodell and Quinn O'Connell had lobbied hard to prevent future Native allotments assigned to the potential pipeline and haul road right-of-way. The finalized act had a clause thwarting such assignments within the proposed right-of-way.

The Alaska Native Claims Act allowed Alaska Natives to select 44 million acres of land. In exchange for surrendering future land claims, the United States would pay the Alaska Natives $462 million over 11 years, plus a 2 percent mineral royalty until it generated another $500 million. To stimulate economic development within the villages, the act established 13 regional corporations and allowed the villages to form local corporations. The regional corporations were to receive the payouts and distribute the funds to their respective villages. The DOI could now lift the land freeze, thus removing one of the barriers preventing the issuance of the pipeline and haul road right-of-way.

Not everyone was happy with the settlement. ASNA believed their fellow Natives were due a lot more. They vowed to continue to fight for full mineral rights beneath Prudhoe Bay.

On the morning of December 29, 1971, Paxton J. Sullivan walked into the Glennallen Land Recorders Office and filed a string of gold claims within the Chitna District. He then drove south on the snowy Richardson Highway and visited the Valdez Recorders Office that afternoon where he filed more claims stretching from Valdez to Tosina. P. J. Sullivan now controlled large sections of the potential Alyeska right-of-way up the Keystone Canyon, over Thompson Pass, and north to Glennallen.

Chapter 9

The Last Hurdles

O n January 11, 1972, the DOI submitted their gargantuan EIS for
the TAPS to the President's Council of Environmental Quality.
Chairman Russell Train accepted the documentation and ordered his
office to immediately begin their review to determine if it fulfilled the
intent of NEPA. Secretary Morton directed his department to keep the
EIS confidential until the Council completed their review. However, environmentalists within the DOI who opposed the project leaked a 48-page
summary report to Wisconsin representative Les Aspin. Representative
Aspin, an ardent opponent of the TAPS project, sent copies of the report
to environmental groups who were also fighting the project. Aspin was
incensed that the EIS stated that the TAPS would increase national security by reducing our dependence on Middle Eastern oil. Aspin demanded
that DOI remove that claim from the document.

A few days later, Bill Arnold sent Harry documents proving he had
revoked Mr. Atkinson's lawsuit and dock permit application. Harry had
Paul Robison review the documentation. Paul confirmed its authenticity
and, with great hesitancy, Harry released the funds in escrow. This caused
a chain of events that materialized Harry's fears on January 27. The Valdez
and Copper Basin News announce that Alyeska had bought the old

Day homestead from Mrs. Oma Belle Day and the A&G Construction Company. Mrs. Day's son, Walter Jr., was the editor of the newspaper. Although the front-page article contained the sensationalized statement, ". . . the largest land sale on record in the Valdez Recording District. . ," it carefully did not state the purchase price.

The *Anchorage Daily News* did that on the follow day. In big black block letters, the title screamed, "$2 million is paid out by Alyeska."

Harry's and Armand's phones began ringing off the hook with land offers. While they took notes on each call, they later found most offers fraudulent. Harry felt some comfort in the knowledge that Jay had secured the available public domain land north of Valdez. However, Harry knew that they had not locked up all the public land and there was one place where they were exceptionally vulnerable to false mining claims—the Middle Fork Koyukuk River valley. Harry had a feeling the miners in this area were fast learners.

Jay Sullivan drove his fledgling right-of-way student, Bob "Silver" Ylvisaker, to his first landowner meeting. Jay's intent was to demonstrate to Bob the proper approach to right-to-way negotiations. This meant adequate preparation before the meeting, an understanding of the project needs, and a logical calculation of fair compensation for an easement or land purchase. Of course, all of Jay's lectures and instruction could not prepare Bob for the infinite variety of human personalities, so Jay reasoned he had to walk Bob through his first negotiation. After that, Jay was going to cut him loose to sink or swim.

Jay had chosen Bob's first assignment with care. Bob would cut his teeth with David Burns. Mr. Burns and his wife lived on their unpatented Federal Trade and Manufacturing claim a mile north of the Sourdough Lodge off the Richardson Highway along the Gulkana River. In 1972, Burns granted an easement to Alyeska along the back western border of his land. Then the pipeline engineers shifted the alignment to the east to improve the crossing of the Gulkana. The new alignment now crossed the front of his property, which also complicated his access from the highway.

Burns had shown every sign of being difficult and Jay couldn't blame him. Burns felt betrayed and believed that Alyeska couldn't care less about the little guy. Jay's discussions with him on his tenuous telephone connection were terse and cut short–either by David hanging up or the line failing. Burns ignored Jay's letters about Alyeska's right-of-way needs. The man clearly wanted to be left alone to live a peaceful existence with his wife in rural Alaska. Jay sensed Burns thought Alyeska was trying to destroy his refuge.

Jay drove with his right hand on the wheel and left holding a cigarette. He took a long drag and said, "Now, Bobby, Mr. Burns will be very uncooperative, to say the least. If we don't get tossed out into the snow, it'll be a miracle."

Jay's declaration rattled Bob. He replied, "Then I don't get it, Jay. Why even waste our time?"

Jay finished off his cigarette and crushed it in the ashtray before answering. "Because we don't have the power of eminent domain. We can't condemn property. So, in our weak negotiating position, we must convince him to sell us what we need and we can't do that behind letters and a telephone. This, Bobby boy, will be the first of many visits with Mr. Burns."

"And how will we convince him?"

Jay turned to Bob with a wicked smile and said, "It's not 'we,' Bobby. It's you."

"Me?" replied Bob with trepidation in his voice. "What can I do?"

"Win him over," answered Jay with authority. "Earn his trust, listen to him, and look for opportunities to help him out. We'll pay him handsomely for the right-of-way. Maybe improve his access to his home. Clear some land for him. We'll never know until you establish a rapport with him. I'll help break the ice, and then I'm shoving you into the lion's cage."

Bob shook his head and said, "You have a strange way of putting things."

Jay slowed the car down and pointed forward as he announced, "Cheer up, Bobby boy, Mr. Burns's abode is directly ahead. All hands on deck!" Jay turned on to a rough plowed road that was marked by an unlabeled mailbox. They drove a little ways until they came to a log home with smoke rising from a chimney.

As Jay stopped the car, Bob asked, "Are they expecting us?"

"I don't know," replied Jay as he opened the car door. "He hung up on me before I could tell him we were coming."

"Great."

Jay straightened his coat and put on his wool hat before trudging up to the front porch. Bob followed reluctantly behind. Jay knocked on the solid, rough-cut lumber door. A minute later, they heard the latch unlock and the door creak open. There stood the sweetest elderly lady that Bob had ever seen. Mrs. Burns wore a full-length dress with an apron tied around her waist. Her silver hair was pulled back in a neat bun. She radiated wholesomeness and health.

Jay took his hat off and held it over his heart and said, "Good afternoon, ma'am. My name is Jay Sullivan and this is my associate Robert Ylvisaker. We are landmen representing the interests of the Alyeska Pipeline Service Company. May we have a few minutes of yours and Mr. Burns's time to discuss our right-of-way needs?"

Mrs. Burns gave them a look and a smile that she knew they would be coming. She stepped aside as an invitation to enter and said, "Yes. Please come inside. I'll get my husband." Jay and Bob entered the home. It was warm and neat. Alaska art adorned the log walls. Family pictures were proudly displayed on the bookcases.

A booming voice from a back room shattered the homey atmosphere. "Who in the hell is it?"

"It's the pipeline men who called you," replied Mrs. Burns.

They could hear some mumbling and cursing as Burns prepared to come into the living room. The door opened and a stocky full-bearded man burst into the room with eyes burning like hot coals. He marched up to Jay and stood with his head cocked back as he looked at him square in the eye and barked, "What the hell do you want?"

Bob was prepared to bolt until he saw Jay struggling to keep the corners of his mouth from bending up. *He thinks this is funny*!

Jay cleared his throat to compose himself and replied, "Mr. Burns, my name is Jay Sullivan. I called you a few days ago about our right-of-way needs."

Unflinching, Burns fired back, "That's right. I remember and the answer is still no. I gave you the easement along the back of my property. You can use that. So, get the hell out of here and take your sidekick with you."

Mrs. Burns put her hand on her husband's forearm and said with a soothing voice, "Now, honey, let's have these gentlemen sit down and rest for a few minutes. They have driven a long ways just to see you. It won't hurt to listen to what they have to say. Please, hon." Her words dampened Burns's anger. He nodded, backed away from Jay, and pointed towards the sofa.

"That's better," said Mrs. Burns with a gracious levity in her voice. "Would you gentlemen like some coffee or tea? I've got a fresh pot of coffee brewing on the stove."

Jay answered with his most humble voice, "Yes, ma'am. Some coffee would go well. Thank you."

Bob replied, "No thank you. I don't. . ." Jay kicked Bob's ankle. Bob glanced at Jay and saw him slightly nod to change his mind. "Oh, on second thought, I would love some coffee. Thank you." Bob would learn that you never refuse an act of kindness during land negotiations.

While they waited for Mrs. Burns to bring the coffee, Jay and Bob avoided Burns's piercing gaze by admiring the paintings of the Alaska Range and moose feeding in a pond. A few agonizing minutes later, Mrs. Burns brought out a tray with coffee and a sugar bowl. "I'm sorry, gentlemen," she said as she offered each a steaming mug, "but we are out of creamer. I hope you don't mind."

"Not at all," replied Jay as he carefully picked up the mug. "I prefer my coffee black. Thank you."

"Oh, black is just fine. Thank you," answered Bob.

Burns allowed them a full sip before launching into them. "Why in the hell can't the pipeline follow their original alignment?"

Jay took another sip, turned to his hostess, and said, "Mrs. Burns, this is very good coffee." Then he addressed her husband. "The engineers determined that the original crossing of the Gulkana upstream was on a cut bank. Thus the river would have eventually undermined the work pad and threatened the pipeline. It would have created a hazard above you. The safest approach would be to shift the alignment east and cross perpendicularly over a stable stretch of river."

"Then keep moving the alignment to the east and miss my property!"

Jay patiently drank his coffee before concisely replying, "Then we would cut right through your neighbor's property. We tried to thread the pipe along the property boundaries to leave your parcels intact."

Jay's answer seemed to mollify Burns. The conversation went silent. Bob could hear a wall clock ticking in the background. Then Burns asked, "How much land do you need?"

"A corridor one hundred feet wide," replied Jay.

"You've got to be sh. . ." Burns caught himself as he glanced at his wife. "There is no way in hell you're getting a hundred feet! Gulp your coffee and get the hell out of here!"

Jay did as he was commanded. As he finished his cup, he patted Bob's leg to do the same. They stood and placed their cups on the tray. Jay bowed his head to Mrs. Burns and said, "Thank you again, Mrs. Burns, for the coffee. It really hit the spot." Then he extended his hand to Burns. Burns stared at it for a second before gruffly grasping it. "Mr. Burns, thank you for listening. I know our project upsets you and I can't blame you for being mad, but I was hoping my associate here, Bob, could come by and discuss it further."

Burns stood and said, "Won't do any good."

Jay took his answer as a "yes". He put his hat on, stepped out on the porch, and walked to the car. Bob and Jay remained silent until they pulled out on the Richardson Highway and drove north. Jay lit up a cigarette and said, "Well, that went better than hoped—no bullet holes and you can come back."

Bob shook his head and said, "Old man Burns isn't going to let me through the door next time."

"Oh, yes he will," said Jay as he took another drag and exhaled smoke out the window, "because you're going to bring them a gift."

Bob gave Jay a puzzled look and asked, "What gift?"

Jay smiled as he turned to look at Bob and answered, "Coffee creamer."

During the early part of 1972, Michael Baker engineers were working hard to design the hundreds of material sites required to build the project. North of the Yukon River, the double demand for non-frost-susceptible gravel to build the pipeline work pad and haul road exacerbated their task.

The material site development usually occurred in the following manner: Geotechnical engineers and geologists directed soil borings and interpreted the core samples. Based on their analysis, the geological team instructed the surveyors to delineate the boundaries of the proposed material site. The Michael Baker civil engineers would then determine the optimum site access and draft a site plan. Environmental specialists and archeologists would visit the site. The environmental staff would note areas of special concern such as wetlands, raptor nests, and nearby water bodies, and develop a revegetation plan to restore the site after the material was removed. The archeologists cleared the site of cultural resources and noted any resources in close proximity that might be affected by the material site development.

The civil engineers finalized their mining plans by incorporating the environmental information. Then drafters developed plats for each site and the entire development package was given to Armand to purchase the gravel.

Depending if the site was on federal or state land, BLM or ADNR received the application. The agencies reviewed each application to ensure its completeness and held it until the DOI issued Alyeska the right-of-way permit. If the site was on private land, Land Field Services negotiated the purchase with the owner.

On March 20, 1972, the DOI release the final EIS to the public. The Council of Environmental Quality had reviewed the document and determined it adequately fulfilled the intent of NEPA. The EIS was enormous. It consisted of six volumes plus tomes of attachments at a federal cost of nine million dollars—not including the Alyeska field work. The EIS preferred alternative was to build a 48-inch oil pipeline from Prudhoe Bay to Valdez with a haul road north of Fairbanks. The EIS stated the purpose of the analysis was to investigate the impacts of granting right-of-way for the project. Secretary Morton announced DOI would issue a formal decision after a 45-day public comment period.

The environmentalists were incensed. The Environmental Defense Fund stated that they had been assembling their own EIS and would have it available for public review within two months. They hinted that their analysis was generating a completely different preferred alternative than the DOI EIS.

Secretary of the Interior C. B. Morton, was a careful man. Never one to brashly announce his intentions or haphazardly execute major decisions, Morton gradually lifted the federal land freeze over a three-month period following the passage of the Alaska Native Claims Act. Slowly, the DOI began transferring State-filed land to ADNR. This land included potential homesteads, possible mineral rights, transportation corridors, and special-use lands such as the future Valdez Marine Terminal.

In April 1972, ADNR sent Armand a notice that the State was offering Alyeska the Valdez Marine Terminal (VMT) land at the appraised value. Armand scanned the enclosed appraisal report and found that the ADNR had assessed the value at $9.175 million dollars–a little less than what Al Olson had quoted. It was a great price and Armand knew Alyeska would pay it. He folded the report back into its envelope and carried it upstairs to Harry's office. Armand felt a little pride in knowing he had just secured an extremely important piece of land for the TAPS project.

As Armand came to Harry's door, he saw him poring over a long strip-map stretched out across his desk. Harry had his head cradled in his hands fully studying the alignment. Armand glanced at the map and saw it displayed the Middle Fork Koyukuk River valley with the proposed TAPS route superimposed over mining claims. Armand had to clear his throat to get Harry's attention.

"Ah, Harry? Did I catch you at a bad time?"

Armand's voice startled Harry out of his focused concentration, "Uh . . . Armand. What's up?"

"Sorry to bother you, Harry. The State's appraisal came in for the VMT property. It's under the ten million that I was quoted earlier." Armand handed the appraisal to Harry.

Harry reached up and accepted the envelope as he said, "That's great news, Armand, but my mind is elsewhere for the moment. I think we have a problem brewing along the Middle Fork of the Koyukuk River. Take a look at this." His finger traced the pipeline alignment through a series of claims. "Do you see these claims? They straddle perfectly across our proposed route. They were staked by John Bullock and Andy Miscovich in the fall of 1969–just before BLM closed the valley for mining claims and just after TAPS gave a presentation in Fairbanks of the alignment. Do you think the timing was a coincidence?"

Armand shook his head and remained silent as he studied the map. Harry continued, "I agree. What's more, neither of these gentlemen presented evidence of mineral discovery as part of their filings. Their claims are pure speculation."

Armand looked up from the map and asked, "So where do we go from here?"

Harry leaned back in his chair and folded his hands behind his head as he replied, "Quinn O'Connell and John Knodell have been in communication with Burt Silcock, the new BLM national director about the situation. I think it's time to raise everyone's awareness of the potential right-of-way conflict and visit the valley. I'm thinking some sort of a joint inspection. What do you think?"

Armand nodded and said, "I think that's a great idea, but we'll need to charter a couple of planes to get in there. And how would we get to the claims? They're several miles from the Coldfoot or Weisman strips."

Harry continued to lean back in his chair and stare at the ceiling for a few moments before he sat up and reached for his phone. "I'm going to call Burt and bounce a few ideas off him. Maybe we can do a full route inspection. He's got several new staff who have never been north of the Yukon."

Harry dialed the Washington DC BLM office and, after a receptionist screened his call, Burt Silcock picked up the phone. "Harry, how goes the right-of-way battle? Are you winning?"

Harry liked Burt. He had dealt with many stuffed shirts in his day, but Burt was a solid man and never put on airs. "Who knows, Burt, how the political winds blow? We'll just keep swinging. Say, Burt, Armand Spielman and I were just talking about a joint inspection of the route north of the Yukon River. We are especially interested in viewing the Middle Fork Koyukuk where the gold claims are staked across our route. Any chance that we could pull off a joint inspection with people from the BLM and Alyeska?"

Burt went silent for a moment before replying, "Harry, that's a capital idea! I've got some guys here who really need to see the alignment before they start throwing their weight around. We could charter an airplane from Fairbanks and fly everyone along the route to Prudhoe Bay and back. How many people from your shop would participate?"

Harry was prepared for the question and immediately answered, "Just two–Jay Sullivan and Armand Spielman. I was hoping you had a couple of mining engineers that could come along and observe the Koyukuk drainage. Any chance of that?"

"Yes," answered Burt, "that's possible. Let me put some feelers out and get back to you. So, you are anticipating some right-of-way conflicts with the unpatented mining claims in the area?"

"You got that right, Burt. I'm thinking we will need a couple of BLM mining experts to determine if the claims are legitimate or if the miners are just trying to make a fast buck."

Burt sighed and replied, "OK. You've got a point. Let me make some calls and I'll get back to you. We should try to make this flight as soon as possible."

"Agreed. Let me know and Armand and Jay will be ready to go. And, thanks, Burt. I appreciate the assistance."

"No problem, Harry. I'll get back to you shortly."

After Harry broke the connection and put the phone back on the cradle, he looked up to Armand and said, "Hopefully, this will bring the right people to look at the problem."

Armand nodded and asked, "Are you thinking these claims might hold up the right-of-way?"

Harry leaned back in his chair and resumed his thoughtful pose before answering, "We'll be going to court over the validity of these claims, Armand. It's as simple as that."

The BLM-chartered Wien Airlines Fairchild F-27 sat ready on the Fairbanks International Airport apron for it passengers on a beautiful late April afternoon. As the men walked in a line to the aircraft, a stewardess dressed in Wien blue and gold colors welcomed each as he came aboard. Since the F-27 could accommodate forty passengers, the twelve men each found a window seat and pulled out their cameras to record the sights. Jay and Armand represented Alyeska. The remaining ten were federal officials from various BLM offices in Anchorage and Washington DC. Noteworthy of the BLM personnel were John Wells, George Neuberg, and Cal Niver. John and George worked for the BLM Mining Division in Washington DC. Cal was their counterpart in Alaska. These men were very interested in viewing the mining claims in the Koyukuk River valley.

The other BLM officials also had responsibilities in the Anaktuvuk Pass and Umiat areas. So, the plan was to fly north over the proposed Yukon River crossing and follow the pipeline alignment to Prospect Creek. From there, the flight would deviate from the proposed pipeline route and follow the winter trail to Bettles. Then they would fly north along the Hickel Highway route up the John River and into Anaktuvuk Pass. They would cross the Brooks Range and descend the North Slope and over Umiat. Then the plane would head north-northwest to Barrow. They would spend the night at the Naval Arctic Research Lab (NARL). The next day they would fly east to Prudhoe Bay and then follow the proposed pipeline route to Fairbanks.

The F-27 took off flawlessly into the deep-blue sky and flew due north over the Fairbanks foothills toward the Yukon River. The plane followed the new haul road from Livengood to the Yukon. Then the pilot slowed the plane and circled above the crossing–giving the men their first good look at the proposed bridge site. They immediately saw that the southern bank was about 75 feet higher than the northern side. Thus, the bridge would slant downward to the north. Although the north side had ample space for staging construction materials, the south side appeared cramped. Alyeska would have to build a staging area about a half of a mile upstream of the crossing.

The plane then continued north over the Fort Hamlin hills and into the rolling terrain of the Kanuti River and Fish Creek watersheds before turning over the intersection of Jim River and Prospect Creek, where the Bettles winter trail began. The Hickel Highway also followed the trail into the Brooks Range.

Fifteen miles farther, the village of Bettles/Evansville appeared on the banks of the Middle Fork Koyukuk River. The large Bettles airstrip provided a refuge for pilots flying along the southern flanks of the Brooks. Here, the plane tilted northwest to the mouth of the John River to start the long climb to Anaktuvuk Pass.

Peeking through the melting snow, the linear scars of the Hickel Highway were clearly visible along the banks of the John River. A 50-foot-wide swath of trees had been cut and leveled to allow winter travel of semitrucks and heavy equipment. The John was still frozen with hints of meltwater around the mouth. However, as the plane headed north, winter still had a firm lock on the land.

Finally, the terrain leveled and revealed wide valley. In the distance, they could see a speck of humanity marooned within a sea of white. This was the village of Anaktuvuk Pass. It was located just south of the continental divide.

The engineers aboard had to wonder about the wisdom of threading the TAPS pipeline through Atigun Pass. In stark contrast to the Atigun, Anaktuvuk Pass had gentle grades on both sides and a wide valley. This is why engineers had selected this route for the Hickel Highway over other Brooks Range passes. The treacherous Atigun Pass required chiseling a perilously steep haul road into the side of an avalanche-prone mountain and there was room for only one pipeline–a future gasline would have to find a different route to cross the Brooks. Anaktuvuk Pass had none of these shortcomings, but it necessitated a longer route and the north-slope section was devoid of convenient gravel sources. Anaktuvuk was also where thousands of caribou annually crossed the range. When weighing the consequences, the engineers chose the shorter route.

The F-27 crested the Brooks Range and headed north-northwest across the frozen white plain towards Barrow. Although the sun shone brightly and high, the vast northern expanse was still frozen and completely snow covered. The brilliant light reflecting off the snow hurt the eyes. In less than an hour, the speck representing Barrow rolled out from the curvature of the earth and steadily grew larger on the horizon.

The plane flew over the new Barrow Airport next to the town. Thick shore ice lined the Arctic Ocean beach. After an uneventful landing, members from NARL met the party with a school bus and shuttled them the six miles up the coast to the research facility. NARL consisted of renovated navy Quonset huts with wooden arctic entries built on the front. The main building that served as a research laboratory, office, and hotel was built on pilings to preserve the permafrost underneath the floor.

As the men filed out of the bus, they could see a flurry of activity farther up the coast next to the old naval airstrip. Cal Niver was particularly interested in the gathering and asked the driver, "Are they landing a whale?"

The man smiled as he answered, "Why, yes, they are. The whole town is up there right now tugging on the block and tackle to pull the bowhead onshore. How did you know?"

Cal laughed and said, "Because I married an Inupiat woman and she told me to keep my eyes peeled for fresh muktuk to bring back."

"Well then," replied the driver, "after you guys get settled, I'll drive you up to the landing party and see if you can fulfill your wife's request."

True to his word, the driver was waiting for them when Jay, Armand, Cal, and two other BLM staffers emerged from the building with cameras in hand. Cal also had a cardboard box lined with paper towels to hold muktuk strips.

When they arrived at the landing, the villagers had slid the enormous 60-foot whale onto the shore ice. Men with six-foot-long blades connected to long poles were standing on top of the animal and cutting long deep slabs of skin and blubber. The Inupiat called the skin connected to the blubber muktuk and they relished it. As the fresh slabs hit the blood-splattered snow, villagers dragged it away from the butchering with meat hooks, cut thin slices off, and handed it to excited family members. Young and old would stuff the muktuk in their mouths and chew enthusiastically.

Cal wanted in on the action and approached a man cutting muktuk pieces from a blubber slab. When Cal had explained his wife's request, the man graciously hacked off a hunk of muktuk that barely fit in his prepared box and weighed close to 20 pounds. Cal strode back to the bus proudly cradling his prize. "Want some?" he asked Jay and Armand.

They both shook their heads no. "Cal," replied Armand, "We don't want to deprive your sweet wife of any muktuk. She should have it all."

Cal cut a sliver off and offered it to Jay. "Are you sure? There's plenty."

"I'm sure, Cal," answered Jay with his hands on his hips, "definitely sure."

The next morning they took off from the Barrow airport and flew over the butchering site. The men were amazed that only a skeleton and large bloody stain remained of the whale carcass. The villagers must have worked all night to complete the task.

The plane headed east along the coast to Prudhoe Bay. The pilots circled the oil field to allow the passengers a good view of the drilling activity. For many, this was the first time they had seen the source of Alaska's oil. Then the plane flew south along the Sagavanirktok River and followed the proposed TAPS route.

An hour later, the plane met the foothills and Galbraith Lake, which was the entry into the Atigun River valley. The plane followed the valley to the abrupt Atigun Pass, which was really only a low point between two peaks. At 4,739 feet, the pass would be the highest point on the pipeline corridor. The men had a bird's eye view of the difficult terrain and avalanche hazards. While Thompson Pass north of Valdez was anticipated to be the most difficult section to construct the pipeline, the Atigun had the dual challenge of building the haul road. In addition to frequent slides that brought tons of snow down to the pipeline route, the blasting to construct a road across the loose shale slopes would trigger massive landslides. There was a high likelihood that men would die here.

The F-27 continued south over the Chandalar Shelf and down the south slopes where the Dietrich River was born. They flew down the Dietrich River Valley until it met the confluence of the Hammond and Bettles Rivers to become the Middle Fork Koyukuk River just north of the historic mining town of Wiseman. Here, the pilot slowed the plane and flew the proposed alignment to the pipeline field camp of Coldfoot before turning around and flying back north to Wiseman. This gave John Wells, George Neuberg, and Cal Niver an unobstructed view of the areas where miners had hastily staked their claims across the proposed pipeline centerline. The men took many pictures of the terrain.

After a thorough tour of the Koyukuk mining district, the plane continued south along the pipeline route to Fairbanks. The trip had been a huge success and enlightened everyone to the challenges that lay ahead.

As the pipeline design matured, the army of Alyeska engineers and technicians were besieged by the endless demand for minute details. For example, government and oil company representatives needed to know gravel site locations and quantities; where the pipe would transition from buried to above-ground support systems; how to span large creeks; and where to access the future work pad. The clamor for data caused many professionals to become myopic–lost in their own specialized world. Few had the capacity and luxury of stepping back from the fray and seeing the whole picture. This sometimes led to conflicts with other projects.

The 1967 flood had left lingering fears within the minds of Fairbanks residents that it could happen again. They transmitted these concerns to Alaska's new statesmen–Representative Nick Begich and Senators Ted Stevens and Mike Gravel. They lobbied congress to secure funding for an enormous diversion dam to move Chena River floodwaters to the Tanana River.

The Army Corps of Engineers studied several locations and settled on a stretch of flat land west of the Moose Creek Bluff–about 20 miles southeast of Fairbanks. In 1971, the Army Corps launched the EIS process. Although Alyeska was aware of the project, its ramification affecting the proposed pipeline route was not fully appreciated until the early spring of 1972 when the Corps published the draft EIS. The large project caught Alyeska by surprise. The preferred alternative was a 6.5-mile-long gravel dam that crossed the surveyed pipeline route. The Chena River dictated the dam location. Thus, the pipeline would have to move.

Alyeska named the six-mile pipeline realignment the Moose Creek Reroute. The Reroute was a one-mile shift to the southwest from the Moose Creek Bluff to Nelson Road, just east of the town of North Pole. The route then followed the section line north to Plack Road, where the reroute met the original alignment.

Although the realignment skirted the proposed dam and followed relatively flat terrain, a major problem became evident. Land Field Services had already secured easements for the original alignment. Thus, they needed to rush back to the field to negotiate right-of-way from new land owners.

Jay Sullivan was already past his eyeballs in priorities. The Fairbanks Reroute was another hot potato heaped upon his back. At first, he was at a loss at how he was going to address the issue. Then a friend and banker, Don Bruce, suggested Jay hire his son, Dick.

Dick Bruce was a genius determined to make his mark in the world, but not quite sure how he was going to do it. Dick had just finished a six-year stint with the army as an intelligence officer stationed in Turkey. He became fluent in Turkish and had excelled in the army, but became disenchanted with the bureaucracy and resigned. Dick had a similar experience with Yale, where he completed three and a half years with honors only to drop out in his last semester out of boredom.

Jay knew Dick was smart, but he initially thought of him as a loose cannon. He seemed brash and full of opinions on various hot topics of the day. However, Dick proved to be a fast study—quickly absorbing Jay's instructions and understanding the options available to secure right-of-way. Jay aimed Dick at the Moose Creek Reroute and launched him. Dick excelled.

Dick Bruce was a small man in his early thirties. He wore his dark brown hair short and combed over. His black-rimmed glasses and collared shirts buttoned high rounded out the appearance of a studious and sincere young man. When he knocked on doors of private landowners, his bookish and nonthreatening demeanor disarmed even the most ardent opponent of the pipeline project.

It took Dick nearly a year to complete all the property negotiations. He meticulously recorded all right-of-way easements and takes. His father was so impressed that he asked Jay for a job, too. Jay hired Don as an appraiser. Thus, father and son became Land Field Service employees.

The early May weather had just exposed bare patches through the snow as Bob Ylvisaker pulled into the Burns's driveway off the Richardson Highway. Two and a half months had passed since his last ill-fated visit with Jay. Bob had sent Burns two letters with maps showing Alyeska's proposed taking along the front of his claim. None were answered. So, Jay directed Bob to pay the Burnses a visit.

Bob felt his anxiety rise as he stopped in front of the log home. His mind raced with frantic thoughts. *Will he shoot me? Yell at me? Tell me never to come back?* Sighing as he turned off the car, he grabbed the large cylinder of Coffee Mate from the front seat and looked at it. "Well, let's see if this gets me through the front door."

He walked on to the porch, hesitated for a moment to gather his courage, and then knocked. A minute later Mrs. Burns opened the door. To Bob's relief, she smiled and remembered him.

"Hello, young man," she greeted as she smoothed back her hair. "I'm surprised you came back after the way my husband shooed you off. I'm sorry, but I don't recall your name."

"Hi, Mrs. Burns. My name is Bob Ylvisaker. I just wanted to follow up on the letters that I sent to Mr. Burns." Bob could see her trying to form his last name on her lips, so he added, "People call me Silver. And, oh yes, here's some creamer. You were out last time."

Mrs. Burns's eyes lit up with surprise as Bob handed her the round white container. "Oh, my goodness! You remembered. Oh, thank you, Bob. We've been without coffee creamer for some time. Please come in."

Jay was right. The simplest gift could open the stiffest door. Bob walked inside and took off his coat. Holding onto the creamer, Mrs. Burns said, "I'll go get my husband."

Bob nodded and spent a few moments looking at the family pictures on the bookcase. The pictures displayed their children at varying ages and their grandchildren, too. Bob wondered what the family thought of the elder Burnses eking out a living in rural Alaska. He suddenly heard a commotion from the back of the house.

"Don't they ever give up? Damn!" Burns bolted into the living room. He looked straight at Bob and yelled, "What the hell do you want?"

Bob instinctively wanted to flee. Burns looked like he was going to rip his head off. Bob managed to say, "Ah, Mr. Burns, I hope you remember me when . . ."

Burns cut him off. "I remember ya. The answer's still no. Move your line. Can you get that through your thick skull?"

"Honey," interjected Mrs. Burns, "please invite the young man to sit down. Then we can discuss the situation over coffee. See, he brought us some creamer! Wasn't that thoughtful?" Her sweet words temporarily silenced Burns. He nodded and pointed Bob to the sofa. Bob promptly complied.

Burns took his chair while his wife busied herself in the kitchen. Then he carefully studied Bob. His stare made Bob squirm. After a few moments, Burns asked, "So, what do you do for a living? Throw old folks out of their homes?"

"Oh, no sir!" replied Bob. "I assist Land Field Services to acquire right-of-way for the Trans Alaska Pipeline System."

"Acquire it? You mean take it!"

Bob shook his head and said, "No, sir. It depends on the property. For privately-owned property we can pay for the land taken. On unpatented land like your claim, we can pay for the inconvenience of the easement and help lessen the impacts to your property."

"Uh, huh," replied Burns, "and how would you do that?"

Bob was encouraged that he was actually having a conversation with Burns. He sat at the edge of the couch and leaned forward as he answered, "Well, I was hoping we could walk the boundary of your property and see what we could do. We would want to make sure you had good access to your home."

"Will the pipe be buried or raised?"

Bob was operating on the edge of his engineering expertise as he replied, "I believe it will be above ground through this section."

Burns shook his head as he said, "We were planning to build a boat access and campground on this claim. What customer in his right mind would want to drive under the pipe to our property? Would you even allow it? What's more, how could anyone see us from the highway with a big fat pipe blocking their view? I don't want anything to do with it!"

Mrs. Burns entered the room with a coffee tray, proudly offering a small bowl of coffee creamer with the other condiments. Bob welcomed the diversion and gratefully accepted the coffee with creamer. After they took a few sips in silence, Burns continued, "I don't see how you can make it better."

Bob nodded and said, "Well, let's go outside and take a look." As they drank their coffee, the three of them changed the subject and discussed the weather, how the highway was deteriorating from frost heaves, and the chances of Senator Stevens being reelected. Bob found the conversation to be open and enjoyable.

Then like flipping a switch, Burns stood up and said gruffly, "It's time we took a little walk. Ready?"

Bob put his cup on the serving tray, nodded his thanks to Mrs. Burns, and answered, "Yes. Please show me your place." They grabbed their coats and hats and walked outside into the spring air. The snow was shallow and crusty from daily thaw/freeze cycles. It crunched under their boots.

They walked up the driveway a few hundred feet until Burns stopped and pointed to a faint survey swath with an occasional sun-faded orange tape tied to trees. "Here is the claim boundary," he announced. "So, you're telling me that your line will go straight down here?"

"That's right, Mr. Burns," replied Bob. He was always amazed how different a real perspective looked versus a map with a line drawn on it. He could see how a 100-foot easement and pipeline would isolate the Burns property.

"Uh huh, so tell me, how you are going give me access to my property?"

Bob suddenly felt at a loss for words. He looked sheepishly at Burns and said, "I honestly don't know, but I can find out."

At first, Bob thought Burns was going to blow up at him, but he studied Bob for a moment and said, "That may be the first honest thing you have said to me. I suggest you find out before coming back here."

Bob dropped his gaze and nodded. Burns sighed and continued in a softer voice, "Bob, I appreciate you coming here. I'm sure it was tough. Let's put this subject aside and discuss other things. Please stay for dinner. I know Mrs. Burns would appreciate it. We don't get that many visitors."

Bob looked at Burns with renewed interest. This was a side of the man he did not know existed. He gratefully replied, "Thank you, Mr. Burns. I would like that." As they walked back to the house Bob thought, *maybe we can work this out after all.*

On May 4, 1972, the Environmental Defense Fund submitted their 1,300-page version of the EIS to Secretary Morton. Their EIS concluded that if a pipeline was built, it should traverse Canada to the continental United States. This alternative would avoid the fragile Prince William Sound and the supertanker traffic along the productive environments of southeast Alaska and British Columbia.

The DOI EIS had analyzed the Canadian route and decided it had roughly the same environmental impacts as the Valdez option. Timeliness was the deciding factor in choosing a preferred alternative. DOI estimated the Canadian route would take two to six years longer. Thus, the official EIS concluded that an 800-mile-long pipeline to a marine terminal was the preferred option.

On May 11, Secretary Morton announced that he approved the EIS and intended to grant the federal right-of-way permit to Alyeska. In a carefully crafted statement, Morton stated that he had "gravely" considered two alternatives—the pipeline from Prudhoe Bay to Valdez and the other through Canada to Midwest US. He said that in his opinion the all-Alaska pipeline would be less environmentally damaging because the route was shorter. Morton also expressed his confidence that the Valdez Marine Terminal and marine shipping would be operated safely.

On the exact day of Morton's announcement, Alyeska Pipeline Service Company printed a full-page ad in all the major Alaska newspapers. It stated that Alyeska was extremely grateful that the DOI had decided to grant the right-of-way permit for the proposed trans-Alaska pipeline. However, Alyeska would not initiate construction until the US District Court of Columbia rendered a decision regarding the claims made in "Wilderness Society et al. versus Morton et al and the Cordova District Fishermen's Union versus Morton et al." Alyeska restated that the company was committed to environmental excellence and pledged the strictest compliance with federal and state construction stipulations.

The ad was Alyeska's attempt to control public expectations. The timing of the article proved that Alyeska had deep connections in the Washington DC DOI office and it had John Knodell's and Quinn O'Connor's fingerprints all over it. Legal terminology and phrases like "et al." indicated that lawyers wrote it.

Another complication arose on July 24, 1972. Chugach Natives, Inc., the for-profit arm of the Chugach Native Association, filed a protest to the BLM about the impending transfer of the 802 acres for the Valdez

Marine Terminal to the State of Alaska. Chugach claimed the property was within the Tatitlek Village withdrawal area, and therefore not eligible for transfer as dictated by the Alaska Native Claims Settlement Act. BLM now had to research Chugach's claim before proceeding with the transfer of this important parcel to the State.

Judge Hart lifted the injunction on granting the TAPS right-of-way on August 15, 1972. Hart stated that the DOI had satisfied NEPA and the Alaska Native land issues were settled. The CDFU concerns were now mute. He believed no other legal issues prevented the project from proceeding.

The environmental groups, however, thought differently. They immediately appealed Judge Hart's decision by claiming the DOI did not comply with the Minerals Leasing Act, which allowed only a 50-foot-wide right-of-way. TAPS needed at least 100 feet for the pipeline and another 100 feet for the Haul Road. The environmentalists believed that Hart had erred in his ruling.

Despite Alyeska's many notifications of caution, Alaskans were ecstatic about the upcoming project. Editorials, radio shows, and political speeches were laced with excitement about the impending economic boon. People begin buying real estate, building apartments, and erecting businesses to serve the future workforce.

Then Alyeska did something unforeseen and troubling. They began to lay people off. The pipe-coating work at the three pipe yards was complete. Most of the surveying was done. The future construction camps and airstrips were secure. Alyeska could continue their engineering work in faraway places such as Houston. The company decided to hunker down and wait. They ran other newspaper ads apologizing for the layoffs and promised to rehire employees as soon as the project was fully approved.

On October 6, the US District Court of Appeals in Washington DC agreed with the environmentalists' appeal. While the Appeals Court concurred with Judge Hart that the DOI had correctly completed the NEPA process, the Court believed the government was not in compliance with the Minerals Leasing Act. Therefore, either Alyeska had to shrink their right-of-way requirements or Congress had to amend the Minerals Leasing Act. The project had hit another legal roadblock. John Knodell and Quinn O'Connell immediately contested the Appeals Court decision to the US Supreme Court.

Shortly afterwards, Alaska's economy faltered. Many residents had overextended themselves. Foreclosures became common in Fairbanks. The State imposed hiring restrictions and cost-cutting measures. Citizens clamored for their Alaska delegation, Representative Nick Begich, Senator Ted Stevens, and Senator Mike Gravel, to get the project approved. This would prove to be a difficult task for the delegation.

On October 16, 1972, Representative Begich and his aide, Russell Brown, accompanied House Majority Leader Hale Boggs of Louisiana on a twin-engine Cessna 310. A seasoned pilot, Don Jonz, was flying them to a campaign fundraiser in Juneau. The plane suddenly vanished during the flight from Anchorage. With vast ocean stretching beneath their flight path, Alaskans assumed the men had crashed in the Pacific.

The US Coast Guard, navy, and air force activated a massive search for the four men and their airplane. After 39 days of fruitless searching, the Department of Defense called off the rescue. The plane and its occupants had disappeared without a trace. Years later, the accident prompted Congress to pass a law mandating emergency locator transmitters in all United States civil aircraft.

In November, Alaska proceeded with their state elections and Begich, who had been missing for two weeks, beat his rival, Don Young of Fort Yukon, for the congressional seat. The Alaska court declared Jonz and his passengers dead on December 29, 1972. This declaration caused Alaska to hold a special election on March 1973. Young won the election and became the new lone Alaska representative.

All members of Alaska's delegation were new, untested, and without seniority. Alaska had elected Mike Gravel as their senator in November 1968. After Alaska's other senator, Bob Bartlett, died, Governor Hickel appointed Ted Stevens to fill Bartlett's seat in December 1968. Alaska held a special election in 1970 and elected Stevens to finish the remainder of Bartlett's term. Then he won the senate seat in the regular 1972 election. Thus, Gravel and Stevens had essentially the same tenure; less than four years. Representative Young had only a few days of experience. However, this freshman delegation was about to receive help from the most unlikely country on the planet–Libya.

Chapter 10

The Perfect Storm

After being so close to attaining the right-of-way permit, the TAPS project sank to a new low in April 1973 when the Supreme Court refused to hear Alyeska's appeal. The pipeline was pinned within a legal logjam. Thus, out of desperation, Alyeska exercised its only option—lobbying Congress to amend the Minerals Leasing Act or create a new law that would permit a wider right-of-way.

As Alaska's economic doldrums extended during the protracted legal battles, Fairbanks's real estate market tanked. Businesses collapsed. People were hurting. Fairbanks's 18,000 residents hunkered down and persevered through an exceptionally cold February of mostly -50° F temperatures. During this stressful and depressing time, the town again expressed its resilient nature of 1967 and dared to consider an extravagant and frivolous venture. The City of Fairbanks thought it was time their Lathrop High School, home of the mighty Malemutes, had a football team.

Named after early Alaska businessman Austin E. "Cap" Lathrop, Lathrop served most of the Tanana River Valley with the exception of the smaller Monroe Catholic and Eielson Air Force Base high schools. A large bus system transported students from faraway communities such as Ester, North Pole, Fort Wainwright, and Fox. Thus, Lathrop's student body swelled to about 1,600.

Many of the Fairbanks businessmen had come from the Lower 48, where football was a deeply ingrained tradition. To them, it was unthinkable to have a local high school the size of Lathrop without a football team. The newspaper and evening radio talk shows frequently discussed the subject. The discussions always came down to cost—and it was staggering. Lathrop did not have a football field, gear or uniforms to outfit at least 30 players, or a coach. To complicate matters, most games required travel to Palmer, Anchorage, and Kenai—distances ranging from 300 to 500 miles each way. Critics screamed, "Where would the money come from?" Still, Fairbanks residents began to slowly develop solutions to these vexing problems.

The football field was solved by expanding the Growden baseball field. Growden was home to the Fairbanks Goldpanners—a semiprofessional baseball team. Fairbanks had built the field in 1960 from salvaged box seats from the defunct Seattle Sick's Stadium. By moving the east outfield wall, the football field would just fit. However, players would have to endure bare ground where the bases, running lanes, and pitcher mound were located. Portable bleachers would be dragged into place along the field and spectators could always pile into the baseball stadium seats.

Businesses stepped forward with donations. Some secured surplus equipment from Lower 48 schools. Fairbanks Air and Wien Airlines promised steeply reduced rates to shuttle the team to Anchorage. Then the search went out through the community for a coach and the City found one—Bill Culpepper. Born and raised in Texas, Bill had coached football at Texas Christian University. He and his family had moved to Fairbanks to accept a job as a counselor and wrestling coach at Lathrop. Unfortunately, they arrived just in time to experience the 1967 flood.

Undaunted, Culpepper plunged into the community as a volunteer for the Fairbanks Youth Football League. He sat on the board of directors and coached teams. This provided Bill an opportunity to see local talent sprouting from the neighborhood and track their development. The youth leagues were extremely popular and helped spark interest in a varsity team. The community knew that there was not a more qualified man to be found who could coach Fairbanks's inaugural team.

Jay Sullivan had never lost his love of the game and had helped Culpepper coach a few teams. So when Bill accepted the coaching post, he immediately contacted Jay for help. Jay invited Bill to join him at the Petroleum Club to discuss the details. After drinks were served and small talk was finished, Bill brought the conversation to a head. "I can't pay you," said Bill with his slight Texan drawl, "but I would really appreciate your help."

Jay chuckled as he downed his first bourbon on ice and replied, "Never figured I would get a dime. So, is the high school team gonna happen?"

Bill answered as Jay raised his hand to the waitress and signaled for two more drinks, "Ninety percent sure. The school board still has to sanction it and the Cook Inlet Football Conference has to accept us as a member. I should know by mid-July if it's a go."

Jay shook his head and said, "That doesn't leave you much time to assemble a team and train them. When is the first game?"

Bill took another swig and forcibly exhaled as he answered, "August 25. Damn, Jay, this stuff will rot your guts out!"

"Naw," Jay replied, "a couple more and you'd think you had a new perspective on life. So, by the time you sign boys up, get them outfitted, and start training, you will have—what, about two weeks before your first game? You are playing against some established teams in Anchorage. This isn't going to pan out well."

Bill got a serious look on his face as he leaned towards Jay and said, "That's right, Jay. The deck is stacked against me. Everyone's looking for a miracle and they ain't gonna git it. This is why I need your help. I need you to look over the team as they practice and help me place them in their correct positions. But, mostly, Jay, I need you to scout the Anchorage teams for me. I know you live in Anchorage, so I was hoping you could attend a few games while you're home and report to me what you see."

The waitress arrived with their new drinks. Jay let her serve them before lifting his glass as a toast. "Here's to a successful football season, cheers!" They clinked their tumblers and threw back their drinks. Jay was glad the bourbon was good because he had a hunch that the football season would not be as smooth.

In the spring of 1973, Congress went to work sculpturing the Trans-Alaska Pipeline Authorization Act to sanction the right-of-way for the project. Infighting occurred immediately and split the Senate in half as they considered the House bill. Environmental groups relentlessly lobbied their senators to push a Canadian option. Their hope was to stall the project for years until it curled up and died. Senator Walter Mondale submitted amendments to delay the pipeline project until the Canadian alternative could be thoroughly studied. The Senate soundly defeated these amendments. Other senators worried that the oil companies would sell the Alaskan oil on foreign markets. For many senators, the only reason they supported the bill was to guarantee another source of oil besides the unstable Middle East. The Senate agreed to insert a provision into the bill that required presidential approval for any exports of Alaskan oil and the Congress had the power to reverse that decision.

While the Senate was debating these issues and developing solutions, another menace began to permeate through the congressional halls. The environmental opposition was preparing a lawsuit claiming the Department of the Interior had not fulfilled the intent of NEPA. Since there was little case law defining NEPA, this was a real threat. The suit could tie the project up in the courts for years.

Help came from the most unlikely person—Alaska's freshman Senator Mike Gravel. Gravel submitted an amendment to the pipeline bill that would limit judicial review of the project. Furthermore, permits granted for the project were not subject to challenges related to NEPA. The opposition screamed like they had just been gutted. Major newspapers and magazines declared Gravel was trying to diminish the most significant piece of environmental legislation in our century. Another argument presented was that Congress had circumvented the Constitution by preventing judicial oversight. Gravel countered by stating that he was only setting time limits on possible legal actions.

The controversy raged until the Gravel amendment finally came to the Senate floor for a vote on July 17, 1973. The Senate split into a 49–49 tie. Vice President Spiro Agnew broke the tie by casting his vote in favor of the amendment. The final authorization bill went into Senate and House committees to hammer out compromises between the House and Senate versions. Congress expected to vote on the bill in late October or early November. Based on the Senate's split on the Gravel amendment, everyone expected a close vote and no one knew which way it would go.

Well, it was worth a try, thought Harry as he read Mr. John Bullock's reply. The previous year, Harry had sent a legal-looking letter to Bullock offering $15,000 to buy his claims that straddled the proposed pipeline route. Harry even had David Henderson sign it. Bullock politely refused and stated he would entertain an offer that more closely reflected the true mineral value of the properties. Harry snorted when he read that line. He could just imagine what his perceived value was.

Harry knew this meant they were going to court to disprove the validity of the claims. Jay thought Alyeska had a good case because when he inspected the sites, he did not discover any evidence of mining or test holes. Still, court proceedings were expensive and incredibly time consuming. If he could avoid legal action, he would, but the handwriting was on the wall. Not only was Bullock preparing to fight, but his cohorts, such as Guy Rivers and Harry Leonard were joining him. Even Dr. Stolting of the Mount Si Project was filing bogus claims along the Richardson Highway.

Suddenly, Harry became aware of the irony of the situation. Here he was fighting false mineral claims across the proposed pipeline right-of-way. Meanwhile, he had authorized Land Field Services to file over a hundred false gold claims north of Valdez to encumber the land. Harry collapsed in his chair as he contemplated the twist of events. "How did things get so complicated?" he moaned. And Harry knew in his heart that things would get worse when construction started.

On a beautiful summer day, Bob Ylvisaker turned off the Richardson Highway onto the familiar access road leading to the Burns homestead. Bob had grown to love these people over the past year. He still had his quarrels with Burns, but Bob realized that their arguments were not personal. Each exchange ended in a stalemate and Burns always invited Bob to stay for a meal. For a young man accustomed to sporadic dinners, this was a welcome treat, as was the engaging conversation afterwards. Bob always left feeling uplifted.

Today was different. Jay had given him a draft book to take to his negotiations with the Burnses. The draft book was a leather-covered checkbook. Jay had shown Bob how to insert a stiff sheet of plastic under the first check blank. Each check had an original sheet and a blue duplicate. Jay had told Bob that if he wrote a settlement check for the Burnses, he must make sure he only tore off the original. Alyeska would need the duplicate for their records. Jay gave Bob a settlement range that he was authorized to issue. If Bob was successful, he was to report back to Jay. Jay would contact Armand or Harry and relay the amount written. They would contact the bank and authorize the payment.

Bob knew that the draft book meant Alyeska had raised the ante on a settlement. As Bob drove down from Fairbanks, he had mused about what this meant. Was Alyeska growing impatient with his negotiations? What would happen if he didn't settle?

He pulled in front of the cabin and saw Burns pushing a cart of cut logs to a woodshed. Bob jumped out and yelled, "Hi, Mr. Burns!"

Burns let go of the cart handles, lifted his cap off his head, and wiped his brow as he said, "Silver! What brings you here on this fine day?"

Bob walked over to shake his hand. "Oh, I thought we could pick up where we left off about getting an easement."

Burns wagged his head as he shook Bob's hand and replied, "You are a persistent fellow, I'll give you that. So, what do you have in your left hand?"

"Oh, this?" replied Bob as he held up the draft book. "It's a checkbook. Alyeska has authorized me to issue you a check to compensate you for an easement."

Burns's friendly face became very solemn. Then he spoke with carefully chosen words, "You know, Bob, there are things in this world you can't buy." An awkward moment passed before Burns motioned with his head for Bob to follow him. They walked in silence to the back of his claim along the Gulkana River.

They stood quietly watching the river flow. Then Burns spoke, "My wife and I filed our claim on this land because we fell in love with its beauty and tranquility. We thought others would feel the same way and would want to camp and enjoy the view. If that oil line crosses the front of our property, it will destroy what we hold dear. Money won't restore the land once construction starts." Burns turned to Bob to emphasize his point as he continued, "I can't be bought."

Bob suddenly felt embarrassed to be holding the draft book. He nodded and returned his gaze at the river. After a few more minutes of silence, Bob said, "Well, I should probably mosey on down the road."

"I'll walk you back."

They made their way back to the car. Bob shook Burns's hand and said, "Please tell Mrs. Burns hello from me."

Burns nodded and replied, "I'll do that." Bob smiled, got into his car, and drove slowly away. He could not help but feel that something dark and sad had passed between them. As his wheels hit the Richardson Highway, the sadness increased when he realized Burns had not invited him to stay for dinner.

On July 20, 1973, the *Fairbanks Daily News Miner* printed, "First Lathrop Football Team Set." It was official. Principal Phil Sword announced Fairbanks was going to have a high school football team. He had authorized Bill Culpepper to move quickly to secure his assistant coaches. Sword had hoped Bill would hire only within the ranks of the existing Lathrop staff. Bill responded by bringing Gene Cole, the high school gymnastics coach, onto the team. Then he convinced Sword to allow him to reach into the community and grab a successful youth football coach as his other assistant.

Bill had his sights on a 21-year-old dynamo named Dan Beardsley. Dan had come to Alaska in 1970 with his stepdad to find seasonal work. Willing to do anything, Dan worked summers from 1970 to 1973 washing dishes at the Chatanika Lodge, helping miners stake claims, working at Curry's Corner, and fighting fires. He always managed to scrape up enough money to fund a semester or two of college in the Lower 48 before making his way back to Alaska to work again.

In 1970, Dan played football for the University of Florida. He made the freshman squad as a defensive end. Dan was under six-feet tall and used his speed to compensate for his lack of size. By the end of the season, Dan had badly injured his shoulder and his football playing came to an end.

But football was in his blood and Dan couldn't shake his love for the game. He satisfied his need by coaching Fairbanks Youth Football during the summers. In 1971, Dan coached the mighty Cowboys and took them to second place in their division. The next year, Dan's Cowboys took first place and traveled to Anchorage to play the city's first-place youth team. The Cowboys lost by a questionable safety call (two points). However, Fairbanks was impressed with their youths' performance and Culpepper took a great interest in Dan's coaching abilities.

When Bill called Dan and offered him the assistant position, Dan turned him down. He was working for the Department of Highways as a surveyor on the Elliott Highway from Chatanika to Snowshoe. He also had purchased a mobile home in the Birchwood Trailer Park off 4.5-mile Steese Highway. For the first time in Dan's life, he had a mortgage. In addition to this debt, Dan had visions of vacationing in Australia for the winter. Thus, he was motivated to make money this summer—not coach football.

But fate dealt another hand to Dan. The Department of Highways decided to wrap the survey project up by September 1. Dan could see the handwriting on the wall. He was not going to be able to fund his Australia trip and decided to make the best of it. So he called Culpepper back and told him that he would take the position if Bill could find him a part-time job. Bill said he would ask his friend, Bill "Billy Bob" Allen, at the Alaska Bank of the North to get Dan something to tie him over. With that, Dan took a leap of faith and filed for an early release from the Department of Highways. The Department granted Dan the release just in time for the start of the two-a-day football practices on August 12.

The Cook Inlet Football Conference mandated that each football player must have at least two weeks of practice to develop the necessary physical conditioning before playing a sanctioned game. Football teams usually compressed two practices a day into this two-week period. The two-a-day practices were a football tradition to quickly bring players into shape, sharpen playing skills, and teach the offense and defense formation and plays.

Culpepper tightly managed the training sessions. Practice started at 8 a.m. sharp with heavy penalties for being late. The two-hour practice consisted of endurance running and countless sprints, endless calisthenics, and drills.

The three-hour afternoon practice started at 3 p.m. and interspersed football skills and strategy with the physical training. During both practices, the coaches drove the players to run the dirt hills behind Lathrop High School. A huge dust cloud always hung over the practice field at the end of the day.

Dan arrived on his first day with his sun-bleached hair almost reaching his shoulders. He was experimenting this year with the new long-hair look of the early 1970s. Dan had not cut it since January. Culpepper was slightly taken aback by his appearance, but dismissed his hair length as a young man's one-time statement to society. Jay, however, was appalled. When Culpepper introduced Dan, Jay could barely mask his displeasure and told Dan that he had a Joe Namath look.

After the rocky start, Dan and Jay developed a mutual respect for the other's football knowledge. Dan concentrated on coaching the defensive backs and Gene Cole focused his efforts on the offensive backs. Jay assisted Bill Culpepper with the overall practice and filled in as a linemen coach until someone permanent could be found.

Sixty-eight boys signed up to play. By the end of the first week of two-a-days, 55 remained. Culpepper thought this was normal attrition, but still wished he could have at least 60 players to start the season. Injuries always took a toll.

Midway through the second week, the team manager poked his head into Culpepper's office and said, "Coach. There's a guy who just came in from the bush who wants to play."

Bill pushed away from his desk and asked, "What position does he play?"

The manager replied, "He said offensive guard and defensive end."

"Alright, then," answered Culpepper. "Have Coach Sullivan talk to him. Make sure he knows that he's entering the season late. All starting positions are taken."

"Right-o! I'll tell him." The manager pulled away from the office and motioned to the boy standing behind him to follow. "I take it you heard the coach?"

"I heard," said the boy as he followed. "I want to try anyhow."

"Suit yourself. Here's Coach Sullivan." Jay was standing at the end of the locker room studying a play sheet on a clipboard. The manager stopped in front of Jay and addressed him. "Coach Sullivan, this guy just got into town. He wants to play. Coach Culpepper asked if you would check him out."

Jay looked up from his board and evaluated the kid in front of him. He stood slightly over six feet with a floppy, unbalanced mop of hair and skinny as a rail. He wore black-framed glasses and had a determined set to his mouth. He looked like a scrapper.

Jay carefully swallowed, held out his massive hand and said, "I'm Coach Sullivan. What's your name?"

The kid grabbed Jay's hand with surprising strength and replied, "Mike Travis, sir."

Jay smiled and asked, "How come you're starting so late?"

"I flew in from Galena two days ago. I got here as soon as I could, but I was at a remote camp and I couldn't get a plane any quicker. Sorry."

Jay was intrigued, "So where exactly were you?"

Mike replied, "Melozi Hot Springs. It's about 30 miles north of Ruby."

Jay was familiar with the Melozitna River and Ruby and knew he must have been in a very remote corner of Alaska. He looked Mike up and down said, "Didn't they feed you out there?"

Mike smiled and replied, "Yes. People made fun of my appetite."

"So, what position do you play?"

"Offensive guard and defensive end."

Jay coughed to cover his laugh. "OK. How much do you weigh?"

"150."

He's lying, thought Jay. "Do you have a physical with a doctor's OK?"

Mike presented Jay with a one-page doctor approval. "Yes. I got my physical yesterday."

Jay was impressed. He took the doctor's approval from Mike, opened the folded page, and read it. Although the doctor approved Mike to play football, it did contain the following note, "Student appears to be underweight, but not malnourished." Jay refolded the note and slipped it into his clipboard before continuing, "OK, Mr. Travis. The manager will outfit you with some gear. Conference rules are you must practice for two weeks before we can play ya. The guard spots are all taken. Maybe you know them? Willie Ault and Tom Richards are the starting guards. Randy Turner is the backup."

Mike answered, "I know Willie. He's a year ahead of me in school. Tom and Randy are in my class and they're my friends."

Jay nodded as he continued, "Then I suggest you focus on special teams. Ever done that before?"

"Yes. Both kickoff and receiving."

"Good," said Jay as he wrote a note on his clipboard. "Go find some gear that fits and I'll see ya on the practice field. Welcome aboard."

Mike smiled and said, "Thanks, Coach. I'll do my best."

After the two-a-day practices ended, the demands on Dan Beardsley lessened and he suddenly had some free time to look for a part-time job to supplement his meager income. Dan reminded Culpepper of his promise to contact Bill Allen. True to his word, Culpepper spoke to Allen, who responded by offering Dan a job as a collection agent for the Alaska National Bank of the North.

Dan cringed at the thought of collections, but he was strapped for cash. Thus, he reluctantly accepted the position. He started his job early each day by reviewing the list of receivables. Then he started calling customers who were behind on their credit card and loan payments. Each call was contentious and grated on his nerves. He worked until 2 p.m. without a break. Then he ran to Lathrop to start the afternoon football practice. Dan knew his employment situation was temporary, but he was uncertain where he was going to find good stable work.

As Dan entered the locker room one afternoon, he saw Bill Culpepper through his office window talking with a young massive man. Bill looked up, spotted Dan, and waved him over. When Dan entered the office, Bill introduced him. "Dan, this is Tom Pierce. He will be our new lineman coach. Tom played some ball for Ohio State. Tom, Dan is our defensive back coach."

Dan and Tom evaluated each other as they shook hands. Tom was about six-feet tall with a thick neck and chest and a crew cut–all the hallmarks of a lineman. He looked down at Dan and sneered as he said, "I guess I will be coaching the big guys and you got the small ones."

Dan squeezed Tom's hand tighter as he replied, "You mean I got the quicker guys and you got the slower ones."

Culpepper watched the exchange with some anxiety. He wasn't anticipating friction between his assistants. "Easy boys. Save it for the games. Tom, I'll introduce you to the team and get you set up." Dan and Tom released their grips and took a step back from each other. *I'm going to have to watch these two*, thought Bill.

Dan and Tom nodded to each other as they left Culpepper's office. Dan walked over to Jay and said, "I met your replacement. I bet he's not as good as you."

Jay grinned and replied, "Why, Danny boy, what on earth do you mean? You think he's rough around the edges?"

Dan stuck out his chin and declared, "I think he's full of himself."

Jay put his hand on Dan's shoulder and said, "Maybe so, but he'll sure free me up to concentrate on scouting. I've been neglecting my business, too. For my sake, let's make this work. What do you say, Danny?"

"Sure, Jay," answered Dan. Intrigued, Dan continued, "By the way, Jay, what is your business?"

Jay looked intently at Dan for a moment before replying, "Land Field Services. We perform surveys and right-of-way negotiations for TAPS. We got a lot on our plate right now. My people are stretched thin. I need to spend more time with them."

Dan responded off the cuff, "My stepdad taught me how to survey. I worked on a highway survey crew this summer north of Fairbanks."

Jay nodded, "That's what I hear. We better get going, Danny boy. The boys are waiting for their practice."

———————————————

The Alyeska engineers selected a route north of Fairbanks that crossed Gilmore Trail, a dirt rural road that followed a ridge north of town, and then descended a steep, but smooth, slope to the floor of the Goldstream Valley. Here, the route met the Steese Highway and followed it north to the intersection with the Elliott Highway. The engineers were pleased with the valley floor because decades of gold dredging had thawed the permafrost to bedrock. The resulting dredge tailings provided a stable foundation to bury a pipeline.

The Fairbanks Engineering (F.E.) Company owned most of the property across the Goldstream Valley and north along the Elliott Highway. Shortly before Armand contacted the F.E. Company, they changed their name to U.V. Industries. The resident manager of U.V. Industries was a lifelong Fairbanks citizen named Dan Eagan. Dan had taken the position from his father and carried on the family tradition of managing the gold holdings. He worked in the old F.E. building off Illinois Street.

Armand and Dan became fast friends. Each was professional and understood the land interests of their company. Dan, though, wanted to educate Armand on the added value of Alyeska's proposed right-of-way take. As they sat back with their steaming mugs of coffee in Dan's antique office, Dan began to describe the land holdings. "Armand, when the gold dredges worked the valley floor, they didn't have the technology to capture small nuggets and flakes of gold. They only got the big stuff. Lots of fine gold either washed out of the screens or fell out of the buckets. U.V. plans to mine our holdings with modern screen plants to capture this gold. So you see, the value of the land is more than the surface. There is a residual gold value, too."

"OK," replied Armand as he nodded, "then I assume you have calculated the residual gold reserves?"

Dan took another sip of the steaming coffee and answered, "Yes. We have assays of our patented mining claims including your proposed right-of-way corridor."

Armand pressed the matter, "So you have proof of mineral content for all 133 acres we want to purchase?"

"For the most part, yes."

"OK," continued Armand, "my company will need to verify any residual gold claims before they will agree to compensate you for the loss. Will that be a problem?"

Dan took off his old frayed F.E. cap and rubbed his short hair. Armand could tell he was stalling for time as he thought about it. Finally, he responded, "It shouldn't be, but we'll need a confidentiality agreement between our companies. OK?"

Armand nodded and replied, "I understand. That won't be a problem. I'll take a crack at the agreement and run it by you before we finalize it. In the meantime, you should start compiling your data for our review."

"Will do," said Dan. Then he leaned towards Armand and asked, "So, are your engineers pretty sure of their route? I mean, it's not going to vary much, will it?"

Armand couldn't see where Dan was going with his questioning. "From what I am told, they like the stable ground and are confident of the route. Why do you ask?"

Dan leaned back in his chair, took another sip, and replied, "Because I'm thinking of drilling along your centerline and collecting soil samples. It will bolster our claims."

Armand nodded as he stood and finished off his coffee. "I think that is prudent." He put down his cup, extended his hand to Dan, and said, "Thank you for the great cup of coffee. We'll be talking frequently over the next months."

"You are welcome," replied Dan as he stood and shook Armand's hand. "Look forward to it."

No one on the Lathrop football team noticed the beautiful fall day in Anchorage on September 29. Under crystal-clear skies, the West High Eagles were murdering the Malemutes. Midway through the fourth quarter, the score was 67 to 0. Nothing had gone right for the Malemutes. The Eagles seemed to anticipate every play and their offense ripped through the Malemute defenses. The feeling of crushing defeat hung over the Lathrop team—a far cry from the elation they had felt from last week's win over Palmer.

Just when it seemed the score couldn't get any worse, West scored another touchdown and an extra point. The score was now 74 to nothing. Culpepper dutifully signaled for the kickoff receiving squad to take the field. Mike Travis slipped on his helmet and trotted out to the field for what felt like the thousandth time. During the years he had played football, he had never occupied the field so much as a special teams unit. They seemed to be constantly punting and receiving kickoffs.

Mike was one of three blockers for the kickoff receiver, Sam McCormick. Sam could run like the wind if he could get an open field, but Mike and his fellow blockers, Rick Redick and Roland Costillo, were having a hard time knocking a hole in the Eagle pursuers.

The West High kicker raised his hand signaling that he was ready. The referee blew his whistle to start the clock and the Eagle line rushed forward. The kicker sent the ball flying high and long–the worst possible combination for special-team blockers. The ball landed on the 10-yard line and began to roll to the end zone. Mike, Rick, and Roland fell back to protect Sam. Rick yelled, "Let it go! We'll take it on the twenty."

The ball stopped six inches short of the goal line.

Someone wailed, "Oh no!" Mike looked up to see the entire West line coming down upon them. Rick was the first to snap out of his disbelief. "We got to get out of here! Let's go!" He picked up the ball and started sprinting forward. His movement drew the tacklers to him. At the last possible second, Rick turned, pitched the ball to Sam, and dove into his opponent. Rick hit him at the knees and sent him tumbling over the top.

Roland cleaved the next man at the ankles and sent him flying. Mike gathered speed and launched a side-fly block taking out two players. A hole opened up and Sam shot through it. He twisted and weaved his way to the 45-yard line before an Eagle brought him down by a shoestring tackle. His run was Lathrop's best play of the game.

As Mike jogged off the field, Culpepper pointed to him and said, "Nope. I want you to play guard. West is finally pulling their first-string team. You might as well get some playing time, too."

"Yes, sir," replied Mike as he spun around and ran to the huddle. He wished he could be happy about being on offense, but he knew that he was playing for all the wrong reasons.

Coach Dan Beardsley was smoking mad. "What an ass! If I get the chance, I'm going to paste that West coach right across the jaw! He should have pulled his starters long ago."

Jay patted Dan's shoulder and said, "Now, now, Danny boy, we can't have you slugging the West coach. What example would you set for the team, eh?"

Dan retorted, "Well, I'm sure not going to shake his hand!" Jay just smiled.

Neither team advanced the ball. The score remained 74-0 at the end. The nightmare game was over. The Lathrop coaches directed their players onto the bus for waiting showers and an F-27 Wien Airlines plane ride from Merrill Field back to Fairbanks.

The following week, Lathrop lost their final game of the season to the Chugiak Mustangs 39-16. The coaches milled through the locker room and said their goodbyes to the players. Mike shook Coach Beardsley's hand and said, "Thanks for everything, Coach. I enjoyed getting to know you."

Dan nodded, causing his shoulder-length hair to swing as he replied, "Likewise, Mike. Have a good school year."

When the gear was put away and the last player had left, Bill Culpepper presented Dan with a check for $600. Although this sum was a pittance for his time, Culpepper informed Dan he had to split it with Gene Cole and Tom Pierce. Thus, Lathrop High School paid the assistant coaches $200 for two and a half months of work. Dan stuffed the check into his front shirt pocket and thanked Bill for the coaching experience.

Financially, Dan was in a world of hurt. He had only a part-time job at the bank and he loathed it. He was facing a hard winter in Fairbanks and he was strapped for cash. He needed stable full-time employment. Thus, the next afternoon as he sat in his lonely mobile home contemplating his predicament, Dan suddenly acted on impulse. He picked up the telephone and called directory assistance for the Land Field Services office number. Then he placed a desperate call to Jay. The receptionist answered and transferred him to Jay. Jay picked up immediately.

"Danny boy," Jay answered with a cheery voice, "what a pleasant surprise. To what do I owe the pleasure of your call?"

By Jay's tone, Dan could visualize that Jay had a smile across face. Jay's voice also betrayed that he knew the answer to the question. Dan cleared his throat and said, "Uh, Jay, I was hoping you and I could talk about a possible position with your firm."

With a teasing tone, Jay replied, "Why, Danny, I understand Bill Allen has taken a shine towards your collection skills. How could I possibly rob Mr. Allen of such a talented employee?" Jay let Dan's jaw drop open before continuing, "Just joshing ya. How about lunch tomorrow at the Petroleum Club? Meet you there around noon?"

Relief flooded across Dan's face as he answered, "Noon sounds good, Jay. I'll see you there. Thank you." Jay said goodbye. As Dan hung up, he suddenly became aware of his hair brushing his shoulders. *I better get a haircut before lunch tomorrow,* Dan thought. *I don't think Jay likes it and I need a job.*

Dan met Jay at noon in the Petroleum Club. He thought he looked sharp with his hair cut to ear length and wearing a sport shirt and slacks, but Jay never commented on his appearance. As was customary for Jay, he ordered drinks before discussing business. Dan wasn't much of a drinker, but accepted the bourbon on the rocks as an initiation rite. Jay saluted and threw back his drink like it was water. Dan took a sip and almost gagged. When Jay raised his hand and signaled to the waitress for two more, Dan knew he had lost control of the afternoon.

Jay now turned his attention to more pressing matters. "Dan, I'd like to bring you on our team and train you to acquire right-of-way. Your survey background is a big plus and will help you understand the proposed pipeline corridor needs. Interested?"

Dan thought this was a dream come true. "Yes! I am very interested. How long do you think your TAPS contract will last?"

The waitress brought the second round of drinks. Dan had barely dented his first. Jay gratefully accepted his fresh glass and took a more controlled swig before answering, "Two, maybe three years. If you're thrifty, it should pay for the rest of your college education."

Dan could barely contain himself. In his excitement, he swallowed a gulp of bourbon and it ripped the breath out of his lungs. He needed a minute to compose himself.

"Easy, Danny boy," Jay said with a laugh, "if you work for me, you've got to pace yourself. Are you all right?"

With tears streaming from his eyes, Dan nodded as he suppressed a cough and asked in a wheezing voice, "What would my starting salary be?"

Jay brought his tumbler to his lips and said, "Oh, I was thinking $1,400 per month. How does that sound?" Jay studied Dan's surprised face as he took a drink.

Dan was astonished at the offer. He would make double what Bill Allen paid him and a two-year job would be the longest steady employment he'd ever had. Dan lifted up his glass and said, "I gratefully accept!" He threw back the rest of his drink so hard that the ice cubes ricocheted off his teeth.

Jay returned the toast by replying, "Welcome aboard!" Later that evening, Dan couldn't recall eating lunch.

Dan arrived a week later at the Land Field Services company to begin his new career. Shirley Pippen met him at the door with a gracious smile and hearty hand shake. "Welcome, Dan. Jay told me to expect you. Let me introduce you to the gang." Shirley turned to the office and yelled, "Hey everyone, Dan's here. Come over here and meet him." Dutifully, they all complied. When they gathered around Shirley's desk, she began the introductions.

"OK. First we have Beth Feeney, my assistant." Beth was the same age as Dan. She was tall and slender with long brown hair. She gave Dan a shy smile and offered her hand. Dan gently took it and said hello.

Shirley continued, "And this character is Bob Ylvisaker. If you can't remember his last name, just call him Silver."

Bob greeted him enthusiastically, "Hi ya, Dan! Welcome aboard." Dan could tell that they were going to become fast friends.

"And here's the Bruces, Don and his son Dick." Dan cocked his head sideways out of curiosity as he evaluated them. To Dan, they seemed out of place, but strangely in sync with each other. Don was dressed in shirt-and-tie business attire while Dick wore a turtleneck sweater and slacks. Each exuded a sense of professional competence as they shook Dan's hand and nodded hello.

Shirley appeared pleased at how the introductions were going. She reached around Don and pulled a small man in front of Dan. "And, finally, this is Keith Christenson. He provides the legal support." Keith quietly smiled as he shook Dan's hand.

"Good to meet you, Keith," said Dan.

Keith mouthed, "Same here."

Shirley put her hands on her hips and proclaimed, "Well, there you have it. Here's the group of scoundrels you got yourself mixed up with. The door's there if you want to chicken out."

Dan looked at the smiling faces staring back at him, shook his head, and replied, "Nope. I'm in it for the long haul."

Shirley shook her blonde curls and said, "I figured as much. You look like you belong here. You had your chance to run. Now you need to see the boss." She escorted Dan to Jay's office, which adjoined the main room. "Here you go, Jay. I tried to shoo him off, but he insisted on staying. He's yours to corrupt."

Jay turned in his chair, extended a 20-dollar bill to Dan, and said, "Welcome aboard, young fella. Now go get a haircut and report back to me."

Dan's jaw dropped in surprise. He almost sputtered that he just got one, but caught himself and awkwardly accepted the 20. Then he said, "Thank you, Jay. I'll be right back." Dan's right-of-way training had begun.

In 1969, Libya's new revolutionary dictator, Colonel Muamer Qadaffi, demanded 50 percent participation of profits from companies pulling oil from his country and raised the price of Libyan crude by 40 cents per barrel. Qadaffi's actions were unprecedented–never before had an owner-country set such audacious terms with one of the seven major producers or with the smaller independent companies. The world, especially America, had developed an insatiable appetite for cheap oil. It fueled their cars, heated their homes, and provided electricity. No producer could simply refuse to deal with Qadaffi and walk away from the tremendous Libyan reserves. The oil market was too lucrative to ignore and the cost of retrieving oil from Libya was much lower than from Iran or Saudi Arabia. The oil companies could absorb the price increase and still make an enormous profit. However, the producers were afraid of the pattern that would be set if they dealt with this wild revolutionary.

Then Colonel Qadaffi raised the stakes in June 1970 by threatening to nationalize the developed fields and ordered a cutback in production. The producers realized they could lose their entire investment in Libya. One by one they agreed to Qadaffi's terms.

The other members of the Organization of the Petroleum Exporting Countries (OPEC) watched with rapt interest and began to flex their muscles. By early 1973, the oil producers were complying with some sort of revenue sharing and quotas within every OPEC nation.

The revenue sharing and increased wellhead prices for crude were an economic boon to OPEC. However, the Arab countries were still politically and culturally separated. The Egypt/Israel Six-Day war in 1967 and the October 6, 1973 Yom Kippur War changed this. As they watched US-backed Israeli forces swat down the Egyptians and then the surrounding Arab nations, OPEC realized that they held the keys to controlling alliances. The United States had failed to develop domestic sources of oil to meet their country's gargantuan demand. Thus, the US economy was vulnerable to foreign manipulation of the country's petroleum sources. OPEC decided to yank the US chain and cut off their source of oil in a bold attempt to stop US intervention in the Arab/Israel conflict.

Qadaffi sowed the seeds of a US embargo in August 1973 when he nationalized 51 percent of the Libyan oil field in recognition of the fourth anniversary of their country's revolution. Then Qadaffi doubled the price of Libyan oil.

Shortly afterwards, Egypt's President Sadat visited Saudi Arabia's King Feisal and asked for help with deterring American support for Israel. King Feisal promised that if the United States did not reduce their arm supplies to Israel, the Persian Gulf would restrict the sale of oil to them. On October 16, OPEC, led by Saudi Arabia, announced a 70 percent increase in crude oil prices and a 5 percent decrease in production.

President Nixon ignored the shot across his bow. On October 19, he requested Congress to appropriate $2.2 billion in emergency aid to Israel. The request triggered a collaborative OPEC response. Libya immediately announced it would cut all oil shipments to the United States and other countries supporting Israel. The rest of OPEC quickly followed and joined a total oil embargo to the United States on October 20. Crude oil prices shot up from three dollars a barrel to over twelve dollars. In response, the United States stock market tanked.

Within a week of the embargo, the American public began to feel the effects of restricted oil supplies. The United States soon consumed the limited storage of refined product causing outlets like the neighborhood gas stations to close. Mainline filling stations connected to one of the seven oil producers remained open, but lines formed over a mile long to refuel cars. Some denser populated areas alternated refueling to cars with even or odd license plate numbers to reduce waiting lines. Thugs even hijacked a gasoline tanker truck to sell the fuel on the black market.

The Texas and Oklahoma oil fields and offshore American production platforms could not meet US demands. Outraged Americans demanded Congress find a solution and political eyes turned toward Alaska to save them. Suddenly, all political misgivings and concerns about the Trans Alaska Pipeline project miraculously dissolved. Congressional debates concluded within two weeks of deliberation. House and Senate committee conferences quickly hammered out their differences. Then on November 12, three weeks after OPEC levied the embargo, the US House of Representatives voted on the Trans-Alaska Pipeline Authorization Act and passed it overwhelmingly, 361 to 14. The next day, the Senate passed the act 80 to 5. President Nixon wasted no time. He signed the bill into law on November 16, 1973.

The Trans-Alaska Pipeline Authorization Act had two main provisions. First, the act directed the Secretary of the Interior to grant a right-of-way permit across federal Alaska lands. The second provision granted the TAPS construction materials priority under the Defense Production Act of 1950. Originally, Congress had created the Defense Production Act for government projects during a state of war, but politicians feared certain grades of steel might be in short supply when construction began, and thus needed protection. Nothing would prevent the nation's securing another source of crude oil. TAPS was the first private project to be protected by this act.

Other features of the Trans-Alaska Pipeline Authorization Act were less apparent, but had wide-reaching ramifications. Free-lance reporter James Roscow interviewed Quinn O'Connell and John Knodell and asked for their opinions on the act. Quinn smiled and replied, "The act in itself was unique. It was well written, but the fact that Congress thought it had to pass it at all is unique in itself."

Then Quinn pointed out the act's unique features. First, the act directed the Secretary of the Interior to formulate an affirmative action plan with goals set for Alyeska to hire minorities—especially Alaska Natives. TAPS was the first private project that the federal government required to implement this program. Another unique feature was mandating Alyeska to fund a federal oversight program that would monitor the construction and operation of TAPS.

John noted that the act established an oil-spill contingency fund to cover spills occurring during construction and pipeline operations. The fund was established by an initial Alyeska payment and maintained by a barrel tax on oil flowing through the pipeline. "The liability applies," said John, "on land or on sea. So the fund still applies to Alaska oil even if it is spilled in California waters." Thus, Alyeska's liability reached beyond Alaska.

Quinn expanded on this theme and described the act's prohibition of tankers discharging their oil-contaminated ballast water before arriving in Valdez. It directed Alyeska to treat the ballast water at the oil terminal before loading the ship with crude oil. "Normally, the Secretary of the Interior would not have any right to challenge these vessels," said Quinn. "This is using a right-of-way permit over federal lands to accomplish a result out in the middle of the ocean."

Later when Alyeska constructed TAPS, regulators and the public would remember Quinn's use of the word unique.

On December 3, 1973, Jay Sullivan filed several Affidavits of Annual Labor at the Valdez and Glenallen Recording Districts. These documents presented proof that Jay was still developing his gold-mining claims along the proposed TAPS centerline. Eventually, ADNR would require mineral assays to prove the viability of his claims. Then ADNR would discover his ruse and nullify his claims, but Jay figured he only needed to hold this land for one more year. By that time, the State would have issued their right-of-way lease.

Chapter 11

Setting the Stage

On January 8, 1974, Governor Egan signed an agreement with the U.S. Department of the Interior to cooperate with environmental surveillance of the TAPS construction. The agreement included opening an office for state and federal pipeline inspectors.

Harry Brelsford knew this action was the forerunner to issuing the federal right-of-way permit and it caused him to fret about undiscovered mining claims along the proposed pipeline alignment. Harry wanted nothing to complicate or delay the approval. Egan's agreement spurred Harry to push Land Field Services to finish the walking tours. While Jay's team had walked the alignment through populated areas and sections where mining was prevalent, there was a stretch of the proposed route near Paxson and south of the Mount Si Project where no inspections had occurred. This section was within the Alaska Range and, in some places, above the tree line. This time of year the area was entombed in deep snow with frigid temperatures and limited daylight. Despite these harsh conditions, Harry wanted that section searched at once.

Jay responded by sending the youngest and hardiest members of his team—Bob Ylvisaker and Dan Beardsley. Jay outfitted them with snow-shoes and Arctic gear and instructed them to work in pairs. "When the temperature falls below -30°, things fall apart in a hurry," counseled Jay. "Stay together and break each inspection up into two-mile sections. Don't push it. Take your time and it will all work out."

Then Jay gave each a pistol and holster. Bob got his .44 Magnum and Dan his .38. Jay continued, "These are not for bears, although you may run into an obstinate moose claiming the trail. These guns are for signaling in case you need to flag someone down for help. Remember, three shots in a row is the universal signal for help. If someone hears you, they will respond the same."

Neither Dan nor Bob had any prior experience with trudging through the Arctic wilderness. They listened intently to Jay's instructions and nodded. Jay studied them for a minute. Their innocence obligated him to enforce something. Whenever Jay had something important to say, he would hug his chest, lean back in his chair, put his chin down, and stare at you. He assumed this posture as he spoke sternly to the young men standing in front of him. "Of course, you would be signaling only to be rescued, not to each other because you're not splitting up, are you?" The men shook their heads. "Good! Stay together and you'll be fine. Now go get'em!"

Bob and Dan shook Jay's hand before loading up and driving south on the Richardson Highway to the Paxson Lodge. Stanley Brown, the lodge owner, set them up in their rooms and fed them dinner. Dan knew Brown's son, Stan, from Fairbanks Youth Football and inquired about him. Brown appreciated Dan's interest and proudly told him that Stan was attending high school in Washington to take advantage of their established football program.

"That's a shame," replied Dan. "Lathrop sure could use him next season."

As he watched them eat, Brown appraised Dan and Bob's situation and became concerned. These young men appeared eager and were in good shape, but they seemed to lack experience. Brown glanced at the thermometer through the dining room window. It read -35° degrees Fahrenheit. The temperature had dropped five degrees in the last four hours and it was still going down. Brown felt compelled to say something.

"Boys," said Brown as Bob and Dan were finishing their dinner, "we need to have a talk about safety." They both stopped and looked up from their meals at their host. "That's right. Listen up. Tomorrow morning, it's going to be colder than -40°. Mark my words. At that temperature, you screw up and you're dead! Understand? Everything you do is gonna take four times as long. So take your time. If you get into trouble, make your way to the highway and flag someone down. If you leave someone behind, get to me and I'll form a search party with the locals. Understand? No heroics out there."

Dan and Bob looked at each other, then back to Brown before nodding in unison. Brown had done what he could to get through to them. He sighed and said, "Well good. Better get a good night's sleep. You guys only got a couple of hours of daylight to work with. Better make the most of it."

The next morning was - 45. Mr. Brown gave each man a thermos of hot coffee and some sandwiches. "Before you guys head out, you better show me on a map where you're going." Bob pulled out an USGS topographical map of the area and pointed to a stretch ten miles south of the lodge where they would start. Brown nodded and said, "OK. Got it. Be careful. See you tonight."

Dan and Bob drove south along the Richardson Highway before finding a plowed pullout close to their first section. Here, they put their gear on and left the car running. It was too cold to shut it off while they were gone. Bob glanced at his watch. It was nine o'clock and the morning was still pitch-black with no hint of dawn.

Their first steps off the road indicated that this was going to be a long and strenuous day. Even with snowshoes, they sank to their knees in the fluffy, dry snow. This required lifting the next foot high above the surface while supporting the weight of the snowshoe, boot, and two feet of snow. Then as they committed to the next step, their snowshoes plunged forward into the deep snow as they repeated their stride to move the next foot ahead. This process quickly tired them and forced them to take turns breaking trail. The brush further hampered their progress. Sometimes they shined their flashlight ahead to navigate through the maze of trees.

They moved slowly up the long hill. Two hours later, they struck the pipeline survey swath. Exhausted, they bent over with their hands on their knees and drew ragged breaths of frigid air into their lungs. The sun had just broken the horizon, but its rays had no warmth. Their perspiration froze on their foreheads and caked their face masks.

"You OK, Bob?" gasped Dan.

Bob tried to answer, but he settled for a nod. They both knew they were in trouble. They were spent and they had not started their inspection. Finally, Bob said, "Let's take a coffee break." Dan nodded and they took off their canvas day packs and fished out their thermoses. The hot coffee hitting the ice-cold cup created a crackling sound and quickly cooled the liquid. They managed to get a couple of good swallows before the coffee became chilled. Then they drained their cups in the snow and repacked before trudging forward.

The flatter terrain and daylight eased the travel, but they still had to bushwhack through the snow. They finally reached their two-mile goal three hours later and were totally exhausted. The low temperature and snowshoeing through the deep snow had sapped their reserves. Dan tamped the snow down around them and they rested while drinking the remainder of the coffee and eating Brown's sandwiches.

Bob recorded the information from the survey marker where they had stopped and then they started trudging back. They were pleasantly surprised to find that the snow had hardened under their trail, which greatly eased their return trip. When they finally reached their car, they threw their snowshoes and packs in the trunk and jumped inside. The heat immediately had a healing effect. The ice melted off their eyelashes and thawed their faces and hands. When they took off their stocking hats, they laughed at each other's hair—matted down with spikes.

They drove back to the lodge as the sunset glow disappeared under the southern horizon. Their headlights shown through exhaust plumes from the sparse traffic, suspended over the road by the frigid weather. Brown was waiting for them. He helped them refuel the car and then plug it into a headbolt for the night, so that the block, oil pan, and battery heaters would keep the engine warm enough to start the next morning. Then he fed them a hot meal. The men wolfed it down.

When they were finishing up, Brown asked, "How did it go today, guys?"

Bob wiped his mouth and said, "It was cold and tough. We inspected only two miles today."

"And that's all you can hope for," snapped Brown. "Breaking trail on snowshoes is tough enough. Throw a hill or two into the mix with limited daylight and gawd-awful cold, and you got all you can handle. Be thankful that you got two miles."

Dan nodded and said, "Well, that means we're going to be here for a while."

"Fine by me," answered Brown. "I've got a Yamaha team coming in here tomorrow to test their new snowmachines in cold weather. They'll be operating them up and down the airstrip for a few days. You guys would fit right in." Dan and Bob smiled weakly at their host. They were too tired to say anything and they just realized they had weeks of grueling work in front of them.

The next four days were almost identical. Each day started with the two men leaving the warm lodge in the dark. Then they drove to an area where they could park their idling car. This sometimes required shoveling a pullout along the road. They would gear up and start the arduous climb uphill to the pipeline alignment, inspect the route for two miles and return totally exhausted. Bob especially was feeling physically beat. His whole body ached in protest. Dan was becoming impatient and wanted to pick up the pace. The cold was draining them. Thus, by the fifth day, Dan and Bob were starting to look for ways to speed up the inspections. Unfortunately, they found one.

It started innocently. Dan noticed two recently plowed access roads leading from the Richardson Highway to the ridgeline where the pipeline route followed. They were separated by about four miles. Dan drove up the southernmost road and found that it led to an Alascom microwave tower. The road intercepted the survey line at the top of the ridge. They couldn't believe their luck! *No more crawling a mile up a hill today*, they thought as they jumped out of the car and geared up.

They snowshoed south for two miles to where they had stopped on the previous day. Although the travel was still strenuous, they finished their inspection hours earlier than normal and with energy to spare. The fortuitous access road had given them an easy day.

When they got settled in the car, Bob and Dan reveled in their good fortune. Then, as many young men's misfortunes begin, Dan had a flash of inspiration. He turned to Bob and asked, "Bob, do you have that USGS topo? Let's take a look where we're at."

Bob fished the map out of his backpack and handed it to Dan. Dan unfolded it and ran his finger along the Richardson Highway until he found the microwave tower road. "Here's our location. See? And this must be the next access road we saw plowed only four miles north of here." Dan turned to Bob and continued, "Do you know what that means? We could double our inspection distance. I could drop you off here at the top of the second access road and I'll bring the car back to here. We would meet in the middle and then walk back to the car. How does that sound?"

Bob rubbed his chin and said, "But that would mean splitting up. Jay told us not to."

Dan's patience was wearing thin. He smoothed his hair back and replied, "Look. I can understand not splitting up if we have to break a trail uphill, but we are talking about traveling on a ridgeline along a marked trail. We can't get lost, we'll double our distance, and we have no hills to climb. OK? Are you with me?"

Bob couldn't refute Dan's logic and he wanted to finish this torturous walking tour as soon as possible, but he had given Jay his word that they wouldn't split up. Since Bob was fourteen years older than Dan, Jay had leaned on Bob to be the responsible adult. The mature reply would be to say no, but Dan voiced a very persuading case and, as Dan pointed out, the risk was low. Against his better judgment, Bob said, "Yes."

"Great," answered Dan as he refolded the map and prepared to drive back to the lodge. "You'll see. It will be a piece of cake." Somehow Bob didn't think it would be that simple.

Dan and Bob started the next day with high hopes of doubling their distance with minimal effort. They prepared to leave the lodge at ten in the morning–about two hours later than normal because they were confident they would start and finish in the short daylight hours. The six-member Yamaha team was just finishing their breakfast when Dan and Bob were walking out the door. The men wished each other a good day.

Dan and Bob secretly envied them. They seemed to be having a great time working on their machines and racing them up and down the airstrip. Then the team always capped their day with drinks at Brown's bar before dinner. Dan and Bob would drag into the lodge beat as the Yamaha team raised their cups in salute. *Why can't we have a job like that?* thought the Land Field boys as they trudged to their cold car each morning.

However, today was going to be different. Dan and Bob were going to have an easy day covering lots of territory with no hill climbing. They might even beat the Yamaha boys to the bar tonight.

When Dan dropped Bob off at the top of the ridge, dawn was breaking over the mountains, but it was still very cold. The lodge thermometer had read -35°. They waved to each other as Dan slowly backed the car down the access road to the highway.

Bob watched him go for moment before shouldering his backpack and trudging south. He had taken only a few steps when a sharp branch snagged his snowshoe. Annoyed, Bob jerked his snowshoe free and repositioned his step. Another wooden dagger pushed through the shoe webbing and held it fast. It took him a few minutes to understand what was happening. To save time, the surveyors must have chain-sawed the brush into three-foot-high stubs. The survey crew had probably swung their saws in diagonal arches as they quickly progressed forward producing a swath of tall pointed sticks. The snow barely covered the tops.

Bob looked for an alternate route, but the thick brush on each side of the survey swath precluded parallel travel. He was forced to continue down the trail. Each step was agonizing and frustrating. Sharp branches snagged his snowshoes during every step. At this rate, his supposedly leisurely trip would take all day. *I hope Dan has easier going,* thought Bob as he struggled forward, *or we're gonna be here all night.*

Dan parked the car in a wide spot on the microwave access road. He grinned as he thought about how well his plan was working. *I can't imagine why Bob had any reservation.* He slipped his snowshoes on, buckled the bindings, and took a quick look around before stepping on to the survey line and starting north to meet Bob. Within three steps, he got hung up on a sharp stick. "What the –" Dan struggled to get out and finally managed to shove his next foot forward and pry his back snowshoe free. His next step became snagged too. Suddenly, Dan lost his smile and realized this section was cut differently than the other parts on the line.

Dan took a deep breath of frigid air and struggled forward. A spear hidden beneath the snow impaled his next step. His anxiety rose as he fought free and planted his other snowshoe ahead. He encountered the same impediment on each step. Yanking his snowshoe free required great effort and strained his muscles. He doggedly pressed on and stopped exhausted after twenty minutes. He was dismayed to see he had progressed only 200 yards. At this rate, it would take all day to cover two miles.

But Dan knew he had no choice. Bob was coming and there was no way to tell him to abort. Dan put his head down and soldiered on.

An hour into his trek, Bob was spent. He bent over and braced himself on his knees as he drew in ragged gulps of air. His perspiration froze like hoarfrost around his facemask and hood. The brush closed around him and prevented him from determining his position. His progress had been at a snail's pace. He had a feeling that he hadn't covered more than a half a mile. "I'm getting too old for this," Bob croaked as he slowly stood and stretched his aching back. Then he gathered his resolve and took another step forward. This time a large pointed stick shoved high above the webbing. Bob lost his patience and yanked his left snowshoe free. The shoe's laminated wooden hoop stressed for the last time behind his foot and snapped. Bob tumbled forward into the snow.

As he slowly picked himself up, he realized that he was in terrible trouble. Without snowshoes, he would sink up to his hip in snow. His progress was going to be even slower. He didn't want to turn back because that would force Dan to march the full four miles through these horrible conditions and then they would still have to find their way back to the car. Bob slowly shook his head as he realized he had no choice. He had to continue.

But first he had to rest. He stamped the snow around him and formed a comfortable place to relax. He pulled out his thermos and poured a cup of hot coffee. Then he ate one of Mr. Brown's sandwiches. After 15 minutes, he started to get cold and knew he had to start moving again. He repacked his gear and moved his left binding forward so he could use part of his damaged snowshoe. The modification worked, but caused him to drag his left foot. He was just starting to move when he heard the gunshots–three in a row.

Bob quickly threw off his pack and retrieved Jay's .44 Magnum. He chambered a shell, pulled back the hammer, and fired. He repeated the process two more times. Then he waited. No response. Despite being cold,

Bob felt the deeper chill of dread slither down his back. *Dan must be hurt!* Now he had no alternative but to move forward and find his partner. He knew if Dan couldn't move, he would not last long in these temperatures.

Dan's groin muscles started to burn as he struggled to take the next step. The sharp sticks had snagged his snowshoes again. He braced himself and yanked the back shoe forward. He felt something pop in his inner thigh and searing pains enveloped him. "Oh, no!" he moaned. "Not now!" His right groin muscle gave out, rendering his leg useless. Dan flopped onto his back to rest and think. He was stuck about a mile into his trek. He couldn't go forward and to stay put was not an option. He would freeze to death by the time rescuers found him. He would have to crawl back to the car.

He needed to signal Bob that something was wrong. Dan pulled the .38 pistol from his pack, pointed into the air, and fired three times. The shots rang in his ears and deafened him. He sat quietly for a few minutes and waited to hear Bob's reply, but his hearing was still severely compromised. He knew he would not hear Bob's shots.

Dan painfully took off his snowshoes and lashed them to his pack. Then he turned and slowly fought his way back to the car through the deep snow and sharp sticks. His right groin felt like it was on fire. He hobbled and crawled, not daring to stop. Hours later as the short daylight waned, he stumbled to the idling car.

Dan drove to where he had left Bob with the wild hope that he had hiked back. Darkness had completely fallen when he reached the ridge. His headlights revealed only their tracks from hours earlier and Bob's one set of snowshoe prints disappearing down the survey swath. Dan felt his anxiety rise as he considered his situation. It was dark, very cold, he was injured, and he had lost his partner on an extremely difficult stretch on land. This was the first time in his life Dan had felt vulnerable. He was in over his head and it hurt his ego to admit it, but he knew what he had to do. He had to find Brown and ask for help. Then Dan remembered the Yamaha team. *Yes! Those guys would be aching to use their machines to find Bob.*

With the decision made, Dan backed down the access road to the highway and drove to the Paxson Lodge. Brown was serving drinks behind the bar when he saw Dan limp into the lobby. The scared look on his face told him something was wrong. He quickly told the Yamaha team to quiet down and pointed to Dan. The laughter died when they saw Dan's condition. Dan took a deep breath and told the men what had happened. In an instant, they whirled into action. Brown organized the Yamaha team into a search party. He pulled out a map and showed them how to access the survey line. They would bring snowmachines up the microwave tower road and head north along the swath.

Dan watched the men as they flew out the door. As the door slammed shut, Dan asked Mr. Brown, "What can I do?"

Brown turned and said, "You can drive the highway to see if he stumbles out, but before you do, I want you to call your office and tell them what is happening. Understand?"

Dan nodded and watched Brown leave. Then he took a deep breath and went to the telephone. This was not a call he wanted to make.

Beth Feeney answered, "Oh, hi, Dan! How's it going down there?"

"Not good," replied Dan. "Is Jay there?"

"I'm sorry. He's at a property negotiation. Can I help?"

"I wish you could," answered Dan. "I lost Bob. Mr. Brown organized a search party to find him. I'm going to drive the highway and look for him, too."

Beth put her hand to her mouth and gasped, "Oh, my God! How did that happen? I mean, you guys were together, weren't you?"

Dan felt a wave of guilt wash over him. He pushed it down and said, "Just tell Jay as soon as you can, OK? I'll call back later when I have more news." Dan hung up before Beth could reply. Then he returned to his car and drove south on the highway—hoping beyond hope that he would see Bob.

Bob's endurance had hit a wall. As he stood weaving, Bob felt the comforting fingers of exhaustion enfold him and lure him to lie down. His body told him it would feel so good just to stop and take a little nap.

He almost succumbed, but at the last moment, he shook himself awake and forced himself to think. Sleep meant death and Bob wanted to live. He gathered his reserve and strained forward to take another step.

Complete darkness had fallen and stars shone brightly across the sky. In another situation, the scene would have been awe inspiring. Bob felt his way forward. The moon had not risen yet, so it was difficult to see the brush. Suddenly, Bob saw light twinkle through the trees on his right side. At first he thought it was his imagination–mirages created by a tired mind. Then he saw light again moving in a straight line below him. Then he recognized it. It was headlights from a car traveling on the highway about a mile downhill. Bob stopped, stared at it for a while and thought, *I can't go on much further. I could make it to the highway and get help to find Dan.* To help him decide, Bob tilted back his head and yelled, "Dan!" Only silence replied. *That's it. I'm going down.*

Bob turned and stepped off the ridgeline. The hillside was steep, which helped him move forward, but the snow was deep–past his waist in places. He held on to scrawny black spruce trees to keep him from pitching forward. After making good progress, Bob reached the bottom of the hill. Then the real work began. Bob waded, swam, and struggled through the brush and deep snow towards the highway. Each step was an agonizing effort. "I'm gonna make it. I'm gonna make it," he chanted repeatedly to himself. He dared not stop now. He was beyond exhausted.

Suddenly, he broke free of the brush and found himself standing on top of an eight-foot cut bank overlooking the road. The glare of a headlight caught him in the act of swaying on his feet before pitching forward and tumbling down to the ditch. The car locked its brakes and skidded to a stop.

Bob was too exhausted to get up. He heard a car door open and boots running toward him. "Bob! Bob! Are you OK? I'm here, Bob!" It was Dan. Bob felt Dan grab his coat and start lifting him out of the snow.

Dan dragged Bob up to the road and laid him on his back over the snowbank. Then he carefully brushed the snow off Bob's face. Bob looked up to him and croaked, "Dan. You're OK. Thank, God. I was so worried about you."

Pangs of remorse ripped through Dan as he lifted Bob to his feet. He choked back tears as he replied, "I'm just fine, partner. Let me help you into the nice warm car." Bob stumbled into the passenger seat as Dan threw his pack into the back. The car's heater felt heavenly. Dan got into the driver's side, pulled Bob's hood, facemask, and gloves off, and searched for signs of frostbite. He was relieved to find none.

Bob closed his eyes and asked, "Are we going back to the lodge now?"

"No," answered Dan as he pulled a U-turn on the highway. "We've first got to tell the Yamaha boys that I found you. Otherwise, they'll be searching for you all night."

Bob nodded and asked, "What time is it?"

Dan glanced at his watch and answered, "Eight o'clock. You've been outside for ten hours."

"Feels like a hundred," replied Bob. Then, after a moment, Bob asked, "Does Jay know what happened?"

Dan started braking to turn on to the microwave access road before emitting a simple, "Yup!"

Bob swore under his breath and muttered, "There'll be hell to pay," before exhaustion smothered him and he fell fast asleep.

On January 23, 1974, US Department of the Interior Secretary Rogers C. B. Morton issued the right-of-way grant for the pipeline across federal lands. With much fanfare, the Alaska congressional delegation, representatives from the seven Alyeska owners, and DOI officials flanked Morton as he signed the document. The 100-page grant contained a detailed description of the pipeline corridor and attached a list of technical stipulations. The grant allocated a 54-foot-wide corridor for buried sections of the pipeline and a 64-foot-wide right-of-way for above-ground sections.

After the signing, Alyeska handed Morton a $12.25 million check to reimburse the government for federal funds expended to complete the Environmental Impact Statement and supporting technical studies. In response, Morton told the press that this was the first time the DOI had required reimbursement from the permittee for required environmental and technical studies. He went on to announce that the DOI also required Alyeska to cover federal costs of construction supervision and monitoring pipeline operations.

Morton then described how the right-of-way permit would work. To ensure compliance with grant stipulations, the DOI would authorize pipeline construction in sections. Alyeska had already designated eight construction sections. Morton stated that each authorization required a formal application that was accompanied by a detailed plan to conform to the grant's environmental and technical stipulations. Morton said retired major general Andrew Rollins would be the DOI authorized officer to approve each segment's application. Morton stressed that Rollins would have complete DOI authority to suspend any project activity that he believed would threaten public health, environmental safety, or wildlife and fish populations. Rollins's office would be situated within the new pipeline surveillance office.

The DOI did not grant the Haul Road right-of-way at this time. Since the State of Alaska would eventually assume responsibility for the Haul Road, the DOI determined that the road right-of-way should be transferred directly to the State. This would be done in the near future.

The federal grant stipulations mirrored the DOI Environmental Impact Statement Record of Decision. The Record of Decision contained the environmental commitments necessary to approve the right-of-way grant. The main grant principles were: (1) employ all practicable means and measures to preserve and protect the environment; (2) balance environmental amenities and values with economic practicalities and technical capabilities; and (3) manage, supervise, and implement the construction, operation, maintenance, and termination of the pipeline system in accordance with sound engineering practices to the extent allowable by state-of-the-art technology.

The DOI also granted right-of-way across all unpatented claims on federal lands for mining, trade, and manufacturing. However, the DOI provided an opportunity for any claimant to sue for rightful compensation in federal court, provided that the claimant could prove a lawful property claim and value lost.

The federal grant did not allocate areas for material sites, construction camps, and staging areas. Alyeska would negotiate these lands with the BLM on a case-by-case basis. BLM always required a restoration plan before approving the temporary use.

Although Alyeska did not have the State and Haul Road rights-of-way, the federal approval was a huge victory and the impetus for committing construction funds. Alyeska reactivated the dormant construction camps and began staging supplies and equipment. They constructed a thick ice bridge across the Yukon River and plowed open portions of the Hickel Highway to drag equipment north.

———————————

During the first week of February, Alyeska submitted their application for 250 miles of State pipeline right-of-way to the Alaska Department of Natural Resources. The application relied heavily on Jay Sullivan's and Armand Spielman's work to regularly update the alignment sheets on file with the ADNR Land Office. ADNR also had to finalize their sale of the land for the future Valdez Marine Terminal.

Shortly after filing for the State right-of-way, John Knodell paid Harry and Armand an unexpected visit in Anchorage. They could tell John had something important on his mind and confirmed their suspicion when he asked to see their land records. Armand led him to a back room where filing cabinets and boxes contained all property negotiations. John looked perplexed as he studied the room before asking, "What happens if you have a fire?"

Armand stroked his mustache and answered, "Then we'd be in a world of hurt."

John nodded as he said, "That's for sure." He turned to Armand and continued, "I want you to build a fire-proof vault to store these records. You could convert this entire room into a storage vault. You'll need the room for the additional records we'll collect by the time the project is over."

Armand stood looking at John in disbelief as he repeated John's directive, "A vault?"

"That's right. The size of this room."

Armand shook his head and replied, "We're on the second floor. Do you realize we would have to reconstruct the floor to support the weight?"

John nodded again and said, "I imagine so. A vault of this size would weigh a lot. Better get cracking. These unprotected records represent an enormous liability to the company."

Armand smirked and said, "Wait until David Henderson hears about this. He'll blow a gasket!"

John's hand cut through the air as he replied, "Leave Henderson to me. This needs to be done now!"

Armand nodded as he thought, *Rank certainly has its privileges.* "OK, John. You clear it with David and I'll get a contractor in here to install it."

John turned to leave as he replied, "I'll talk to him now."

Armand watched him march down the hall. When John was out of earshot, Armand muttered under his breath, "How are we going to fit a bank vault up here?" During the next two disruptive weeks, Armand saw how it could be done.

On March 19, 1974, Armand arrived in Fairbanks to attend a large competitive gravel sale. The auction was scheduled to start at 10 a.m. at the Bureau of Land Management Field Office. Armand had arranged with Jay to have Bob Ylvisaker meet him at the airport and drive him to the event. Bob would then remain by his side taking notes and assisting Armand with the auction.

Armand had attended several BLM gravel auctions in the past two years. They were all boring formal affairs that were sparsely attended. Armand was invariably the only one participating and would acquire the gravel by his first bid. BLM simply went through the motions to sell a public resource to a private concern.

When Armand and Bob walked into the conference room, there was no indication that this sale would be any different from past proceedings. A few people were scattered among the empty seats. Two BLM employees were busying themselves on a low stage. Armand recognized one of the employees–Richard LeDosquet, the Fairbanks manager of the BLM office. Richard would conduct the auction. A large blackboard with a tray holding large pieces of white chalk was positioned behind and to the left of the podium.

Armand scanned the room and identified one of the attendees as Dennis Fradley, a reporter for the *Fairbanks Daily News Miner*. They nodded a greeting to each other. Dennis looked bored to tears. Armand couldn't blame him—nothing exciting ever happened at these meetings. Dennis would return to his desk in a few minutes and report Alyeska spent a few hundred thousand dollars for gravel—o hum! Armand motioned to Bob that they should sit in the front row.

There was one slightly unusual aspect to this sale. This morning would be the largest federal sale of gravel in Alaska that BLM had ever held. Today, BLM was auctioning the rights to 3.4 million cubic yards of gravel along the pipeline route north of the Yukon River. BLM had advertised the auction in the Fairbanks and Anchorage newspapers two weeks before the sale. The advertisements stated that the minimum bid would be 10 cents per cubic yard, or $340,000. Anyone interested in bidding was required to pay a $1,000 participation fee and be an Alaskan resident. Armand satisfied both requirements.

At precisely ten o'clock, Richard LeDosquet knocked on the podium with his gavel and called the session in order. "Everyone, please take your seats. We shall begin the public auction of gravel resources along the pipeline corridor north of the Yukon River. My assistant will write the prevailing bid on the blackboard until the final price is determined. Any questions? Good. Let's start. Do I have an opening bid of ten cents per cubic yard?"

Armand raised his hand and announced, "On behalf of the Alyeska Pipeline Service Company, I do." The BLM assistant wrote 10¢ on the board.

Conditioned by past uneventful auctions, the BLM employees began to consolidate their paperwork while they waited the customary 30 seconds before declaring a successful bidder. Suddenly, a voice rang out from the scattered audience, "Eleven cents!" Several eyebrows shot up. Armand gave Bob a what-the-hell look before careening his neck to see who made the last bid. A casually dressed young man sitting in the middle row had his hand raised.

Richard was clearly disturbed. "What is your name?" he asked the man.

The young man stood and replied, "My name is David Wtipol from Indian, Alaska."

Richard checked his papers and said, "Ah, yes, right here. Mr. Wtipol paid his $1,000 fee and signed the residency affidavit. He is qualified to participate." Richard nodded to his assistant before continuing, "Please register his bid." The man wrote 11¢. "Now, do I hear. . ."

"Twelve cents," interrupted Armand.

"Thirteen," interjected Mr. Wtipol.

Armand's mind started to whirl. Each penny increase meant an extra $34,000 that Alyeska had to pay for the gravel. Armand had no idea how much he was authorized to bid. This had never happened before. "Fourteen cents," announced Armand.

"Fifteen," Mr. Wtipol replied. BLM hurriedly wrote the number on the board.

Here we go, thought Armand. "Sixteen."

"Seventeen."

"Eighteen," Armand countered. The bidding seesawed back and forth until the offer crested at 30 cents per cubic yard—over one million dollars total. Armand grabbed Bob and whispered urgently in his ear, "Call Harry. Ask him how high I can bid. Hurry!"

Bob whirled from his chair and ran out of the conference room to the offices down the hall. He borrowed a telephone and placed a collect call to Harry Brelsford. Much to Bob's relief, Harry picked up on the second ring. "Harry. This is Bob Ylvisaker. Armand is in a terrible fix! Some guy is trying to outbid him for the gravel. Armand wants to know how high he can bid."

Harry had to shake the marbles from head to get his mind wrapped around the problem. "What? Who is this character anyhow?"

Bob answered, "I don't know. Nobody seems to know him, but he's acting very confident. BLM deemed him qualified to bid."

Harry gulped and asked, "How high is the bid now?"

"I imagine they've crested forty cents a yard by now."

Harry let out a whistle before answering, "Well, to tell you the truth, I'm surprised it hasn't happened before now. OK. Tell Armand to go for broke! We can't afford to have someone else control the gravel. Understand?"

"Got it, Harry," answered Bob. "I'll tell Armand. Goodbye." Bob slammed the phone down and ran back to the conference room. The blackboard had "43¢" written across it.

A distressed Armand asked Bob as he slid into his seat, "What did he say?"

Bob looked Armand straight in the eye and said, "Go for broke! Alyeska needs the gravel."

Armand seemed to gather strength from Harry's instructions. He raised his hand and said, "Forty-four cents."

"Forty-five," was the reply. The bidding went back and forth until Armand's bid of 64 cents per cubic yard finally forced Mr. Wtipol to concede. The gavel came down and Richard announced Alyeska as the successful bidder to purchase the gravel for about $2.2 million.

David Wtipol gathered his papers, stood up, and bolted for the door. "Hey! Not so fast!" shouted a man behind him. David turned to see Dennis Fradley with pen and paper in hand chasing him down. "Please! Mr. Wtipol! May I have a moment of your time? I have some questions to ask."

David stopped in the hallway and waited for Dennis to catch him. Dennis smiled and said, "You made quite a splash back there. I am Dennis Fradley with the *Fairbanks Daily News Miner*. I'd like to report the facts of this auction. Please tell me your occupation."

David shrugged and said, "I am a construction engineer, currently unemployed."

Dennis eagerly wrote down some notes. "OK. Why were you trying to drive the cost of materials up?"

David shook his head and answered, "I wasn't. I read the legal notice about the auction in the <u>Anchorage Times</u> and I was shocked at the low price the feds were offering for the gravel. I mean, it was way lower than what we pay in the private sector. So, I thought if I could win the bid, I could resell the gravel to Alyeska at normal commercial prices and make a small fortune."

Dennis had to smile at the man's gumption. He looked at David and asked, "Could you have afforded to pay over two million dollars for the gravel if you were successful?"

David nodded as he replied, "Yes. An outside bank backed this venture. Our business model showed we could generate a healthy return on our investment if we could purchase the gravel for less than sixty-four cents a yard. That was our limit."

Dennis had a few more questions, but David terminated the conversation as he excused himself to leave. "I'm sorry, Mr. Fradley. I've probably said too much. I have to go." Then he strode out the door.

Dennis watched him go and then returned to the conference room just as a stunned Armand was gathering his papers and preparing to leave. He walked up to Armand and asked, "Mr. Spielman, I imagine this was a surprise to have a competing bidder, no?"

Armand stopped, studied Dennis's face for a second as he stroked his mustache, and then answered, "Surprise? How about shocked, dumbfounded, or stunned for a more accurate description of my feelings? Part of me feels that I should have conceded at sixty cents and watched him squirm to pay two million dollars."

Dennis smiled and asked, "Why didn't you?"

Armand pointed at Dennis's chest and answered forcefully, "Because we needed the gravel to build the project. Alyeska could not afford to have someone else control it."

Dennis nodded and continued, "Do you think the system should be changed to prevent this sort of thing from happening again?"

Armand's eyes flared as he answered, "Absolutely! We can't have single-minded fortune hunters driving the cost of gravel up with no consequences." Armand then turned to Bob, motioned for him to follow, and they marched out of the conference room without uttering another word.

The next week, Harry Brelsford had a discussion with Curtis McVee to change the bidding requirements. After this exchange, BLM changed the bidding procedures to restrict the use of the gravel for the construction and maintenance of the Trans Alaska Pipeline System and the Haul Road. In addition, BLM required a 50 percent nonrefundable deposit of the minimum total value of the gravel before the party was eligible to bid. These two changes eliminated future profiteering.

The State of Alaska and the Fairbanks and Anchorage Chambers of Commerce posted notices in the major national newspapers warning citizens that there were no unlimited employment opportunities in Alaska. Alyeska even published and distributed a brochure titled, "The Truth about Pipeline Jobs in Alaska" to discourage job seekers. There were two reasons for the notices. First, Alaska did not want impoverished and desperate families crawling into the state looking for work. They would drain the communities' limited resources. Then the families would be trapped in a cold and remote country that was far away from their homes.

Secondly, Alaska was just emerging from two brutal recession years. The project delay caused by years of legal wrangling had destroyed the local hopes and dreams generated in 1969. Property values had dropped. Unemployment was high. Bankruptcies were common. Alaska wanted their residents employed first before outsiders.

However, the ads did little to discourage the influx of people seeking employment. First, the US border guards at the Alaska/Canadian border noticed a steep increase in Lower 48 people entering the state. Then communities saw their rental vacancy rates plummet. Housing costs began to rise. Businesses began to hire people to meet increased demands.

Then school enrollments skyrocketed. In many cases, the students were crammed into buildings far above their occupancy limit. The Fairbanks North Star Borough school board was forced to consider emergency measures to alleviate overcrowding such as double-shifting— having two separate school times in the same building.

Lathrop High School was the most visibly impacted. The school was already at full capacity when the influx started. The school board announced that, starting in the fall, Lathrop would have two sessions. The kids bused from the rural areas would attend in the morning and students from the city would have classes in the afternoon. To save money, athletic teams would consist of students from both sessions.

The rise in population quickly overwhelmed the Fairbanks utilities. The Fairbanks Municipal Utility System announced that a new telephone hookup would take up to three months to install. Several months later, they would revise their estimate to six months. The aging coal-fired electrical plant was operating at full capacity and engineers worried what would happen next winter when the demand would skyrocket. The Fairbanks wastewater treatment plant was in the same predicament. Its old infrastructure barely accommodated the local waste load before discharging into the Chena River. The plant needed major upgrades to handle increased volumes.

Anchorage, Fairbanks, and Valdez noticed vehicles with out-of-state license plates were starting to fill their streets. Not all the vehicles were owned by families. A high proportion of newcomers were single men looking for a chance to strike it big. Following these men were the schemers trying to milk them for every dime they had. Hastily erected strip bars, gambling clubs, and prostitution sprouted in the communities seemingly overnight. With them, crime shot up. The pipeline boom had all the trappings of humanity–and the pipeline construction had not started yet.

In early March, Alyeska awarded a contract to the joint venture of Manson-Osberg/GHEMM Company to build the Yukon River Bridge. Since the crossing was crucial to the Haul Road and pipeline construction, the joint venture also had to provide an immediate means to transport equipment and supplies across the river. They would do this by operating two 100-ton-capacity hovercrafts with a backup tug and barge.

The bridge construction and hovercraft operations required large staging areas along the river to temporarily store equipment, building materials, and supplies, and maneuver the hovercraft. This was not a problem on the north bank because the terrain was mostly flat. However, the south side consisted of steep banks. The only level land on this side was located about half a mile upstream of the proposed bridge crossing. Unfortunately, this proposed staging area was a Native allotment owned by Bill and Poldine Carlo, and Bill was notoriously hard to find.

The Manson-Osberg/GHEMM contract had wicked liquidated damage clauses for both sides. Alyeska demanded the hovercrafts be operational soon after the ice left the Yukon. The joint venture required access to the staging areas by April 15. The failure to provide services or access carried steep penalties that both parties wanted to avoid. Ben Anderson called Harry Brelsford and explained the situation. Then Harry immediately called Jay.

Tipped off by Shirley Pippen that something serious was afoot, Jay skipped the usual banter as he came online. "Good morning, Mr. Brelsford. How may I help you?"

Harry went directly to the point. "Jay, the Yukon Bridge contract requires Bill and Poldine Carlo's allotment for a staging area. Ben Anderson just told me that heavy liquidated damages will be imposed if we don't provide the contractor the staging area by April 15. I need you to get it, pronto!"

Jay fell back in his chair, closed his eyes, and began to rub his massive balding head. He could visualize exactly where the property was located. He and John Pate had negotiated a lease from the Carlos years ago for staging the ice bridge. It was the only flat ground for miles along the southern bank of the Yukon. They had no choice but to deal with them again. "OK, Harry. I know the Carlos from the last time we negotiated a lease. I am fairly certain that I can find Poldine, but Bill is always tromping through the woods. He may be hard to locate."

Harry's voice rose almost to a shout as he replied, "Find him, Jay! The entire Haul Road construction is held up until we get that lease. I don't care if you have to scour half of Alaska. Find him!"

Jay thought, *finding Bill is half the battle. Getting him to sign a lease is a whole other story.* "OK, Harry. We're on it. I'll keep you informed on our progress."

"Thank you, Jay," answered Harry. "I don't mean to sound so dictatorial, but this is of the utmost importance."

"I understand, Harry. Goodbye." When Jay hung up the telephone, he remained in deep thought for a moment before whirling into action. "Shirley!"

Shirley came running, her blond curls bouncing. "Yes, boss!"

"Shirley, please pull the Carlos file. I need you to write up a lease to use their allotment for another four years and hand me their contact information. I will need to pay them a visit as soon as you finish the lease."

Shirley nodded and replied, "Top priority, boss?"

Jay gravely nodded as he answered, "Double top priority, Shirley."

Late that afternoon, Jay was driving down the snow-filled streets of Fairbanks to the Carlo home. He had failed to contact Bill or Poldine. So, he called their daughter who worked for the Fairbanks Native Association. She located her mother at a friend's house and arranged for a meeting. As Jay had feared, Bill was somewhere in the Alaska bush— out of touch with civilization and no one knew when he would return.

Jay stopped at the small house, grabbed his portfolio with the new lease, and walked up to the arctic entry. He stepped inside and knocked on the door. Poldine opened the door with a wide smile, "Mr. Sullivan! Linda told me you needed to see me. Please come in."

"Thank you," replied Jay as he took his hat off and stepped inside. Jay was always conscious of his massive size intimidating others. When he needed sweet persuasion, he would try to assume the meekest demeanor as possible. He quickly took off his coat and boots and carefully made his way into the living room. Then he gently sat down on the couch hoping it wouldn't creak.

Poldine was a short Athabascan woman with dancing eyes. She was filled with life and loved adventure. Pictures of her family boating down the Tanana and Yukon Rivers adorned her walls. She seemed to be thrilled with Jay's visit. "Coffee, Mr. Sullivan?" she asked.

"Yes, ma'am," replied Jay, "that would taste good on a day like this. Thank you." Jay could smell the fresh pot brewing in the kitchen.

Poldine whirled off and came back shortly with two steaming cups. "Here you go. Now what was it that you wanted to discuss? I think Linda told you that her father is somewhere down the Rampart Canyon trying to salvage our barge that got stuck in the ice. Last fall, I told Bill it was too late to bring that thing up the river. But, no! He just wouldn't listen. Now he has to pay for his stubbornness."

Jay smiled as he took a sip of coffee. "Wow! This is good, Poldine. Thank you. I didn't know Bill was on the Yukon. Any guess when he might return?"

Poldine laughed and replied, "Oh, goodness gracious no! Bill could be gone for a week or a month. He loses track of time when he's in the bush. Is there something that I can help you with?"

Jay nodded and pulled out his satchel. "Yes, there is, Poldine. Alyeska needs to lease your allotment again. This time we need it for four years as we begin to build the Haul Road and pipeline. I drafted up the lease."

Jay handed to document to Poldine. She carefully opened the folder and stared at the lease for a few moments before replying, "I'm afraid, Mr. Sullivan, that Bill needs to look at it. Sorry, but it wouldn't be right to sign it without his approval."

I was thinking the same thing, thought Jay. He rubbed his head a few moments as he contemplated the problem. Suddenly, a flash of inspiration flared in his head. Jay looked at Poldine with a huge smile and asked, "Mrs. Carlo, would you be game for a helicopter ride?"

Poldine put her hands to her face and exclaimed, "A helicopter ride? Oh my! I've never been in a helicopter. I don't know what to think. Where would we go?"

"I was thinking we could pay Bill a surprise visit and show him the lease. What do you think?"

Poldine's enthusiasm slightly faltered as she envisioned dropping down on her husband unannounced. She looked at Jay and said, "If we do this, better let me get out of the helicopter first."

Her comment puzzled Jay and he asked, "What do you mean?"

Her answer was direct. "Otherwise, he'll shoot you."

The high overcast sky was heavy with dark snow clouds as they crested the White Mountains and began their decent into the Rampart Canyon along the Yukon River. Dan Beardsley sat in the front right seat of the Bell Jet Ranger. Mrs. Carlo sat directly behind him and was totally enthralled with the helicopter. Dan would periodically glance behind him to see her smiling face framed in a large headset. She was grinning ear to ear as she gazed over the remote terrain. Even the occasional downdrafts didn't faze her.

Dan still felt uneasy at how Jay had thrown him in the helicopter and told him to get Mr. Carlo to sign the lease. As Jay closed the aircraft door, he sternly told Dan that this was payback for almost killing Bob. Now, here he was flying unannounced to a remote location on the Yukon River in the middle of winter with a blizzard threatening. To top it off, Carlo was known to shoot first and ask questions later. "Great," muttered Dan as the helicopter turned downstream and low over the frozen river.

They flew another five miles when they spotted a barge near the north bank. Several men were pulling on block-and-tackle rigs that were anchored into the shore to slide the barge free of the river's icy grip. Dan saw a large hole in the river ice where the men had chiseled around the barge. Poldine thumped Dan on the shoulder and pointed excitedly to the barge. He could see her trying to frantically tell him that was her husband below, but she forgot to push her talk button on her intercom.

Dan thumbed his talk button forward and told the pilot, "She says that's her husband's crew. We found them."

The pilot nodded and calmly replied, "Hold on." He laid the helicopter into a steep bank and buzzed the barge. The men scattered like wild cattle. Dan snapped his head back to see a couple of them grab rifles.

Oh, good! That'll stir them up. The pilot abruptly reduced speed and dropped them gently on the ice.

"A little maneuver I learned in 'Nam'," said the pilot as he quickly began his shutdown procedures.

Dan looked out the canopy to see four men standing a short distance away. Two had rifles at the ready. Poldine was going nuts in the back trying to release her harness and open the door. Dan took off his headset and motioned for her to remain calm. "You have to wait until the rotor stops," he shouted over the whine of the turbine. "Then I'll help you."

After a few agonizing minutes, the rotor finally came to a halt. Dan jumped out, opened Poldine's door, and helped her exit the helicopter. She ran straight to the men who appeared stunned to see her.

"Poldine!" shouted the older man with a rifle, "What's wrong? Has something happened to the kids? Why did you fly out here?"

Poldine smiled and ran up to her husband with outstretched arms as she said, "No. Nothing to worry about, Bill. Alyeska flew me here to discuss leasing our allotment again. This young man has the lease and needs to talk with you." They embraced. Dan could tell Carlo was relieved to hear there was no emergency. A fresh snowflake bounced off Dan's face and it reminded him that they had very little time.

Dan cleared his throat and said, "Uh, Mr. Carlo, may I have a little of your time?"

Bill looked over Poldine at Dan, narrowed his eyes, and spat, "Why is it you guys are always in such a big hurry? Could this not have waited until I got back? Must you risk my wife's life over a lease?"

Dan felt embarrassed and dropped his eyes. "Please sir. May I show you the lease?"

Bill released Poldine and shoved his hand to Dan. "Let me see it," he said. Dan handed him the folder. Bill took off his gloves, opened the file, and quickly scanned the document. "Looks similar to the last one. How do I know you guys will clean up my property when you're done?"

Dan replied, "I understand we restored it last time and built you an access road to your property."

"That you did," replied Bill as he continued to read the lease. "Well, I see Alyeska still likes lawyer gobble de gook." Bill handed the lease to his wife and said, "Poldine, have our lawyer look at this. Then we'll talk when I get back to town."

Dan felt his hopes sink. "When will you return to Fairbanks?" he asked.

Bill grimly held Dan's gaze for a moment before answering. "We almost have the barge to the riverbank. Another day's work and then we're done. It will take us two days to get home. So, I'd say five days from now if I don't shoot a moose on the way back."

Dan nodded. He knew this was the best he could do. "OK. I'll call five days from now. Thank you, Mr. Carlo." Dan shoved his hand forward and Bill reluctantly shook it. "We better get going. It's starting to snow."

The Carlos embraced again. Dan motioned for the pilot to start his takeoff procedure. Dan and Poldine walked back to the helicopter and strapped into their seats. As the pilot spooled the rotor, snow began to fall. Poldine waved goodbye to her husband as the helicopter lifted and turned east.

The pilot flew up the river for a mile to gain altitude before heading south towards the White Mountains. However, they encountered near-whiteout conditions at only 500 feet above the terrain. This forced the pilot to fly back to the Yukon and continue following the river. Dan heard the pilot say over the intercom, "Don't worry. I'll just fly to Rampart Village and then follow the Minook to the Elliott Highway. Done it many times before. I know this country like the back of my hand."

Right, thought Dan. *Famous last words. Now, I'm really worried!* He continued to strain his eyes forward to see through the streaming snow.

A few minutes later, they flew over the tiny village of Rampart. The pilot banked south and followed the Minook Creek drainage through the mountains. Dan felt his anxiety rise as he looked at the towering terrain around them. He keyed his microphone and said to the pilot, "You realize that the mountains are much higher than we are, right?"

"Yep!" was the reply. "I've got this. I'll just follow the creek to the pass and drop down. . ." The mountain suddenly loomed in front of them and filled the entire canopy. The pilot wrenched the helicopter to the left and dropped to the valley below. Dan swore their landing skid scraped the slope. "Whoa!" exclaimed the pilot. "Where did that come from?"

Dan shook his head in disbelief. They had just skirted death. The pilot slowed the helicopter to a snail's pace and crept up the Minook. Dan turned in his seat to check on Mrs. Carlo. Her eyes were wide with terror.

A few minutes later, they squeezed through the pass and dropped down the valley to the Elliott Highway. The ceiling lifted enough to stay clear of the terrain and trees. Upon crossing the road, they followed it to Fairbanks. No one said a word when they exited the aircraft.

Five days later, Dan called the Carlo house. He was relieved when Carlo answered the telephone. "Mr. Carlo, this is Dan Beardsley from Land Field Services. I met you at your barge last week on the Yukon."

Bill Carlo's voice was frosty as he replied, "Yeah, I remember you. I hear you almost killed my wife!"

How does a guy answer that? "Um, we encountered some bad weather on our return. The pilot should have been more careful. I am very sorry for any distress it inflicted upon Mrs. Carlo."

Bill went silent for a moment before answering, "Well, it shook her up a bit. I don't think she'll want to go flying in a helicopter anytime soon."

I can't blame her! Neither do I. Dan swallowed and said, "Yes sir. I was hoping we could discuss leasing your allotment. Did your lawyer get a chance to review it?"

"Yes, he did," replied Bill. "Why don't you call Lyle Carlson and set up an appointment for all of us to discuss it? I'm free most of the week."

Dan was elated! *Progress*, he thought. "OK. Thank you, Mr. Carlos. I'll do that as soon as we hang up."

"Sounds good," concluded Bill. "We'll see you then."

"Good bye, Mr. Carlo." Dan hung up the telephone and looked up to see Jay staring at him.

"You look chipper," said Jay with a smile. "What'd he say?"

Dan shrugged as he replied, "Well, he's still upset about us almost killing his wife. But, other than that, he told me to make an appointment with his lawyer to hammer out the lease details."

"Uh, huh," answered Jay, "and who's his lawyer?"

"Mr. Lyle Carlson."

Jay nodded and said, "I know him. Be careful. It's not beneath him to try to slip something past you. Harry is chomping at the bit for that lease. The deadline is coming up in a few days on the liquidated damages clause. Try to schedule that meeting ASAP."

Dan nodded his understanding and Jay left him alone to work it out.

Two days later, Dan met with the Carlos at Mr. Carlson's office. Carlson exuded an air of confidence over the meeting. Dan knew he was in a weak negotiating position. Alyeska needed the lease, there were no alternatives, and time was short. Carlson smiled at Dan like a cat ready to pounce on a canary. *He knows something*, thought Dan.

Dan swallowed hard, smiled, and opened the meeting by saying, "Thank you, Mr. and Mrs. Carlo and Mr. Carlson, for meeting with me today. On behalf of Alyeska Pipeline Service Company, we would like to lease the Carlo Native allotment to stage our construction of the Yukon River Bridge."

Carlson gravely nodded and said, "You are welcome, Mr. Beardsley. I have had a chance to review the draft lease you gave Mr. and Mrs. Carlo, and found it—how shall I say it—lacking."

Here we go. He steeled himself and asked, "Um, Mr. Carlson, can you elaborate on your findings?"

Carlson steepled his fingers together and spoke through them. "We believe that the amount of yearly compensation that Alyeska proposed was rather paltry. We were hoping for something more commensurate with the strategic importance of the property."

Dan exhaled forcefully and replied, "OK. And what, pray tell, is more commensurate?"

Carlson smiled as he tapped his fingers together and said, "Perhaps $6,500 per year."

Dan put his poker face on and said, "OK. I will need to go back to Alyeska for approval or present to you a counteroffer."

Carlson continued to smile as he replied, "That will be fine. Let's reconvene in, say, two weeks?"

Dan lost his cool and blurted, "Two weeks! I was thinking this afternoon."

Mr. Carlson sagely nodded and answered, "I see." He turned to Bill and Pauline and asked, "Do you feel comfortable with such a rapid pace? Will you need more time to scrutinize the amended lease language?" The Carlos stated that they were comfortable with the proceedings.

Carlson turned to Dan and said, "Well then, I eagerly await your amendment."

It's all show, thought Dan as he stood. He put out his hand to shake on the details. They all returned it. "I'll be back in a few hours, Mr. Carlson," said Dan as he gathered his papers. He rushed out the door and back to the Land Field Office where he called Harry and got his approval for the yearly compensation. Dan amended the lease and gave it to Carlson' secretary. It was all he could do for the day.

Harry called the next day and demanded to talk with Dan. With deep trepidation, Dan took the call, "Good morning, Mr. Brelsford. How may I help you?"

Harry wasted no time getting to the heart of the matter. "I'll tell you how you can help me, young man. Get that Carlo lease. That's how! The liquidated damages start tomorrow. Do you know what that means? Big bucks quick!"

Dan swallowed and said, "I understand, Mr. Brelsford. I'm meeting with the Carlo lawyer late this morning. He is supposed to have the Carlo signatures on the lease."

Harry went silent for a moment before replying. When he did, his voice was like steel. "Dan, I need that lease in my possession before the close of business today. Understand? You have my full authorization to charter a plane from Fairbanks to Anchorage if you can't get on a commercial flight. Am I making myself clear?"

Dan hated to be bossed around. He calmed himself and said, "Yes, sir. Perfectly. I'll see you this afternoon. Goodbye, Mr. Brelsford." As he hung up the phone, he assessed his feelings and found his feathers ruffled. *I'm doing my best.* Dan got his coat and prepared to visit Carlson again. *Why can't Harry understand that?*

Dan drove to Carlson's office and found him waiting. He handed Dan the signed lease as they sat down at Carlson's table. "I believe you will find everything in order," said Lyle Carlson as he watched Dan skim the document.

Dan was relieved to see the Carlo signatures, but to his dismay, he noticed the payment schedule had been altered. "What's this?" Dan asked.

"Oh, that," replied Carlson with a smile, "I simply corrected the document to reflect our agreement."

"Uh, looks like you added another $6,500 payment up front in addition to the yearly amounts."

Carlson nodded and said, "Merely compensation for the inconveniences Alyeska imposed on the Carlos and my time to rectify it. Of course, if you object, I can revise it and try to find the Carlos to approve it. I believe Mr. Carlo had to return to the Yukon for some urgent business. It may take a week or two to find him." Then Carlson leaned forward and added, "I'm sure the GHEMM Company joint venture would be interested in knowing about this development, hmm?"

He knows! "I'm sure this is fine with Alyeska, Mr. Carlson. I was just surprised at this development. I'll make sure Alyeska executes it at once."

Carlson gave Dan a triumphant smile and said, "Excellent! I look forward to receiving the first payment promptly."

Dan was disgusted with Carlson's treachery. Dan didn't even shake his hand as he jumped up and said, "Well, I've got an airplane to catch. Thank you for your time, Mr. Carlson." He ran out the door and headed to the airport. By his estimates, he should just make the early afternoon Wien flight to Anchorage.

During March and April 1974, BLM coordinated the transfer of the Haul Road right-of-way across federal lands with the State of Alaska. By the third week of April, they had hammered out the details and Charles Herbert, Commissioner of the Alaska Department of Natural Resources, sent draft leases to each owner of the Alyeska Pipeline Service Company. The leases stated that Alyeska agreed to build a haul road within a 220-foot-wide right-of-way to secondary highway standards as defined by the American Association of State Highway Transportation Officials. The State expected Alyeska to maintain the facility until the Alaska Department of Transportation and Public Facilities took over the road management. The lease anticipated the State takeover to occur in the early 1980s.

On April 23, the ADNR issued the State Certificate of Public Convenience and Necessity. Herbert granted the certificate without following the formal application procedure because the Alaska legislature had determined the TAPS project was eligible for the certificate when they met in a special session in the fall of 1973. The significance of the certificate was two-fold. First, it granted Alyeska the right to build the pipeline and haul road across State lands—regardless if unpatented state mining claims existed. Jay Sullivan's gold claims evaporated with the stroke of a pen. Secondly, if Alyeska encountered a private entity that refused to negotiate essential land for the project, Alyeska could petition the ADNR commissioner to condemn the required right-of-way. This was a huge tool for Alyeska to use to prevent a deadlock in property negotiations.

The Alyeska owners quickly agreed to the lease terms and notified ADNR to finalize the agreement. ADNR responded by stating they would initiate the lease by the next week. Alyeska jumped the gun by starting the haul road construction on April 29. BLM transferred the haul road right-of-way to ADNR on May 2, 1974. ADNR incorporated the right-of-way into the lease and issued the State pipeline and haul road agreement to Alyeska on May 3.

With the federal and state right-of-way in hand, the TAPS project exploded. Alyeska issued major contracts to hasten the construction of the Haul Road. They also began constructing camps in Delta Junction south of Fairbanks, Isabel Pass in the Alaska Range, and Tazlina along the Copper River. Since Fairbanks was located centrally to the project, Alyeska decided to place all construction management there. Ben Anderson's offices in the Polaris Building were overwhelmed. They needed much bigger space quickly.

On May 6, Alyeska signed a lease with Fort Wainwright, the army base next to Fairbanks, for twelve old buildings. In addition, Alyeska secured an option to lease seven more buildings if needed. Alyeska's intent was to renovate the buildings into a construction headquarters. The refurbishment became a huge project of its own as Alyeska underestimated the amount of work required to modernize the structures. It would take almost a year to complete the work.

The stage was set for the largest private construction project ever attempted since the completion of the trans-continental railroad.

Chapter 12

Construction Begins

J ay opened the staff meeting by pointing to the map pinned to the wall. The group had assembled around folding tables and chairs in their new spacious office in the basement of the Polaris Building. Although rough, the Land Field Services employees could now spread out their projects and move without tripping over each other. "People," began Jay, "the Nordale Realignment and the Gilmore Trail Crossing are now our top priority." Jay's finger traced the new alignment crossing the Nordale Road and extending northwest to Chena Hot Springs Road. "The geotechnical investigation found the soils in here were frozen muck. The engineers doubted that the material would support an elevated pipeline with thermopiles. By offsetting the alignment by several hundred feet, the engineers found soils that they can work with. Unfortunately, we need to get back out there and acquire the new right-of-way."

Jay looked at Dick Bruce and said, "Sorry about that, Dick. I know you worked hard to get the old alignment easements."

Dick shrugged, smiled, and said, "Job security, I suppose. We'll get on it. Does Alyeska have the new route plotted yet?"

"That's the spirit," replied Jay. "Yes, Ben Anderson said he would deliver the new plan sheets to us today. Don, I need you to pull the title reports and figure out what properties are affected. Then give us a rough estimate of value."

Dick's father, Don, nodded and answered, "No problem. I'll get on it as soon as the alignment arrives." Don was wearing his customary suit and tie. He held his pen like a cigar and nibbled at the end as he leaned back and draped his arm around the back of his son's chair.

"Good," continued Jay. "Now here's where I think we're going to have the most problems." Jay's finger rested on the Steele Creek Road/Chena Hot Springs intersection. "From here, up Steele Creek Road, and across Gilmore Trail. This section has all the hallmarks of real nasty conflicts. At the intersection, we have a group of gentlemen who are trying to make the world believe they are building a high-class subdivision. They will want top dollar for every foot of right-of-way we get from them. Then we got established home sites up the road and south-facing view lots on top of Gilmore Trail. Yep. We'll have our hands full in these areas."

Jay continued, "Don and I know many of the characters we will have to negotiate with on the property takes. So we took a guess at the parcels the pipeline will cross and wrote a little bio for each owner. You know, their personalities, family ties, and occupation. I don't have to remind you that our thoughts are highly confidential. Anyhow, the narratives should help you prepare before you knock on their doors."

Jay looked around the room and found everyone looking at him attentively. "Good. Now let's discuss the procedure for negotiating compensation." Jay held up a long, thick checkbook protected by a black hard cover. "I know some of you have used this draft book before, but Alyeska has developed an official procedure to track costs. I need to review it with you, so we can minimize any discrepancies and misinterpretations."

Jay held the book so everyone could see it and flipped the cover open. "OK. Notice each check blank has a duplicate sheet behind it. You must make sure the plastic separator is underneath the duplicate before you write on the check–like this, see? Otherwise, you'll ruin the checks below." Jay demonstrated by sliding the thick plastic sheet under the first check set.

Jay continued, "Now, this is how the process will work. First, Don and I will determine the value of the property or easement that you will acquire. We will also give you a value range that you are authorized to negotiate. If you are successful in reaching agreement within that range, then write out a draft and hand them the original check. Then tell them that you must authorize the draft. The authorization will take two days to complete. You must point out to them that the check is good only at the Alaska National Bank of the North. Got it?" Jay looked around the room and saw only nods.

"Great! Now let's go through the paperwork once you return from a negotiation. Here is the draft authorization form." Jay held up a sheet of paper. "You must fill it out completely with the property owner's name, the legal description of property, mailing address, and the draft amount. Then attach a copy of the acquisition agreement. Shirley or Beth will fax it to Anchorage for Armand's or Harry's approval. Understand?"

Jay scrutinized the young faces looking back at him. *They seem to understand.* Then Dick slowly raised his hand. "Yes, Dick," acknowledged Jay, "what's on your mind?"

Dick smiled and asked, "What if we can't reach an agreement? What is the process then?"

Jay replied, "Good question. People, I want to be clear that we must make every effort to reach a settlement with each landowner. Each one of you must document every meeting, telephone call, and offer presented. In the event of an impasse, we must be able to demonstrate to a judge that we did everything possible to meet the landowner's needs. Understand?

"Good. Now, in the remote possibility that we fail to reach an agreement, I will work with you to establish an administrative record of negotiations and then we'll send it to Harry Brelsford. He will petition the Commissioner of Natural Resources for an eminent domain determination. Let's try to keep these situations to a minimum, people. Eminent domain proceedings are expensive, time consuming, and, frankly, generate a whole lot of bad feelings in the community. We don't want a bunch of angry property owners along the pipeline right-of-way. Things tend to explode when that happens."

Jay looked around the room and all he saw were eager faces staring back. Don exuded an air of confidence. Dick, Bob, and Dan had the let-me-at-them looks. Shirley and Beth seemed supportive and willing to do anything to help. "All right people –." A knock at the door interrupted Jay.

Shirley got up and opened the door. A man walked in holding several full-sized alignment sheets. Jay recognized him as a Michael Baker drafter and addressed him, "Ah, right on cue! I presume these are the Nordale Realignment?"

"That's right," replied the man has he plopped the rolls on the folding tables in front of the group. "This is the latest and greatest."

"Outstanding!" bellowed Jay. "Now we can get to work." The drafter nodded and promptly left. The Land Field Services crew unrolled the sheets and huddled around the table as they studied them. Jay's finger traced the new alignment as he pointed out some features. "OK. So, the Michael Baker boys shifted the alignment northeast from its original location. See how it crosses Nordale Road further up? And here's a tight spot. We'll be crossing Chena Hot Springs Road on the west side of the Steele Creek Road intersection. Do you wanna handle that negotiation, Danny boy?"

Dan stuck his chin out and said, "Sure, Jay. I'll give it a shot."

Jay stared at him for a moment and then said, "OK. You got it. The experience will be good for you." Dan could tell by the look in Jay's eyes something monumental had just happened, but he was at a loss to fathom what it was.

Dick Bruce stopped his car at a house in south Fairbanks. He adjusted his tie and checked his appearance in the rearview mirror. Then he grabbed his satchel off the passenger seat and exited his car. Yesterday, he had called George Harkness and briefly discussed Alyeska's need for additional property due to the realignment. Harkness seemed interested, but appalled that the pipeline realignment would carve a 150-foot swath through his land. The original alignment would have crossed along the southern boundary and not interfered with future plans. Dick knew he would have a challenge to convince Harkness to part with a substantial amount of land—nearly 10.5 acres.

Land Field Service's file on the Harkness parcel stated the property was actually family-owned with one of the members recently deceased. Registered owners were George Harkness, Walter Harkness, Katherine Harkness Coon, and the estate of Keith Harkness. Dick knew he would have to reach a consensus of all parties before he could finalize any deal. He believed that might be difficult because of two issues—the estate of Keith Harkness had not been settled and the surviving Harkness members had an inflated sense of the property's worth.

The Harkness property was one lot west of the proposed Nordale Road alignment. The Department of Highways was still designing the new Nordale Bridge across the Chena River. Thus, the land north of the river had no roads. A person needed a riverboat to access the Harkness property. Therefore, Jay and Don had valued the property at $400 per acre. Dick had a gut feeling that this price would be a hard sell.

Dick walked to the door and knocked. A minute later, George answered. He was dressed in blue jeans and a flannel shirt. His face was expressionless. He greeted Dick with a simple, "Yes?"

Dick gave George his best professional smile and said, "Good morning, Mr. Harkness. My name is Dick Bruce. I'm with Land Field Services. I called you yesterday about acquiring some of your property for the Trans Alaska Pipeline System."

George gave Dick a sigh and said, "Yeah, I was expecting you. Please come in and we'll talk about it. I got to be honest with you. I'm not too keen about parting with that much property. I doubt the rest of family would want to sell it, either. They wanted me to hear what you've got to say before deciding."

"I understand, Mr. Harkness," replied Dick. Secretly, Dick was thrilled to be invited inside the house. He had just cleared the first hurdle in negotiations—get past the door.

George led Dick to the kitchen and motioned him to sit at the table. Then he walked over to the coffee percolator. "It just finished perking. Would you like a cup?"

Dick nodded and answered, "Please. Thank you. That would taste good this morning." George poured Dick a stemming mug of coffee and handed it to him. Dick was not much of a coffee drinker, but the aroma and warmth were pleasant. He gently sipped it.

George sat across from Dick at the table and took a swallow of coffee before saying, "OK. Show me what you got."

Dick immediately opened his satchel and retrieved a map depicting the Harkness parcel and the proposed pipeline right-of-way. He spread them on the table. "As you can see, Mr. Harkness," began Dick, "when we cross the Chena River, we'll start making our way to the northwest towards Chena Hot Springs Road. Our alignment shifted to the west to miss very poor soils north of your property. That's why I'm here talking to you now. We'll need to take more than we first anticipated."

George studied the maps for a moment before asking, "How much will your total take be?"

Dick disliked beating around the bush. He replied, "About ten and a half acres."

George whistled softly at the figure. Then after a moment of silence, he asked, "What were you guys thinking it was worth?"

Again, Dick was direct. "Four hundred dollars an acre for $4,200 total."

George sneered at Dick and replied, "Four hundred dollars an acre. You've got to be kidding. This is riverfront property. It's prime land! We aint gonna part with it for $400 per acre. No sir!"

Dick had anticipated Harkness's reaction. "Mr. Harkness, you are right about the property bordering the Chena River, but currently it's isolated. You can access it only by boat. This is why it's valued lower than property with land access."

George pointed to the Chena River on the map and said, "The Department of Highways plans to build a bridge and road just upstream of our property within the next two years. The property will have land access."

Dick shook his head and answered, "True, but a property's value is determined by its condition during negotiations—not by anticipated developments."

George placed both hands flat on the table and stared straight at Dick as he shouted, "Bull! Our property is worth more and you know it! If you guys can't give us a decent shake, then we'll tell it to a judge. I'm sure he'll think the way we do."

Dick could tell his meeting was over. They were at an impasse until cooler heads prevailed. He began to fold up his maps as he replied, "Very good, Mr. Harkness. Thank you for your time. We'll double-check our valuation and touch base with you later."

"Yeah," responded George as he rose from the table, "you just do that." Dick nodded as he gathered his satchel and shook George's hand goodbye. When he walked out the door, Dick had a feeling that he would never set foot in that house again. Alyeska would have to pursue eminent domain proceedings.

———————————

Being a landman for most of his professional career had conditioned Armand not to panic when he received distressing telephone calls about vexing land problems. He had never understood why people called the land office when a project went awry. Armand thought they called because they knew he understood the nuances of the property owner-ship and history. Or maybe, thought Armand, they called because he negotiated final acquisition deals, which often were contentious inter-actions that required problem solving. Whatever the reason, he had participated in solving a wide variety of conflicts and he thought that he had heard them all—until now.

The Valdez Marine Terminal camp manager called Armand with a distressful discovery. While building the new construction camp, the dozers leveling the old Fort Liscum parade grounds had uncovered a buried cache of rifle and field artillery ammunition. Fearing an explo-sion, the men scurried from their equipment and cleared the area. All work stopped until someone could figure out what to do. According to the camp manager, that someone was Armand.

"What the hell do you want me to do?" replied Armand.

"Why, I want you to call someone to get rid of this stuff," answered the manager. "We can't be building a man camp with live shells below us."

Armand swore under his breath before answering, "Well, the way I figure it, the army buried the stuff there. So, the army can come get it. I'll give Fort Richardson a call and see if they can send someone out."

215

"Now you're talking, Armand! Great idea. I knew you were the man to call. Let me know when I should expect them. Thanks." The manager hung up and left Armand flapping in the wind. Armand cradled the telephone for a few moments to gather his thoughts before calling his secretary and asking her to find the phone number for the Fort Richardson bomb squad. A few minutes later, Armand placed one of the most unusual telephone calls of his life.

The bomb squad arrived at the camp site two days later. They removed the ammunition and detonated it at a remote site.

On July 10, 1974, the much-awaited land package arrived at Armand's office from the Alaska Department of Natural Resources. It was the sales contract for 857 acres for the Valdez Marine Terminal, 497 acres for Pump Station 1 in Prudhoe Bay, 27 acres for Pump Station 8 south of Fairbanks, and 10 acres along several mountain tops for communication sites along the pipeline route. The total sale price for this property was $9.175 million. The offices of Governor Egan and the ADNR Commissioner had finalized the sale terms three weeks earlier on June 24.

Alyeska was now authorized to begin shaping the mountains and hills to build the gargantuan tank farm that would receive the Prudhoe Bay crude oil and construct the docks required to moor the super-tankers that would transport that oil. Valdez's population boomed and quickly outstripped all available housing. The terminal construction camp soon became its own city. Around the clock, heavily laden trucks carrying supplies, construction materials, and pipe roared up and down the narrow Richardson Highway. The Valdez Marine Terminal was finally in full construction.

On a hot Fairbanks summer day, Armand entered the old F.E. Company office next to Illinois Street. Dan Eagan had been expecting his visit and greeted Armand with a large smile and said, "Good to see you again, Armand. Looks like you are building a pipeline."

Armand grasped Dan's hand and replied, "We're trying. We still have some blank spots in the right-of-way that we need to acquire. A good hunk of it is your property. By the way, are you ever going to move that junk dredge in Fox so we can build our line across the lot? The center-line goes right over the top of it."

Dan gave Armand a look of mock surprise and answered, "Why, do you mean Dredge Number Eight? I'll have you know that old dredge is in good working order. We could fire it up tomorrow and recover huge gold nuggets under it." This was an exaggeration, but it made a good story and set the stage for a lively property negotiation.

Armand rolled his eyes in fake disbelief and said, "Now you're going to tell me that there is a fortune in gold right down our proposed alignment and U.V. Industries wants top dollar for those old beaten-up mining tailings."

"Well, Armand," replied Dan as he directed Armand to a solid polished wooden table, "there's gold there and those old beaten tailings make very good pipeline beds, no? Come take a look at what I plotted along your alignment." Dan had laid several large sheets across the table. "Based on the survey data that you gave me, I plotted our mining claims that would be affected. As you can see, we have sixteen continuous patented claims that we believe would be rendered useless with your pipeline buried within them."

Armand studied the claims. There was nothing symmetrical about their alignment. If bought in their entirety, the right-of-way width would vary between 100 and 350 feet. "How much property are we talking about here, Dan?"

Dan pointed to a small table in the corner of the summary sheet. "Total comes out to just shy of 133 acres."

Armand scanned the summary table and saw the parcels varied between 0.5 acres and 47.5 acres. The claims had Alaskan names like Number 18 Below Discovery Creek, Number 17 First Tier, Twin Claim Placer, and Wild Goose Association Claim. Armand looked up and asked Dan, "So, what are you thinking your land is worth?"

Dan face became serious as he stroked his chin and thought for a moment. Then he said, "We've got some assays of these tailings. The recoverable gold varies from claim to claim. I am going to have to do some figuring."

Armand shook his head and said, "Why don't you just give me an average worth per acre? Then we can multiply the total take by that value. It would be a whole lot simpler and we wouldn't have to haggle over each claim. So, we would pay a little more for claims that have little gold and less for your hotter properties. As long as the average price is within reason, I think we can strike a quick deal. What do you say?"

Again, Dan retained his serious poker face and stared at the plots for a moment before replying, "I guess that would work. When were you guys thinking about building your line through this area?"

Armand answered, "Alyeska needs to have all properties acquired by early next year. We would like to break ground next June."

Dan looked at Armand and said, "OK. We'll have an average acre cost by December. I have to coordinate with our corporate managers in Salt Lake and New York."

"Thank you, Dan," replied Armand. "We should just make our deadline if we could settle by then."

Dan Beardsley saw the handwriting on the wall. The South Slope Subdivision right-of-way purchase, located west of Steele Creek Road, was not going to be cheap or easy. He sat at his office table reading the Fairbanks North Star Borough platting files spread before him. To Dan, the evidence was obvious. The owners of the property had rushed the platting approval to establish the subdivision before Alyeska could finalize their intended alignment. Clearly, the owners, Kenneth Ringstad, John Butrovich Jr., Duane Hall, Bill Stroecker, and William Waugaman wanted to create the perception that this property was a valuable and thriving subdivision. Thus, they would be eligible for huge compensation if Alyeska needed to buy their lots for the pipeline corridor.

At first look, the South Slope Subdivision looked very inviting. The lots averaged just over an acre in size with easy access to Steele Creek and Chena Hot Springs Roads. The lots sloped to the south and were elevated so that they would receive the precious low-angle winter sun. Each lot had large birch trees that indicated that the soils were permafrost free. They also had a tremendous view of the Tanana Valley and Alaska Range.

However, Dan noticed a potentially troubling aspect to the plat. The subdivision had no covenants or restrictions on future development. Thus, lot owners could build any type of structure on their lots. An owner of a beautiful expensive home might discover a neighbor building a far less comparable structure next door. Not only would the shack negatively impact the ambiance of the neighborhood, but it could also lower the market value of the prestigious home.

Dan observed this exact scenario beginning to unfold in the South Slope Subdivision. In their haste to establish the subdivision, the owners had sold several lots on the east side of Steele Creek Road to a religious sect. The church members built four geodesic domes and sprayed the exterior with urethane insulation. The church lots were located at the entrance to the subdivision and were highly visible from Chena Hot Springs and Steele Creek roads. Dan shared the opinion of many residents who frequently traveled the area that the domes were a blight on the countryside–thus lowering the value of the subdivision lots.

The proposed pipeline route required partial and full takes of 15 lots on the west side of Steele Creek Road for a total of 18.5 acres. Dan approached the subdivision owners about purchasing these lots. As he anticipated, they wanted top dollar for each lot plus compensation for perceived diminished value of the adjacent lots. The partners were looking for total compensation between $400,000 and $500,000.

Dan tried to explain that since the subdivision had no permafrost, Alyeska planned to bury the line through their subdivision. When revegetated, the crossing would have no visual impacts to the surrounding lots. However, Ringstad, Butrovich, Hall, Stroecker, and Waugaman were unconvinced and stuck to their original inflated price and demands because they believed that they were in a controlling position.

Dan documented his coordination with the South Slope owners and his offers to purchase the properties. Then he handed his file to Jay. Jay reviewed Dan's work and concurred that Dan had tried to reasonably negotiate a fair price with the owners.

Jay smiled as he said, "Looks like we got a little conspiracy going on. Do you know the background on these guys?" Dan shook his head and Jay continued, "Ringstad is a real estate developer and probably put the subdivision package together. Butrovich was a state senator and president of the senate in 1967 and 68. He even ran for governor against Egan in 1958. He's a highroller. Stroecker is the money man. He is the president of First National Bank of Fairbanks and Hall and Waugaman are on the bank's board of directors. These guys make a tight little group."

Jay closed the file and said to Dan, "Yep. It's time to send this documentation to Harry. I'm sure he'll agree that condemnation is the logical course of action." Jay looked at the file for a second as he thought about the situation. Then he shook his head and continued, "It's a shame they got so greedy. They would have gotten more from your offer than what the judge will give them."

Dan cocked his head and asked, "When will condemnation proceedings occur?"

Jay put his hands behind his head and replied, "Next spring. And that doesn't leave us with much time before construction." Then Jay smiled before continuing, "You are gonna love this process, Danny boy. It will be a learning experience." Dan looked back at Jay with the feeling that he only had an inkling of what was to come.

———————————

August 1974 was a challenging month for Armand. It started with a telephone call from the Fairbanks Alyeska office on the afternoon of August 1. Two armed men from the mining town of Wiseman had driven a large bulldozer across the uncompleted haul road and blocked traffic. Their names were Harry Leonard and John Bullock and they were upset that Alyeska was going to build a road and pipeline over their mining claims. When construction workers approached them, Leonard and Bullock told them to "take a hike" and they were going to tear up the road if construction continued.

The construction workers pulled back and Alyeska called the state troopers. The troopers flew to the Coldfoot construction camp, which was located about 120 miles north of the Yukon River. Then they drove

15 miles north to Wiseman. When the troopers confronted the men, the miners drove their tractor off the road. Then the troopers gave the men a warning and advised them to seek restitution in court.

The next evening, with pistols strapped to their hips, Leonard and Bullock barged into the Coldfoot manager's office and repeated their threats. The camp manager told them that if they continued to threaten their crews, he would get a court order barring them from the project boundaries.

Armand assured everyone that Leonard's and Bullock's claims were unpatented. In other words, the miners had hastily staked potential mining claims ahead of the project and had not proved to the federal government that gold existed in concentrations that warranted mining it. Jay Sullivan and BLM mining engineers had investigated the claims during the summer and found neither man had performed any development work over the past four years on the properties. Armed with this information, Armand and Harry Brelsford were willing to go to court to prove that the mining claims were a sham.

On August 9, President Nixon resigned over the Watergate scandal. Vice President Gerald Ford replaced Nixon in the oval office. John Knodell and Quinn O'Connell assured Armand and Harry that the Department of the Interior was stable and no major changes were foreseen. Armand was uneasy over the government shakeup. He did not want any change that could stall or prevent his office from completing its task.

Earlier that year, Jay Sullivan had provided Armand with undeniable proof that Alyeska had built the Coldfoot construction camp and airstrip on the unpatented mining claims of Andy and Verda Miscovich. Jay researched the federal claim files for the area and found that the Miscovichs had filed their claims many years before. Although the Miscoviches had not proved that substantial gold concentrations existed on the property, they had dutifully tried to work their claims. Unlike the Leonard and Bullock claims, the Miscoviches could easily prove that their mining interests were legitimate and active.

In the vastness of Alaska, Armand knew mistakes sometimes happened. He had received a permit from the Alaska Department of Natural Resources to construct the camp and airstrip. Jay had told him that the area was first settled as a mining town named Slate Creek in 1899. Five years later, prospectors had struck gold in the Hammond River area. The miners moved north and formed the community of Wiseman.

There were many stories of how Slate Creek was renamed Coldfoot. One story stated many young fortune seekers would reach Slate Creek after weeks of arduous travel and get "cold feet" about spending the winter in remote Alaska. They would catch the next barge drifting south and head back to civilization.

Another story claimed the name change was more recent. When Alyeska surveyors first shot the pipeline alignment next to the camp, they found that they were traversing an old cemetery. When they cut the dense brush, they stumbled upon a partially opened grave with a skeleton foot sticking out. The surveyors wrote the name "Cold Foot" in their survey notes. The name for the area stuck.

There may have been some validity to the latter story because the original pipeline alignment did cross the old Slate Creek cemetery. Harry Brelsford learned of the discovery and demanded that the Michael Baker engineers find another route to miss the property. The final alignment shifted east and archeologists confirmed no graves were located within the proposed right-of-way.

During the spring of 1974, Armand began calling Andy Miscovich at his Fairbanks home about buying his Coldfoot claims. Andy wanted top dollar for the property–way more than Armand was willing to pay. Armand then pulled this trump card and asked Andy if he had ever heard of the Federal Multiple Use Act. Armand's question invoked a serious retort from Andy.

"That's a bunch of hogwash!" yelled Andy. "I've looked at it and it doesn't apply in Alaska."

"No, Mr. Miscovich," replied Armand, "it does apply and if we can't come to an agreement, I'll have to file for eminent domain." Andy abruptly hung up.

The stalemate continued into August of 1974 and Armand was beside himself. The Miscoviches had temporarily relocated to their mine on Clara Creek for the summer. Clara Creek was about two miles north of Coldfoot and, thus, the Miscoviches had limited communication with the outside world. Armand had to resolve the situation soon or follow through on his threat of condemning the property. Then help came from the most unlikely person–William King Fish Arnold. Bill unexpectedly called Armand's office in mid-August. A stunned Armand answered, "Mr. William Arnold! What do I owe the pleasure of this surprise?"

"Mr. Spielman," began Bill with formality in his voice, "I believe once again we have a common business interest."

"Really?" responded Armand. "And what, pray tell, would that be?"

"Mr. and Mrs. Andrew Miscovich."

Armand went silent. *Here we go again*! It took him a few seconds to get his wits about him. Then he replied, "I see. And what business with the Miscoviches are you referring to?"

King Fish Arnold answered as if he was talking to an errant student, "Now, now, Mr. Spielman. No need to be coy. Mr. Miscovich has confided in me about the details of Alyeska's trespass. He has also provided me with copies of your past transmittals. Before the Miscoviches moved to their mining site for the summer, Mr. Miscovich tasked me with reaching a settlement with your company."

Armand was awash in conflicting emotions. He was elated to have a chance to rectify the problem, but wary of King Fish Arnold and his use of the word trespass. Armand was still stinging from his last brush with Mr. Arnold over the Day property. He decided to go on the offensive and see how cooperative King Fish was willing to be. "Mr. Arnold, this is delightful news. I know you are fully aware of the Multiple Use Act and its implications. Since you are his attorney, you can explain it to him and hopefully we can reach a deal."

King Fish Arnold appropriately coughed and replied, "I'd be happy to, but Mr. Miscovich is unreachable for the foreseeable future."

Armand let loose with both barrels. "OK, then. I tell you what I'll do. I will put together a document that describes the land Alyeska needs from the Miscoviches and a purchase agreement. Then I will bring it over to your office for you to review. Once we agree on the documentation, we will fly to Fairbanks and I'll charter a flight to Coldfoot. We'll borrow a pickup and drive up to Clara Creek and present it to the Miscoviches. I will have my draft book with me and authorization to write a check up to $100,000. It's up to you to persuade Mr. Miscovich to accept the offer, which will be far more than if we condemn the property and have the State court award the compensation. Do I have your cooperation, Mr. Arnold?"

Armand could hear King Fish blink. After a few seconds, William Arnold replied, "Ah, I believe that would be an acceptable course of action. I look forward to receiving your documentation."

"Very good, Mr. Arnold," replied Armand. "This is my top priority. You will be hearing from me shortly. Goodbye." Armand hung up the telephone and let loose a loud sigh.

"Another challenge, Armand?" Armand looked up to see Harry standing in the doorway smiling at him. "I could hear that moan in the hallway. You really must buck up when you are being shot, Armand. Most people don't like to hear it."

Armand shook his head and said, "Harry, you'll never believe who just called!"

"William King Fish Arnold."

Armand was astounded. "How did you know?"

Harry nodded towards the receptionist and said, "I heard Arnold's name when I was passing your secretary's desk. That's why I stopped in. What's up?"

"Arnold is representing the Miscoviches on the Coldfoot claims. I think he's on board with solving our impasse, but I'm very reluctant to deal with him."

Harry nodded and said, "I understand your misgivings. He must be getting a cut of the settlement. I heard you say that you will give him a draft of the purchase agreement."

Armand replied, "That's right. I will try to get it to him by tomorrow. If we could get this turned around by the end of the month, it will save us the time and expense of condemnation proceedings."

Harry turned to leave, then stopped and gave Armand a parting directive. "Armand, I too want this solved by the end of the month. But we can't be playing cat and mouse games with Arnold forever. If things fall apart, give it to me, and we'll have the property condemned. Understand?"

Armand nodded and replied, "Understood, Harry. I better get to work."

By the close of business of the next day, Armand had assembled a detailed documentation of the Miscovich claims and a purchase agreement. He organized it in a manila envelope and, on his way home that evening, Armand slipped the package under Arnold's office door.

William Arnold called the following morning. "Mr. Spielman, I reviewed the material that you slid under my door last night. I found it well written and complete. I am ready to travel to Coldfoot whenever you are."

"Excellent!" exclaimed Armand. He was secretly relieved that Arnold had found the documentation and purchase agreement acceptable. If King Fish had wanted to nitpick, they could have bogged down for weeks over minutia. "I'll coordinate the charter and our ground transportation. Let's plan for next Monday, August 12, to fly to Fairbanks. We can take the 7 a.m. flight up. Better plan to take the last evening flight back to Anchorage. It's going to be a long day."

"That sounds acceptable, Mr. Spielman. I will meet you at the airport next Monday. Goodbye."

As soon as Armand hung up, he dialed the Land Field Services' number. Shirley immediately picked up. "Armand," she purred, "what a pleasure to hear from you! How may I help you?"

As often as Armand called Land Field Services, he never tired of Shirley's compliments. "Good morning, Shirley. I'll be coming up your way on Monday and I need you guys to schedule a charter to Coldfoot."

"We can do that," answered Shirley. "I'll get my husband Jim to fly you up. Let me put Jay on so you can discuss the details."

Jay came on the line and, after their usual banter, Armand discussed the details of the trip. "So, you see, Jay, we unfortunately have to deal with Mr. Arnold again to solve the Miscovich claims."

"Roger that," responded Jay. "However, this time he knows that not accepting our best offer will lead to condemnation. He may just be the catalyst that closes the deal. I'll pick you guys up at the airport on Monday and take you to Aurora Air Service on the East Ramp."

"Sounds good, Jay. We'll see you then."

Jay met Armand and King Fish Arnold at the Wien gate at 8:15 in the morning. Arnold had a cheery attitude up to the moment he saw Jay. Then he instantly fell back to his customary reserved manner and gave

Jay a token handshake. Jay was unabashed and slapped King Fish across the back like they were old chums. King Fish grimaced at the blow.

Jay was in great spirits. "How was the flight up? What a glorious day! You'll have a fabulous flight to Coldfoot."

Armand smiled and replied, "Good to see you, Jay! It was a beautiful and smooth ride up. We've got our satchels and we're ready to fly on the charter."

Jay nodded and said, "Great! Your chariot awaits. Come on. My truck is parked out front." The three men squeezed into the truck cab with Armand squashed in the middle. Then Jay drove around the airport to the east ramp where several bush pilots operated charter services. Jay drove on to the parking apron and continued to a red and white Cessna 206. The pilot had the cowling open and was reading the oil dip stick when they stopped. Jay jumped out and asked the man, "How's it looking, Jim? Are you about ready to fly?"

Jim Pippen wiped the oil off the stick and slid it back into the engine block before answering. "Yep, Jay. I'm ready to go. Are these distinguished gentlemen my passengers?"

Jay motioned for the men to come forward before introducing them. "They sure are. This is Armand Spielman and William Arnold." Jay let each man shake Jim's hand before continuing with a little jibe. "Now, Jim, I want you to know Armand is my boss. So if you have to leave someone behind, it better be Mr. Arnold." Accustomed to Jay's humor, Jim smirked, but King Fish only scowled. Jay slapped Arnold across his back and said, "Only kidding, King Fish. Jim will get you there and back in one piece."

Then Jay became serious and gently took Armand by the arm and said, "Uh, Armand, I need to have a quick private word with you before you leave."

Armand became alarmed at Jay's demeanor. He knew Jay well enough to know that he had something important to tell him. "What's up, Jay?" he asked when they were out of earshot.

Jay put his hands on his hips and asked, "Did you hear about Mark Ringstad's antics over the weekend?"

Armand shook his head and replied, "No I didn't. He's been threatening some type of action over the past few months. What did he do?" Ringstad was upset about the Alaska Department of Highways relocating Johnson Road across his property. He blamed Alyeska for the realignment because the new Pump Station Eight was being built on the ridge that the road followed. The construction site required the road to be moved around the pump station. Ringstad claimed that only federal government employees had the right to use the road. Over the last six months, Armand had exchanged many letters with him and his lawyers. Each letter was testier than the last.

"Well," continued Jay, "he built a barricade across Johnson Road and prevented people from crossing it. The air force discovered it first when their men were traveling to their radar station. Then the Pump Eight construction crews hit it. One of them called me."

"Wow! What did you do, Jay?" asked Armand.

"I called the state troopers. They responded shortly and forced Ringstad to dismantle it."

Armand shook his head and asked, "Why do you think he did it?"

Jay shrugged and replied, "Beats the hell out of me. Anyway, we're headed to court. I'm sure they're filing a lawsuit. We should see it soon."

Armand looked at Jay and said, "August has been a heck of month, hasn't it? First the Wiseman miners tried to block the Haul Road and then Ringstad tries to block Johnson Road."

Jay nodded and replied, "Yep. People are unpredictable. We'll get through it. We better get back to the plane before King Fish starts imagining that we are plotting against him."

As they walked back, Jim had finished his preflight inspection and was ready to load his passengers. "OK, Armand. Ready to go? I need you to sit in the backseat to balance the weight. So, you need to get in first. Then Mr. Arnold will sit up front with me." The men climbed into their assigned seats. Jay stood back and waved goodbye to them as Jim started the engine. Minutes later, they were flying high in the blue sky over Fairbanks and headed north to Coldfoot.

The flight to Coldfoot took about an hour and a half. Jim landed on the dirt airstrip and taxied to the makeshift tower to park. The camp foreman met them and assigned a pickup truck for their use. Jim stayed with the plane and Armand and William drove the two miles north to

Clara Creek. They arrived at the rutted single-lane trail off the Haul Road at about eleven o'clock.

"Better hold on, William," said Armand as he eased on to the trail. "This could get bumpy." King Fish grabbed the stirrup above his door and braced himself as Armand negotiated around the potholes and boulders. After a long, slow mile, they spotted the Miscovich cabin through the woods. Armand pulled into the driveway and turned off the engine.

They sat quietly for a moment as they studied the well-built home. The Miscoviches appeared to be inside waiting for them. Armand had an idea and asked William, "Do you need a little time alone with Mr. and Mrs. Miscovich? I could kick around the property while you explain the situation to them."

King Fish nodded and said, "I think that's a capital idea! I appreciate the opportunity to advise my clients confidentially."

Armand replied, "Great! Have at it. Then come get me when you are ready." Armand watched William Arnold laboriously exit the pickup. He smoothed this sport coat and straightened his tie before walking up to the door and knocking. Andy Miscovich opened the door and greeted him. Armand saw King Fish explaining something to Mr. Miscovich and wag his head towards Armand before entering the cabin.

Armand watched the door close and then sat quietly for a few minutes in the truck before deciding to get out and stretch his legs. The warm summer sun felt good on his head and shoulders, but the heat also brought out the scourge of the north—mosquitoes. Although mid-August was past the peak mosquito season, there were still plenty of those pesky insects trying to get one last blood meal before autumn. Armand swatted at them and finally resorted to applying some mosquito repellent. It helped but the bugs still tried to hit his unprotected neck.

Armand worked his way down to Clara Creek and stumbled upon a gravel dam across the stream. The dam directed the water through a wooden device that resembled a cradle with a rough bottom that looked like a washboard. On closer inspection, he saw carpet had been tacked to the bottom with strips of wood. Armand surmised that the Miscoviches used this device to capture gold, but he had no idea how it worked. He continued to explore the property until he finally had his fill of swatting mosquitoes. He decided to make his way back to the cabin. He glanced at his watch and discovered over an hour had passed. This disturbed him because no one had called for him to come join them. Armand thought, *Have I screwed this acquisition up? What if they won't settle? Condemnation was a god-awful process.*

Armand was filled with trepidation as he walked up to the door and knocked. He heard someone inside yell, "Come on in!" Armand entered the cabin to find everyone seated comfortably in the front room.

Andy smiled and said, "Good to see you, Armand. We thought a bear got you."

Armand walked over and shook Andy's hand as he replied, "Never saw one of those creatures wandering around." Then he extended his hand to Verda and greeted her, "Pleased to meet you, Mrs. Miscovich. My name is Armand Spielman."

Verda stood and graciously offered, "Likewise, Mr. Spielman. May I interest you in a cup of coffee?"

Armand nodded and replied, "Yes, ma'am. That would be fabulous. It's been a long morning." Armand took a seat next to William Arnold. As he accepted the cup of coffee, his eyes spotted the pie plate on the counter next to him. On closer inspection, he saw the gold nuggets piled inside.

Armand tilted his head towards the plate and asked Andy, "Is this what would get out of that box in that dam of yours?"

Andy laughed and replied, "Yep! That is what it's all about. That device you saw is called a sluice box. We run the sediment through it. The gold gets hung up in the riffle board and carpet."

Armand shook his head in wonder and said, "I've never seen so much gold in one spot!" Then Armand took a sip of coffee and turned to Andy to change the subject. "Well, Andy, William and I did not travel all the way here this morning to discuss your gold operation. I trust Mr. Arnold explained our offer to you. Do you have any questions?"

Andy shook his head and said, "Nope. Bill explained it quite thoroughly. In fact, Verda and I have already signed the agreement." He picked it up and plopped it on Armand's lap. "Now, all you have to do is write us a check for your maximum limit and we have a deal."

Armand smiled as he reviewed the signed document. He had a hunch that King Fish would tell the Miscovichs to go for the whole $100,000.

Seeing that everything was in order, Armand retrieved this draft book from his satchel and wrote out a check to Andy and Verda. He detached it from the book and handed it to Andy. Andy glanced at it and then promptly flipped it over and endorsed it. Then he handed it to his wife who did the same. Afterwards, Andy handed it to King Fish who placed it in his wallet.

"Whoa there!" exclaimed Armand. "That money is not yours, Bill."

Andy extended his hand towards Armand to calm him and said, "Not to worry, Mr. Spielman. I have given Mr. Arnold explicit instructions to purchase a new D-8 cat from Northern Commercial Company in Anchorage. My old one here is about ready to kick its legs up and die."

Armand still did not like King Fish handling the money, but what the Miscovichs did with their affairs was their business. "OK. I can't argue with that. Bill, I believe we should start our way back home. We've got some miles to cover."

Armand thanked Mr. and Mrs. Miscovich for their hospitality, loaded into the pickup, and began the arduous trip back to the Haul Road. A half an hour later, they pulled up to the Coldfoot Camp. Jim Pippen was waiting for them in the break room. "How'd it go?" he asked.

"Mission accomplished," answered Armand. "Do you think you can get us back to Fairbanks for the last flight to Anchorage?"

Jim stood, finished his coffee, and said, "No problem. Let's go." The flights to Fairbanks and Anchorage were uneventful. Armand drove home from the airport in the late summer evening with a sense of accomplishment. He had solved one large problem. He savored the moment because tomorrow would bring more challenges.

During the blustery morning of September 30, 1974, 80 people gathered beside the Wien Airline service counter inside the Fairbanks International Airport. A bystander would have recognized many faces in the crowd. Politicians, Alyeska managers, state managers, and reporters milled together and enjoyed amicable conversations as they passed the time. Heavy early snow had postponed their planned ten o'clock flights to the Haul Road ribbon-cutting ceremony. Prospect Camp was struggling to keep the airstrip open during the continuous snowstorm. As an hour ticked by, hopes that the weather would clear plummeted. Bruce Campbell, ex-Burgess Construction Company manager and now commissioner of State Highways, summarized the situation by accusing the Sierra Club of slapping an injunction on sunshine, which produced snow and prevented the ceremony. A few minutes later, Alyeska canceled the trips.

While some disappointed people returned to Anchorage, most decided to participate in Alyeska's backup plan—a mock ribbon cutting on Fort Wainwright. Alyeska shuttled the crowd to Haynes Hall, where lunch was served in the gymnasium and afterwards the ceremony was performed on the auditorium stage. By a series of mountaintop repeater stations, Alyeska broadcasted the proceedings simultaneously to the Prospect and Coldfoot camps and to the linkup site on the Haul Road.

First, Nate Bauer, Alyeska Haul Road project manager, began the ceremony with a prayer asking for God's blessing on the project. Then he asked for a moment of silence to remember the men who died building the road. Afterwards, Harold Kennedy, Prospect Creek section manager, who was at the linkup location, broadcasted a short speech praising the efforts of everyone who built the 360-mile road through adverse conditions within 154 days.

Mr. Bauer then briefly described the construction process and challenges of building the Haul Road. He commended the project supervisors, managers, and workers and stated that Alyeska would present a certificate of accomplishment to everyone in appreciation for a job well done. He concluded his speech by introducing Edward Patton, Alyeska president. Patton reiterated Kennedy's praise of the Alyeska team and workers for completing the job on time. Simultaneously, Kay Eliason read Patton's speech to the attendees at the linkup site.

Then, Bruce Campbell came onto the stage and described the problems encountered building the road. He concluded by saying, "Persistence and reasonableness paid off, though. And we were able to tiptoe through the tundra with no real damaging effects."

The wives of Harold Kennedy and Bruce Campbell tied a ribbon across the stage. Marl Campbell held the ribbon and Vera Kennedy cut it with a large pair of scissors to signify the completion of the Haul Road. At the same time, Deanna Turner, wife of Bill Turner, Alyeska senior project manager, cut the ribbon at the linkup site. Then Art Voss from Coldfoot Camp and Jack Deets from Prospect Camp drove their dozers towards each other and pushed the final gravel cover to connect the road. Fourteen semitrucks loaded with supplies and equipment were staged a half mile south waiting to drive north to Prudhoe Bay. The Haul Road was officially open.

Technically, the 28-foot-wide Haul Road was not completely built. The gravel cover was thin, but the early winter was freezing it fast. Most bridges were temporary structures designed to last until the permanent crossings were built. Trucks had to be ferried across the Yukon River by hovercraft until the river froze thick enough to drive on the ice. The Yukon Bridge was anticipated to be finished by October 1975. Alyeska told the State Department of Highways not to expect the road to meet secondary highway standards until 1980, when the right-of-way would transfer back to the State of Alaska.

On November 2, 1974, Jay Hammond narrowly defeated Bill Egan as Alaska's next governor. Two unusual factors caused the election to be highly controversial. First, people identified Hammond, who was an Alaskan bush pilot and looked the part with his thick beard and stout build, as a conservationist. This confused and split the traditional Republican Party base. Egan, a Democrat, was pegged an industrialist, which ruffled the feathers of his party. During this confusion, a substantial third-party candidate, Joe Vogler, stepped into the ring and declared his candidacy under the Alaska Independence Party. Vogler was a Fairbanks miner and real estate developer with an open contempt for the environmental movement. His plain and common-sense talk pulled voters from both sides. When the dust settled and the final tally of votes certified, Hammond had eked out a win.

For Armand, Hammond was the third governor to take office while he struggled to attain the right-of-way for TAPS. Each change meant new land managers would be assigned posts, new policies and priorities would be implemented, and reeducation of new staff would be needed. Armand hated political change—especially when they were so close to building the pipeline.

Chapter 13

The Final Push

Near the end of January 1975, Armand found himself staring out his office at the cold, snow-covered Chugach range. He was exhausted from five and a half years of unrelenting work. The experience had been fascinating and challenging, but he had reached his limit. Alyeska had received the majority of their right-of-way permits. The remaining work consisted of countless small easements and property takes for the pipeline construction, access roads, and materials sites. Jay's people were adequately handling this workload. Thus, the time was right for Armand to consider stepping out of the project and returning to his old position with ARCO.

When Armand came to this conclusion, he stood and walked immediately to Harry Brelsford's office. Harry was just hanging up his telephone when he spotted Armand at the doorway. He could tell by the look in Armand's eyes that he had something important to discuss. "Come on in, Armand. What's on your mind?"

Armand nodded, entered Harry's office, and closed the door behind him. *Wow! Must be important*, thought Harry. Harry remained silent and let Armand get comfortable. He wanted Armand to speak when he was ready.

Armand looked at Harry with a steady gaze and said, "Harry, I believe it's time for me to gracefully return to my old position with ARCO."

This announcement took Harry by surprise. He knew Armand had been unusually contemplative these past weeks, but he did not realize the extent of his disillusionment until now. Harry calmed himself before replying, "I see. I didn't know that you were burning yourself out. Do you really need to leave? I mean, we could find you some qualified help to help you with your duties."

Armand shook his head, "No, Harry, I'm done. I've been pushing hard for years. Now I can see the light at the end of the tunnel. Jay's group can take it from here."

Harry's shoulders slumped forward as he accepted Armand's resignation. He knew Armand was right, but he was going to miss him. They had been through a lot together. "OK, Armand. Obviously you have been thinking about this for a while. I have enjoyed working with you these past five years. It won't be the same without you."

Armand replied, "I have enjoyed working with you, too, Harry. You are a good man with sound judgment. I don't know what I would have done without your advice."

Harry looked down to conceal the wetness around his eyes. After a few moments, Harry got control of his emotions and was able to continue. "OK, then. Have you given any thought about an orderly exit? I would sure like you to train a replacement, but I seriously doubt if there is anyone out there with your experience."

Armand smiled. He was pleased that Harry was taking his resignation as well as could be expected. "Actually, I was thinking Jay could find someone to work here in Anchorage. Then Alyeska could use the contract employee as long as we need him. I could show him the ropes and Jay and you could supervise him."

Harry rubbed his jaw as he thought about Armand's idea. "Yes, I think that might work. Please contact Jay and discuss it with him. Are you working on any major negotiations at this time?"

"Just one, Harry. The U.V. Industries gold claims in Fox."

Harry nodded and answered, "All right, Armand. Then let's plan on you finishing that acquisition before throwing in the towel. I'll try not to slide anything else on your plate. We'll save that for your replacement."

Armand stood relieved and shook Harry's hand before he left. He was thankful that Harry was a compassionate and understanding man. Now he needed to call Jay and tell him to start looking for someone to help Harry. Armand's great adventure was coming to an end.

On March 6, Armand walked into Dan Eagan's office in Fairbanks. Dan greeted him with fresh-brewed coffee. "Armand! Good to see you again. I trust your flight up here was uneventful."

Armand enjoyed visiting Dan in his old F.E. Mining office. They had developed a good honest friendship during their negotiations. Armand shook Dan's hand in earnest and replied, "Good to see you, too, Dan. I flew Alaska Airlines this time. Marvelous flight. You could see for hundreds of miles around us."

Dan nodded, "Yeah. I love the Interior in March–crystal-blue skies and bright sunshine." Dan then motioned to the table as he handed Armand a mug of coffee, "Well, I've got each claim's metes and bounds described. There are sixteen patented claims. Here is the list. We need to discuss a condition that we are going to insist on including in the agreement and the company has determined an average price per acre."

Armand picked up the list and began to review it. "Good. Looks like you have been busy, Dan. What condition do you want in the purchase agreement?"

Dan pointed to a claims map showing the proposed pipeline alignment and replied, "It has to do with access, Armand. Alyeska needs to provide us a way to cross the pipeline and develop the claims adjacent to the new pipeline right-of-way."

"I can understand that," answered Armand. "Since the pipeline will be buried in this area, I'm sure we can come up with an engineered crossing that can support heavy equipment. I have no objection to U.V. Industries' request."

"That's great, Armand. What kind of purchase agreement were you thinking to use?"

Armand rubbed his chin and replied, "I was thinking of writing a special warranty deed that will include an exhibit that describes the metes and bounds of each claim. The deed would contain a reservation that preserves your access to your abutting properties. How does that sound to you, Dan?"

Dan smiled and said, "Sounds good. I think that's a very logical approach. Now all we have to discuss is the average cost per acre."

Here's where the rubber hits the road, thought Armand. His face became serious as he looked Dan in the eye and asked, "That's right. What were you guys thinking?"

Dan took a swallow of coffee before answering, "We were thinking $5,000 per acre. How does that square with you?"

Armand let out an audible sigh of relief. He was expecting a much higher amount, which would have led to terse negotiations, and God forbid, condemnation proceedings. Dan's price was fair and close to what Armand had estimated. Armand knew he could convince Harry that this was a good settlement price, too.

Armand reached out his hand to Dan and said, "OK. It's settled. Five thousand dollars an acre."

Dan seemed to be relieved too. He grasped Armand's hand and shook it. "Deal. Will you take the first crack at the purchase agreement?"

"Yes," replied Armand. "I will have to run it by the corporate attorneys. They'll probably want to contact your attorney to ensure all the proper words are included. Then we can cut a check to U.V. Industries and have the agreement recorded."

Dan suddenly became a little agitated. "Uh, Armand, there's something I should tell you."

"Oh, what's that?" asked Armand.

"We are changing our name. By the end of the month, we'll be known as the Alaska Gold Company. "

Armand shook his head and answered, "Things never stay the same, do they, Dan? OK. All the more reason for my corporate lawyers to contact yours. We'll make it happen."

Jay Sullivan quietly began searching for a replacement for Armand. He knew that he would never find a true substitute–a person with decades of pipeline right-of-way experience. So, he focused his search on individuals with a good work ethic and a positive mental attitude. Fortunately, Jay stumbled across a promising applicant that was residing in Anchorage. His name was Warren Krotke.

Jay had become reacquainted with Warren during meetings with the Sourdough chapter of the International Right-of-Way Association. Jay and Warren had been instrumental in starting the IRWA chapter in Anchorage. Jay had originally met Warren in 1968 at the Alaska Title and Guarantee (AT&G) office in Fairbanks. They worked together cleaning up the flood mess and reconstructing the AT&G title records.

Warren was in his early 30s, married, and seemed mature beyond his age. Impressed by his sincerity and polite manners, Jay lured him away from the Alaska Division of Aviation, where he performed title research and land acquisitions and hired him as Armand's replacement. Warren began his tenure with Land Field Services working out of the Sullivan house. Jay and Nancy had set up an office in their basement.

After a short orientation, Jay introduced Warren to Armand and Harry. The three men quickly developed a bond and a working relationship. Within a week, Armand and Harry agreed with Jay that Warren could eventually assume Armand's workload. Warren began working closely with Armand and Harry in their Alyeska offices.

Armand spent the final weeks of March completing the special warranty deed that would grant fee simple title of the U.V. Industries mining claims to the owners of TAPS. He connected the Alyeska senior attorney, W.R. Harrison, with the U.V. Industries general counsel, Oliver Gushee in Salt Lake City. Harrison and Gushee hammered out the final wording, which allowed Armand to finalize the deed.

During the last week of March 1975, Armand flew to New York City to hand-deliver a check to Martin Horwitz, the CEO of U.V. Industries. The Alyeska Pipeline check was made out to the Alaska Gold Company for $664,700 to purchase 132.94 acres at $5,000 per acre. Alaska Gold Company executed the deed a few months later and submitted the transaction to the Fairbanks Recorders Office to complete the filing. Alyeska now owned most of the required right-of-way north of Fairbanks.

While Armand was in New York, Dan Beardsley was trying to secure right-of-way across two mining claims in the upper Middle Fork Koyukuk River valley. The owners were Earl Boese and Arctic John Etalook. Earl had a mine on Linda Creek. He had single-handedly built a home and carved out an airstrip on his claim. Every year, Earl recovered a substantial amount of gold from his mine and easily proved his claim to the BLM. The BLM granted Earl a patent for his property. Therefore, Alyeska could negotiate directly with Earl to secure the pipeline right-of-way.

Arctic John's claim was more complicated. On Jay's advice, John and his wife Esther applied to the Bureau of Indian Affairs for a Native allotment. Thus, Alyeska needed the Etalooks' written concurrence and BIA approval before the pipeline right-of-way could be procured.

Dan met frequently with Earl and developed a level of trust. Together, they walked the proposed alignment where it would cross his property. Earl gave Dan suggestions where Alyeska could tweak the route and avoid impacting his mining operations and damaging his runway. Dan forwarded Earl's thoughts to the Michael Baker engineers. They agreed that Mr. Boese's ideas were prudent and realigned the pipeline route. Dan traveled back to Earl with a revised alignment map and a right-of-way purchase agreement that reflected these changes. Earl signed the agreement.

Dan's next challenge was Arctic John. He had tried several times to discuss Alyeska's needs with John, but their meetings always concluded by Etalook chasing Dan off his property. Out of desperation, Dan turned to Earl for help. Earl was happy to intervene.

"Oh, heck, Dan, I know John and Esther well," exclaimed Earl. "I can get them to settle down and talk to you. But the problem is, you would be hard pressed to find them this time of year. I hear tell that Esther is back in Fairbanks and John hotfooted to Anaktuvuk Pass to visit with relatives. I don't know when he's coming back."

Dan absorbed this information and thought about the situation. He couldn't wait for John to return to his allotment. Who knew when that would be and pipeline construction would be starting soon. Dan needed to track him down now. Then a light bulb lit up in his brain and illuminated a desperate idea that dragged suppressed gut-wrenching memories from the forgotten recesses of his mind. Dan could charter a helicopter from Coldfoot and fly Earl and him to Anaktuvuk Pass and track down Arctic John. It was a year ago this March that Dan had almost met his maker on Minook Creek after chasing down Carlo. He had no interest in tempting Lady Luck again—but he had no choice.

Dan looked at Earl and said, "Are you up for a helicopter ride, Earl? I think I can charter one from Coldfoot to take us to Anaktuvuk Pass. Then we could find John and discuss our right-of-way needs. How about it?"

Earl grinned like a kid at a carnival. "Sure, I'm up for that! When are you thinking?"

"How about tomorrow? First light. If this is going to happen, we'll land on your runway in the morning and pick you up before heading to Anaktuvuk."

Earl scratched his neck as he scanned the mountaintops surrounding them. "I reckon that might work," replied Earl. "It's looking like it might storm on us soon. We'll see. I'll look for you tomorrow."

Dan shook Earl's hand, got into his pickup, and started driving south to Coldfoot. He brooded over Earl's words about an impending storm. The same thought kept replaying in his mind. *Why do I keep getting myself into these situations?*

———————

Dan felt *déjà vu* strike him as he shook hands with his helicopter pilot and followed him to the red and white Bell Jet Ranger under the gray-blue cloudy sky. The pilot was clean shaven and wore a baseball cap. Dan thought that he looked normal enough. Then the Coldfoot camp manager told Dan that he was a highly trained Vietnam pilot. *Great*, thought Dan. The army had discharged hundreds of helicopter pilots after the war. All were phenomenal behind a stick, but some had unsuppressed wild streaks up their spines. Helicopter charter com-

239

panies had snapped up many of these men to fly the unpredictable weather and rugged terrain from Valdez to Prudhoe. Dan hoped his pilot could restrain himself from trying to relive an adrenaline-driven war scene on their way to Anaktuvuk Pass.

They flew to Earl's airstrip on Linda Creek. Earl was waiting for them. The pilot got Earl situated in the backseat and equipped him with a headset. Then the pilot took off and headed south to the Hammond River. He followed the Hammond upstream and threaded through a series of tight mountain passes as he gradually worked his way northwest towards Anaktuvuk Pass. The Brooks Range did not possess exceptionally high mountains, but they were rugged. Dan looked down at the knife-edged peaks with trepidation.

As the pilot methodically negotiated the terrain, Dan noticed the clouds were pushing lower. The pilot responded by slowing the aircraft. Suddenly, snow fell thickly from the sky creating a whiteout. The pilot brought the aircraft to a hover and then turned to retrace their route. A wall of white prevented them from retreating.

We're trapped! Dan spun in his seat and saw Earl's face etched with fear. Dan thumbed his intercom and asked the pilot, "Now what?"

The pilot coolly replied, "We're going down." He gently lowered the helicopter until the ground emerged about a hundred feet below them. "Now we'll follow the drainage south until we clear this storm and then we'll try to find a way back north."

Dan shook his head and said, "No! Take us back. This isn't worth it. We'll try again when the weather is better." Dan turned and saw Earl nodding in agreement.

Pilot answered, "OK. Have it your way, but I still think I can make it to Anaktuvuk."

Dan was in no mood for heroics. He replied with a simple, "Home." The pilot nodded and flew low until they eventually left the snowstorm. He followed the drainage to the John River. Here he flew downstream to the Koyukuk River, which he followed upstream past the village of Bettles and continued to the Haul Road. Then he turned north to Linda Creek to drop Earl off.

The pilot shut the engine off and helped Earl out of the helicopter. Earl looked like he was happy to be home. He took off his cap, wiped his brow, and said, "That was a heck of ride, Dan. Can't say I want to do it again. I'll see if I can find out when John is returning to his claim."

Dan shook his hand as he replied, "Thanks, Earl. I appreciate the help. Sorry for the rough trip."

Later that evening in Coldfoot, Dan heard a knock at his door. Puzzled by the unaccustomed intrusion, Dan warily opened the door. There stood Earl grinning from ear to ear. "Earl!" exclaimed Dan. "What are you doing here?"

Earl replied, "I just found out that Arctic John will be in Fairbanks tomorrow."

Dan cocked his head in curiosity and asked, "How do you know that?"

Earl laughed and said, "I heard it on the Trapline Chatter radio show." At 9:20 p.m., KJNP in North Pole, Alaska amped up their transmitting power and broadcasted messages to residents in the Alaska Bush. In rural Alaska, this was the only form of communication with major Alaska towns. Everyone in the Alaska bush listened to the nightly broadcasts. It was like eavesdropping on a massive party line. Everyone knew everyone's business.

Dan smiled and said, "Thanks, Earl. Now I feel like a true Alaskan."

On March 27, 1975, Alyeska laid the first section of pipe and held a celebration to commemorate it. They chose a short section across the Tonsina River north of Valdez. Senator Ted Stevens and Alyeska Vice President of Project Management Peter DeMay were among several dignitaries in attendance to witness the historical event. Jay Sullivan had managed to wrangle an invitation from a Michael Baker manager and drove down from Fairbanks to participate.

Although sunny, the weather was still nippy with a biting breeze. Most attendees wore parkas and all had white hard hats. The Tonsina was flowing choked with ice. The ground was frozen solid.

When the equipment lined up to carry the pipe, the section foreman narrated the installation for the crowd. Using a megaphone, he explained, "As you see, the cranes are working in unison to sling the pipe in place. We dug a trench earlier to accommodate the pipe."

Twelve side-booms (bulldozers with side-mounted cranes) worked together to maneuver the 1,400-foot welded pipe section over the trench. Alyeska had encased the pipe in a waterproof, concrete liner to protect it from corrosion. "The plan is to lower the pipe to the water surface. Then we will place cement counterweights over the pipe to prevent it from floating. After the counterweights are secure, we will continue to lower the pipe into the trench. Then we'll backfill it with gravel and remove the weights."

Jay pulled out his Kodak pocket instamatic camera and snapped pictures of the pipeline installation. As he clicked the shots and wound the film roll to its next frame, Jay smiled at the knowledge that this crossing was one of his "gold" claims. He had managed to hold the land until Alyeska finalized their route.

The foreman lifted the megaphone to his mouth and announced, "They will begin to lower the pipe now." A whistle blew and the operators skillfully lowered the pipe to the river surface. Then large front-end loaders carried the weights over the pipe and put them in place. The weights fit snugly like enormous saddles. The foreman continued, "OK. Here we go! Ladies and gentlemen, this is officially the first buried installation of the Trans-Alaska Pipeline System! Let's give them applause." The spectators clapped as the whistle blew again. The operators responded by smoothly continuing to lower the pipe below the water surface and into the trench. Jay clicked a few more photos.

When the operators' cables went slack, laborers unhooked one side of the slings from the crane cables and the operators pulled the slings from under the pipe. The installation was flawless. Immediately, dozers pushed gravel into the trenches and filled it to the original riverbed elevation. They completed this work within an hour.

The foreman announced, "Now they'll remove the concrete collars." The loaders moved in, attached to the weights, and lifted them off the pipe. "And the installation is now complete. We will repeat this process hundreds of times as we cross rivers and streams from Prudhoe Bay to Valdez. Now people, please accept our invitation for lunch. It will be served in the camp mess hall. I look forward to discussing the construction process personally with you. So, let's . . ."

Jay saw it first before the foreman interrupted his speech. The water began foaming over the trench. Someone yelled, "Get back!" Suddenly, the entire pipeline section erupted to the surface and began to move downstream in the current. The weight of the gravel could not compensate for the empty pipe buoyancy without the counterweights. Men scrambled to latch on to the pipe with their equipment and secure it. The debacle cast a pall over the ceremony. Jay shook his head in dismay as he snapped his final pictures.

The construction crews required three and a half weeks to secure the Tonsina crossing. A year and a half later, inspectors discovered the pipe had suffered damage during the reinstallation, which required replacing it. Thus, the Tonsina River crossing became the first and last TAPS pipeline section to be installed.

While Armand was finalizing the U.V. Industries right-of-way purchase, Land Field Services had their hands full with a tough, burly character named Ray Duncan. Ray and his wife Janet owned a trucking company and property at 9-Mile Steese Highway–the location where the pipeline was going to cross the road. Their property also abutted U.V. Industries and they were keenly aware of Alyeska's negotiations with the mining company. Thus, when Land Field Services offered the Duncans what they assessed as fair market value ($6,660 for 4.8 acres), Ray erupted in a rage, claiming it was pittance compared to what Alyeska was willing to give U.V. "I don't know what you offered U.V.," Ray yelled at Land Field Services, "but I bet it was a hell of a lot more than this!" Negotiations degenerated swiftly after his outburst.

Finally, Jay gave up and submitted the negotiation package to Harry to initiate eminent domain proceedings. The *Fairbanks Daily News Miner* published the Duncan legal notice of taking on April 9, 1975. Because of Ray's volatility, an Alaska state trooper hand-delivered the notice to Ray's trucking business. Ray spotted the trooper getting out of his car holding a crisp envelope and deduced the purpose of his visit. His anger flared and he sneaked out the back when the officer knocked on the front door.

The trooper knocked a few more times before trying the door knob. The door was open, so he walked inside. As he looked around, he called out Mr. Duncan's name and asked if anyone was here. Suddenly, the officer heard a truck pulling up to the front. He walked back to the door to see Ray attaching a tow hook to his squad car. Disbelief froze the trooper for a critical second, which allowed Ray to jump back into his cab and throw the truck in gear.

"Hey! Stop!" yelled the trooper.

"Stop yourself!" screamed Ray through the side window as he dragged the car backwards on the snow. Ray raced toward the highway and then twisted the truck into a tight turn twirling the car behind him like a gigantic game of snap-the-whip. The trooper ran after Ray, but had to jump out of the way when his car came swinging through the air.

Ray peeled his tires forward as the trooper car came out of the arc and shot toward his building. Then he slammed on his brakes and turned sharply causing the car to fly through the air behind him. Ray craned his neck out the window and yelled, "So, you think you can just steal anyone's property by just knocking on their door, huh? I think I'll just grab me a cop car because I can, too. What do you think about that?"

The trooper had enough. He stepped in front of the truck, unbuckled the flap over his pistol holster, and stared straight at Ray. Ray gulped and froze as the officer began to slowly walk forward. When he got to the window, he addressed Ray with the voice of authority, "Mr. Duncan, I'm willing to overlook your transgressions if you immediately unhook my car. Failing to do so, I will be forced to arrest you for threatening an officer and absconding with his vehicle. You will be incarcerated for several days until the judge sorts it out. Your choice."

Ray could tell he wasn't fooling. He shoved the truck in gear and turned the engine off. "Fine," Ray replied as he threw opened his door. "Have it your way."

"Thank you, Mr. Duncan. You will have your day in court to tell the judge how you feel about taking your land for the pipeline."

Ray muttered under his breath as he popped the hook off the trooper's bumper, "Damn sure I will!"

In April, 1975, the South Slope Subdivision condemnation proceedings began. To facilitate the proceedings, the judge recommended using a mutually agreeable master to analyze the potential worth of the proposed right-of-way. A master operated like an arbitrator. Both sides agreed on who would fulfill the duties of a master. This person then independently gathered the necessary information to calculate value and presented his findings to the court. For the South Slope case, the plaintiffs and defendants selected Jeff Cook to be the master.

Jeff was a young, well-known realtor in the Tanana Valley. He was born and raised in Fairbanks. He had completed his bachelor's of Business Arts and MBA degrees at the University of Oregon. Jeff's father, Earl, was a longtime real estate broker and Jeff had worked in the family business since he was teenager. Thus with years of pertinent experience, Jeff was the ideal candidate to be the master.

Jeff visited the subdivision—paying special attention to the homes built within it. He walked the proposed right-of-way and noted possible impacts to existing infrastructure and nearby homes. Then he dove into the borough platting records and researched the development of the subdivision and any special restrictions and covenants imposed on the subdivision.

Jeff Cook submitted his report to the Alaska Superior Court in early 1976. The court had already awarded access to Alyeska to prevent delaying the pipeline construction. The only contention now was how much the land was worth. Mr. Cook's report documented similar properties within close proximity and their assessed values. He also noted the premium potential customers put on south-facing, permafrost-free lands in Fairbanks. Then he focused on the same troubling aspect that Dan had stumbled upon—the lack of covenants that would ensure that only high-value homes would be built in the subdivision.

Jeff noted the construction of the urethane-coated geometric domes at the entrance to the subdivision and believed that the domes lowered the ambiance of the subdivision. Since these unseemly domiciles already impacted the subdivision's desirability, a buried and revegetated pipeline would have little effect on property values. Thus, Mr. Cook assessed the value of the lots required for the pipeline right-of-way to be around $150,000.

The subdivision owners were appalled and balked at the value. They brought their own valuation to the court and vigorously defended a higher price. On November 12, 1976, the Superior Court awarded a final compensation to the owners of $160,237.25, which included interest, costs, and attorney fees. The defendants decided not to appeal the award.

Above Steele Creek Road, Land Field Services encountered another challenge–negotiating right-of-way with Helenka Brice. Helenka was a beautiful, tough, and determined lady with an eccentric wild side. She insisted her name was spelled with a small "h" and pronounced it "e-LEN-ka". At 70 years young, she had a two-way radio installed in her car and frequently demanded the Radio Fairbanks operator to patch her into the telephone network as she careened from her hillside property into town.

Helenka and her husband Luther moved their family to Fairbanks in the late 1950s in hopes of starting a lumber company. They acquired an 80-acre parcel just north of Steele Creek Road in 1961 and formed the Brice Lumber Company. On this property, they built a home, an equipment storage yard, a material site, and eventually an ad hoc orphanage.

Later, Luther and Helenka separated, but Helenka soldiered on and ultimately became the driving force behind the fledgling Brice Construction Company. Helenka first secured land-clearing contracts and eventually grew the company into a small construction firm specializing in remote projects. She was well connected in politics and frequently grabbed the ears of Alaska senators–especially Mike Gravel.

At first, Helenka wanted nothing to do with the pipeline. "Move it!" was her mantra every time a Land Field Services employee would approach her for right-of-way. Frankly, no one could blame her. She had a beautiful parcel that overlooked the Tanana Valley. She put her heart and soul into developing the property. Helenka called it "Brice-in-the-Hills." She wasn't going to lose even a sliver of it.

After several failed attempts to negotiate, Jay launched his secret weapon—Don Bruce. Don was an old-time resident of Fairbanks. Always professionally dressed, he looked and conducted himself as a perfect gentleman. Don exuded respect and calm, which the Fairbanks matriarchs found very appealing. He also knew almost every prominent citizen in Fairbanks including Helenka.

Don called her and asked if he could meet with her at the Brice office. She immediately granted his request. Don arrived on time carrying nothing but his charm. The moment her eyes fell on him, Helenka lost her resolve and accepted his gracious hug. That seemed to set the tone for the meeting. They drank coffee and updated each other on their respective families. Then they exchanged juicy bits of shady information about select residents. As they finished slandering their victims, Don smoothly steered the discussion to Helenka's concerns about a pipeline crossing her property.

"Donald," Helenka explained, "I won't tolerate a pipeline ripping through my property, even if it's buried."

Don nodded with sage concern and answered, "Helenka, I completely agree. Please let me drive you up there and we can walk the route and determine if we can find an alternative. What do you say?"

Helenka appeared hesitant. She clearly looked like she had other pressing matters. Don sensed she was teetering on refusing his request. So he leaned forward, patted her hand, as he said, "Please, Helenka. I would consider it a personal favor if you would." She looked into his eyes and reluctantly nodded. Don gave her his best pleased look and said, "Wonderful! We'll take my car. This shouldn't take too long. I'll have you back in a jiffy."

Don escorted her to his car and opened the door. After she got settled, he whisked her off to her upper hillside home. Upon their arrival, Helenka pointed out the flagged survey line that denoted the planned pipeline route. The survey swath almost bisected her property. Don stopped the car, got out, and gallantly raced around the front to open the door for Helenka. She appeared to enjoy the attention.

Helenka walked into the field and spread out her arms and said, "Now see here, Donald? This is my problem. Alyeska wants 100 feet for their pipeline, but the route here would separate me from accessing my property. The west side would be useless to me. Do you see that?"

Yes, I do see it, thought Don. He turned to her and asked, "So, access is your biggest concern?"

Helenka nodded and said, "Yes, and I need assurance that Alyeska will restore the land the best they can."

Don's mind was wheeling. He sensed they were close to an agreement. All he had to do was to present Helenka with a feasible solution. Don looked into her eyes and found inspiration. "What if we shift the pipeline a little further west so we are not crowding your home and operations? We could engineer a road crossing for you to access the rest of your property. The only drawback would be that we'd still have to accommodate the subdivision road. That would take some more right-of-way to pull that off."

Helenka appeared interested. "How much more?" she asked.

Don rubbed his chin as he thought about the problem then replied, "I like to work with even numbers. So, I'm thinking another hundred feet width. That would make a 200-foot wide right-of-way."

Helenka looked wistfully back at her property for a moment as she considered Don's proposal. As she looked north, she softly said, "I suppose if I refuse, you are going to take it anyway, won't you?" Don remained silent. She sighed and then found her resolve as she set her jaw and turned to Don and said, "OK. I'll do it, but it's going to cost you, though."

Don felt sudden relief, but masked his feelings. He quailed at the thought of taking Helenka to court. She would be a formidable opponent. "Of course, Helenka. I'll put together a valuation and present it to you this week. Thank you, Helenka."

Helenka threw her head back and quipped, "We'll see how you'll be thanking me when we settle on a price. Take me back, Donald." Don leaped at her command.

Shirley got the emotional telephone call in the early morning and immediately transferred it to Jay. The screaming woman on the other end was seething mad and was calling long distance. She first asked for Donald Bruce. Upon hearing that he was not available, she demanded to speak to his supervisor. Jay took a deep breath before punching the holding line and addressing the woman, "Good morning. This is Jay Sullivan speaking. How may I be of assistance?"

"Sullivan!" shouted the woman. "This is Helenka Brice. What is the meaning of giving me a phony check for my land? You swindled me!"

Jay was blindsided by the call and accusation. He shook his head to clear his thinking and asked, "Come again? Mrs. Brice, I haven't a clue what you are talking about. Are you referring to the draft Mr. Bruce cut you last week?"

Helenka blasted back, "Yes! Donald gave me a check that bounced higher than the moon! I want my money now!"

Suddenly Jay had an inkling of what was causing the drama. "Uh, Mrs. Brice, where are you calling from?"

"Why, I'm in Washington, DC," she replied tersely.

"And did you try to cash the draft there?"

"Not me, Mike Gravel did and the Senate Bank refused it!"

Jay fell down in his chair, propped his enormous feet on the table, closed his eyes, and began rubbing his balding head. "So, you gave Senator Mike Gravel your draft?"

"As a matter of fact, I did," answered Helenka. "I endorsed it and gave it to him as a contribution. Why does that matter?"

Jay let out a deep sigh, not bothering to hide his frustration, and replied, "Because the draft is good only at the Alaska National Bank of the North."

Helenka roared back, "Why is it that this is the first that I've heard of this? Do you realize how embarrassed I am?"

Jay calmly replied, "Don told you. It's also written on the draft that it's only redeemable at Alaska National."

"Well," Helenka responded icily, "I am appalled at how your company conducts its business. You should be ashamed!" Then she slammed the phone down and the line went dead.

Jay slowly hung up his phone, put his hands behind his head, and contemplated life. Shirley tiptoed inside and softly asked, "You OK, boss?"

Jay stayed silent for a moment before responding, "You know Shirley, I think it's time for a drink."

"But it's only nine o'clock!"

"You're right," answered Jay as he stood up. "I'll take Bobby with me to bring me back."

On July 1, 1975, Armand officially transferred back to ARCO. His departure created little fanfare. As Armand cleaned out his Bragaw Street office, he saw Warren and Harry bent over a desk in the office across the hall discussing a plat and future right-of-way negotiations. Armand felt a pang of resentment at not knowing what they were discussing, but Harry remained true to his word that he would start sliding new projects to Warren and Warren proved to be a capable man.

Armand sighed and finished removing the last of his personal items and placed them in a cardboard box. He took a last look around to check if he forgot anything and to soak in the memories. A lot had happened within these walls over the past five years.

Armand carried his box into the hall, set it down on the floor, and then went to say goodbye to Harry and Warren. It took them a few minutes to sense Armand's presence and interrupt their discussion.

"Armand," exclaimed Harry, "all set to go back to ARCO?"

Armand stuck out his hand and said, "I guess so. It's been a great ride, Harry. Thank you for being there for me. I have enjoyed working for you."

Harry grabbed Armand's hand and firmly shook it. "Yes, it has been a good ride, Armand. You were a good hand and you rolled with the punches. Thank you for taking the project to construction. Land Field Services and I will mop up the stray pieces from here."

"That's what I figured," replied Armand. He turned to Warren, offered this hand, and said, "You are in good hands, Warren. I'm sure you will do well."

Warren smiled as he grasped Armand's hand and replied, "Yeah. I think we'll survive. Thank you for giving me a chance. I really appreciate the opportunity to work on TAPS."

Armand smiled and squeezed Warren's shoulder. "Well, I guess that's it. If there is nothing else, I'll be on my way."

Harry raised his finger in the air and exclaimed, "Whoa, wait a second! I almost forgot. I've got something for you. Hold tight." Harry walked briskly out of the office and returned a minute later with a thin package. He handed it to Armand and said, "Here you go. A little something to remember your efforts here."

Armand held the paper sheath for a moment before opening it. He found a certificate inside sandwiched between two thin sheets of cardboard. The certificate was printed on a textured paper. An artistic rendering of Alaska rimmed the certificate with light blue and soft brown images of Alaskan wildlife, mountains, and pipeline construction. The inscription read, "Alyeska Pipeline Service Company, in recognition of services rendered, is pleased to present this certificate of appreciation to Mr. Armand C. Spielman, who from March 1, 1969 to June 1, 1975, actively participated in the largest project ever undertaken by private industry, the Trans Alaska Pipeline System." Alyeska President, Edward Patton, had signed the certificate.

They're off by a month, but close enough for pipeline work, thought Armand as he carefully slid the certificate between the cardboard sheets and into the envelope. He held it up to Harry and said, "Thank you, Harry. I'll treasure it."

Harry nodded and replied, "It's the least we could do, Armand. I hope ARCO is good to you."

Armand looked at the two men for an awkward moment and then finally bent down to pick up his box. "I guess I'd better be going. I'll see you guys around. It's a small world." Harry and Warren said their goodbyes again and then turned back to their plats. Armand left them and walked away for the last time.

When Armand reached the ground floor, he turned to the parking lot exit and bumped into David Henderson on the way out. David took a step back and immediately understood why Armand was carrying a box crammed with assorted items. His facial features uncharacteristically softened as he stuck his hand out and said, "Armand, you did a fine job here. I hate to see you go."

Armand laid the box down and accepted his handshake as he replied, "Thank you, Dave. I enjoyed working for you."

"The name's. . ." David stopped himself and then smiled at Armand's deliberate jibe. He patted Armand on the shoulder and said, "See you around, Armand." Armand couldn't help smiling as he picked up his box and continued out the door.

The Middle Fork of the Koyukuk River miners' confrontation that Harry Brelsford feared came to a head during the summer of 1975. After analyzing the careful research of Jay Sullivan and the BLM mining engineers, John Wells and George Neuberg, Harry was convinced that the unpatented mining claims where the pipeline needed to cross were bogus. They appeared to be hastily and haphazardly staked—most after 1969 when the project centerline was roughly surveyed. The claims stretched from Coldfoot to the Hammond River, and in the restricted river valley, Alyeska could not avoid them. Thus, Harry filed for authority and necessity to condemn 114.5 acres in Alaska Superior Court.

The defendants were names well known to Fairbanks residents. They were John Bullock, Ross Harry, Harry Leonard, Les Matson, Yutana Barge Lines, Inc., Guy Rivers, and Howard Sparks.

Judge James Blair presided over the hearing. The court proceedings began during the first week of August. Judge Blair allowed the defendants to present evidence that their claims were valid and economically viable. John Bullock and Guy Rivers presented anecdotal evidence that land nearby produced sufficient gold to warrant mining. People in the court room had to smile when Bullock testified because they remembered his last summer's armed resistance.

Harry submitted the reports of Jay Sullivan and John Wells as evidence that the unpatented claims had no merit. Jay's work showed that no mining activity had occurred on the claims. Mr. Wells' analysis determined that mining these claims was uneconomical because his drilling cores showed that only low-grade ore existed and the gold was found too deep for a bucket dredge to mine.

On August 28, 1975, Judge Blair determined that the condemnation and taking of the Koyukuk mining claims was necessary for public use. The court granted the State of Alaska immediate possession. The court agreed with the Sullivan and Wells reports and determined that the claims were not valid and, therefore, the pipeline right-of-way was not eligible for compensation. The miners suddenly found their claims were worthless pieces of paper. The ruling set up the basis for a future fight in federal court when BLM moved to completely invalidate the claims.

The summer of 1975 found Fairbanks in the middle of a housing crunch. The population had exploded from 18,000 in 1974 to over 80,000 in August 1975. Homeowners were renting a single room in their houses for $800 per month. Tenants had to share a bathroom and a kitchen. Some brazenly rented their pickup campers parked in their driveways on a weekly basis and people gladly paid. Thus, newcomers were always searching for novel ways to meet their housing needs.

Ginger Noteboom arrived in Fairbanks to seek a pipeline job. She planned to stay with her sister and brother-in-law, Janet and Ray Duncan, at 9-Mile Steese Highway until she could find permanent arrangements. During her stay, she met Betty Snyder, a neighbor who proposed a solution to Ginger's housing dilemma. Betty had an 11-by-12-foot, one-room cabin on her property and she was willing to part with it for $200 if Ginger would move it. Janet and Ray agreed to help Betty relocate the cabin onto their property. Thus, Ginger thought this was the perfect solution and paid Betty her price with the promise of returning later that month to move it.

Ray returned to the cabin during the evening of August 25 with a truck and low-boy trailer to haul it to a new foundation that he had built on his property. Janet and Ginger were in the truck cab with him, and their jaws dropped when they found the cabin was gone. Someone had dragged it away.

Betty was just as shocked at the discovery and filed a police report. Ray started pounding on doors in the neighborhood and asked if anyone had seen the theft. Jeff Shelton told Ray that he had come home from work one evening to find it gone. That happened about a week ago. Ray was incensed that someone would steal property so close to his home. He began vigilantly guarding his property and keeping a sharp eye on activities nearby. Unfortunately, one of those activities was the construction of the Trans-Alaska pipeline.

During the first week of September, Ocean Tech surveyors were setting the pipeline centerline and right-of-way limits for the 9-mile crossing of the Steese Highway. Their work caught Ray Duncan's watchful eyes and enraged him because he and his brother George were still battling the eminent domain proceedings.

Ray confronted the surveyors with clenched teeth and fists and screamed, "Get the hell off my property! No one enters until I see some money. Understand! Get out before I blow your heads off!"

The surveyors looked at each other in shock. One man held a machete that he was using to clear the brush for surveying. Ray pointed to the man and asked, "Are you threatening me with that knife?"

The man looked at Ray with disbelief and replied, "What? No! Why are you so spun up?"

"Spun up?" answered Ray. "I'll show you spun up! Take another step, that will be the last thing you ever do! Scram!" The surveyors decided to back away. This big man looked like he meant business.

On September 10, Alyeska brought the right-of-entry case to Superior Court Judge Buckalew. Harry Brelsford retained Mary Nordale, a tough, brilliant Fairbanks lawyer, to represent them. She had honed her skills by helping rugged miners throughout Alaska fight for their land rights. Ray Duncan's fierce stares had no effect on her. She had faced these kinds of men before and knew how to handle them.

When asked to present her case, Mary calmly approached the podium and carefully arranged her notes. Then she folded her reading glasses and placed them before her. Crisply dressed in black shoes and slacks with a white ruffled blouse and a matching blazer, Mary exuded confidence as she addressed Judge Buckalew. "Your Honor, Alyeska's plea is simple. We request the right for peaceful possession of the land that the Alaska Court has granted us. As the worth of the land is in dispute, Alyeska will abide by the valuation determined by the eminent domain proceedings. Until that time, we should not have to stand for people interfering with construction work and threatening our employees."

Mary turned to Ray Duncan and leveled a finger at him as she continued, "This man threatened to blow our contractor's head off. We should not have to tolerate this kind of intimidation." Ray bared his teeth at her, but Mary never quivered. She returned her attention to Buckalew as she concluded, "In summary, your Honor, Alyeska requests a temporary injunction forbidding Mr. Duncan from interfering with pipeline construction. Thank you for your consideration."

Mary gathered her papers and glasses and marched back to her chair with her head held high. As she settled herself, Judge Buckalew addressed Ray Duncan. "Mr. Duncan, I understand you have chosen to represent yourself. Please approach the podium and present your case."

After Mary's graceful and professional performance, Ray looked like a Neanderthal as he lumbered to the podium. He carried nothing with him. Ray grasped the podium with both hands and looked uncertainly around him like he thought someone was going to take a swing at him. Judge Buckalew nodded for him to begin.

"Well, your Honor," began Ray, "I don't know much about courts and all, but I know when I'm being swindled! I know Alyeska is going to get my land one way or the other, but they should have to pay true value for it. Did you know that they paid U.V. Industries $125,000 for their land across the street from mine and they only offered $3,500 for my three and half acres? Now does that seem right to you? And now we're not even settled in court and they're mining the tailings on my property and building a pad. No sirree! They know my land is worth way more than three thousand—more like $300,000! And they have no right to mine my tailings."

Judge Buckalew took off his glasses and rubbed the bridge of his nose before replying, "Mr. Duncan, you must stay on topic. This court is focused on lawful entry onto lands already granted to Alyeska. The issue of the land's worth will be decided in the eminent domain proceedings. So, Mr. Duncan, I must ask you to recount your recent interaction with the Alyeska surveyors."

Ray ground his teeth as he stared at the judge. He obviously was struggling to control his emotions. Then he looked quickly around him and realized everyone was waiting for his response. Ray returned his attention to Judge Buckalew and replied, "I threatened a surveyor because he had a cutting knife and I was intimidated." This produced snorts of disbelief in the courtroom, which enraged Ray. So he added, "But I didn't get my gun or chase after them. Just words."

Judge Buckalew nodded and asked, "Anything more that you care to add, Mr. Duncan?"

Ray shook his head and said, "No."

"Very good, Mr. Duncan, please be seated." Ray looked around him with uncertainty before returning to his chair. Buckalew continued, "Ms. Nordale, do you have any witnesses that you would like to call forward?"

Mary stood and said, "Yes, your Honor, I have the two surveyors that were accosted by Mr. Duncan. I would like each to testify."

The court proceedings lasted two partial days. When it concluded, the court granted Alyeska a temporary injunction forbidding Ray Duncan from interfering with pipeline construction or tailings removal. The court agreed with Mary Nordale that the issue of who owned the tailings should be considered during the eminent domain proceedings and the value of the land would be adjusted accordingly. Ray was angry at the decisions and vowed to contest Alyeska's valuation of his land.

By December 1975, several outstanding issues were resolved. Ginger's cabin was found. Out of either guilt or discovery, a young man called the Duncans and said that he had just heard that he was living in a stolen home. He said that he had found it lying in a ditch along Sheep Creek Road and decided to take it home with him. He moved the cabin to 5-Mile Chena Pump Road, remodeled it, and built a front porch.

Ginger and the Duncans came to the man's home and verified that it was the cabin. Embarrassed, He paid Ginger $250 for it. They left mystified how someone could just pick up a cabin on the side of the road and drive off with it. They decided to let the police sort it out.

By the end of the year, Alyeska had acquired the right-of-way for the entire 800-mile-long pipeline corridor. The right-of-way widths varied depending on the entity granting the authority. On federal lands, BLM and BIA granted a right-of-way width of 54 feet for buried pipeline sections and 64 feet for above-ground sections. ADNR granted 100-foot-wide right-of-way on State lands. The private holdings varied from 54 feet to 300 feet depending on the negotiated purchase or eminent domain decisions.

The following displays the final right-of-way sources:

Federal Government:	376 miles
State Government:	344 miles
Alaska Native-Owned Land:	51 miles
Private Land Owners:	29 miles

Approximately, 149 parcels comprised the 29 miles of private lands. Remarkably, only eight of these transactions required condemning of the property. Most of these occurred between Nordale Road and Gilmore Trail–a stretch Alyeska nicknamed "Condemnation Alley." Alyeska required two other condemnations in the Big Delta area, about 120 miles south of Fairbanks, next to the Tanana River for a construction camp. This limited number of condemnations resulted from Alyeska's and Land Field Services' professional and persistent hard work to keep eminent domain proceedings to a minimum.

As construction progressed, countless temporary right-of-way and access issues would arise, which kept Alyeska and Land Field Services hopping. These issues usually involved developing material sites and building unforeseen support facilities. Both activities required access rights, easements, and small property purchases.

Not everyone was satisfied with Alyeska's right-of-way practices. Ray Duncan took one last swipe at the company when the *Fairbanks Daily News Miner* printed his letter to the editor on December 23, 1975. It read:

The Right Way?

Dear Editor:

After doing business about 20 years in Alaska I find myself ready to quit and leave the state.

Perhaps some of your readers could answer a few questions for me. First of all about the Alaska pipeline. My understanding is this is private enterise. Since when does private enterpise have the powers of condemnation?

If they have this just power, wouldn't they at least have to pay just compensation for property taken?

Instead they take property at about one per cent of the value to us and we are forced out of business and our home. While Alyeska Pipeline Service Co. breaks every law in the land and gets richer and the little people lose everything. If this is right, then I don't want any more to do with the "Great State of Alaska."

Sincerely,
Ray Duncan

Chapter 14

Epilogue

I n August 1976, the US Department of the Interior transferred the land patent for the Valdez Marine Terminal parcel to the State of Alaska. The Alaska Department of Natural Resources staff reviewed it and discovered that the patent recognized only 762.9 acres of the 862.7 acres of the originally requested parcel. Almost exactly 100 acres were missing.

DOI reviewed their documentation and agreed with ADNR. Curtis McVee, State BLM director, approved the revised patent and Bill Moses reissued it to the State of Alaska. On January 28, 1977, ADNR issued the land patent to Alyeska to complete their land purchase for the terminal.

As Alyeska advanced their construction of the pipeline and improved the Haul Road, their engineers realized they had significantly underestimated the project's gravel needs. The sections underlain by permafrost required enormous amounts of gravel to stabilize the melting soil and provide support for structures and equipment. Also, the pipeline paralleled major rivers such as the Lowe, Middle Fork Koyukuk,

Dietrich, Atigun, and Sagavanirktok. Large revetments, groins, and scour aprons were required to protect the pipeline and Haul Road and prevent erosion. These structures required gargantuan amounts of gravel and quarry rocks.

BLM struggled with allocating the mineral rights to Alyeska for their material needs in the Middle Fork Koyukuk River Valley. The narrow confines of the Koyukuk valley necessitated taking resources from the unpatented mining claims in the area. Finally, BLM decided to proceed with invalidating the unpatented mining claims straddling the pipeline and Haul Road. The miners appealed the BLM decision to the Federal Appeals Court in Sacramento, California.

During the first week of March, 1978, the Court provided a venue for miners to plead their cases. Of the original claim owners, only John Bullock and Guy Rivers traveled to Sacramento and protested the BLM decision.

Bullock testified that he had been mining since 1934. He had staked the Middle Fork Koyukuk River claims in 1969. He discovered small amounts of gold on the claims, but did not drill on the property to quantify the resource. Regardless of the lack of information, Bullock believed that his claims were valid and warranted mining. During cross-examination, Bullock agreed that a prudent man would not begin a mining without conducting a drilling program to validate the discovery and determine the most efficient mining method. Bullock also stated that he kept the gold recovered in vials, but did not segregate the results by claim.

William Nordene from Bettles testified on John Bullock's behalf. Nordene was mining on the upper reaches of Emma Creek—about one mile above Bullock's claims. He estimated that his average claim yield was $15.00 of coarse gold per yard of material processed. Mr. Nordene had sold the Middle Fork claims to Bullock and he believed that the claims would produce a similar yield.

Guy Rivers testified that he had done some work on his claims. He advanced three borings with a churn drill to a depth of 92 feet, where he hit quicksand which forced him to stop. Rivers also stated that a fellow miner, Jim Kelley, was drilling nearby in an excavated shaft when the tunnel collapsed, nearly killing him.

The BLM presented the testimony of two federal mining engineers, John Wells and Larry Shafford. These men had worked together collecting data from the 31 contested claims. Wells presented his information first.

John Wells testified that other than some bulldozed access roads on Bullock's property, he did not observe any mineral exploration activity on any of the contested claims. Wells collected surface samples from each claim and even allowed Bullock to choose the sample location from his property. Wells found that gold values averaged $0.0043 per cubic yard.

Then Wells examined Alyeska's drilling logs along the pipeline centerline as it transversed the unpatented claims. The average depth to bedrock was 93 feet and often exceeded 150 feet. Mr. Wells said that these data raised serious doubts whether a bucket dredge could economically mine the claims. His economical analysis showed the cost of dredging to 50 feet to be $0.73 per cubic yard in 1975 dollars. Wells's conclusion was that the claims did not possess enough gold for a prudent and reasonable man to invest labor and capital into mining the property.

Larry Shafford presented his analysis, which corroborated Wells's testimony. Shafford based his economic analysis on $195 per ounce of gold–the January 1970 peak gold price. His findings showed that total mining operating cost would far exceed the value of recovered gold from the contested claims. He also stated that the geology of area indicated that the gold reserves were in the streams above the river.

By the end of March, the Federal Appeals Court ruled that the miners had failed to prove that sufficient gold reserves existed on their unpatented claims to warrant mining. The court agreed with BLM that the cost of mining exceeded the value of recovery. Therefore, the unpatented claims were invalidated. BLM was free to allocate gravel resources to other projects.

David Burns was furious that the BLM had granted a 100-foot-wide right-of-way to the Alyeska Pipeline Service Company. The BLM determined that since Burns's trade and manufacturing claim was unpatented, the federal government was obligated to use the land for the public good. The right-of-way swath covered the eastern front of his claim, effectively severing his road to the Richardson Highway. Alyeska was willing to provide him gated access to his home, but this restriction quashed his plans for developing boat access to the Gulkana River and a campground–the very basis of his claim for the land.

Burns sued Alyeska for trespass in federal court. Alyeska took a step back and analyzed the legality of Burns's trade and manufacturing claim. They discovered that his claim violated two basic restrictions. The claim overlay both sides of the Gulkana River, which violated the constraint that the land claim must be contiguous. In addition, since the Gulkana was a federally recognized navigable water body, he could not claim more than 80 rods (1,320 feet) of shoreline. When totaling the shoreline lengths of both sides of the Gulkana River, Burns's claim exceeded this limit. Therefore, Alyeska countered Burns's suit with a request for summary judgment to invalidate the claim.

On October 22, 1985, Judge James von der Heydt granted Alyeska the summary judgment and ruled that David Burns's trade and manufacturing claim was invalid. Judge von der Heydt also dismissed Burns's trespass claim and any future counterclaims. With the stroke of a pen, the Burnses' dreams of carving out a living in remote Alaska were crushed and they had no legal basis to reside in their home.

Land Field Services' workload began to wind down in the early 1980s. Jay Sullivan eventually closed his Fairbanks office and based his work out of Anchorage with his wife, Nancy. Charlie Parr reopened the Fairbanks office in the early 1990s. Thus, Land Field Services continued to offer right-of-way consulting statewide.

Dan Beardsley took Jay's advice and left Land Field Services in 1975 to finish his college education. He graduated in 1977 from the University of Florida and rejoined the company. Through Jay's encouragement, Dan applied and was accepted in Gonzaga University's law program in 1979. While working summers for Jay, Dan attained his law degree in 1981 and returned to Land Field Services to work in the

Anchorage office. In 1984, Dan left the company to pursue a career in right-of-way law.

Bob Ylvisaker (Silver) continued to work for Jay on the Solomon Gulch Hydroelectric project for Copper Valley Electric Association out of Valdez and Glennallen. Bob then relocated to Anchorage to work out of the Land Field Services office. Silver continued his tradition of celebrating Thanksgiving with the Sullivan family for decades.

Warren Krotke maintained a relationship with Jay while working independently as a land consultant. Don Bruce became an invaluable resource for the Fairbanks North Star Borough Land Department. Dick Bruce moved to Eugene, Oregon and became a right-of-way agent for Lane County.

Jay and Nancy provided right-of-way consulting services until 2005. They gradually decreased their workload and began to spend more time at their cabin on Flathorn Lake–a remote site about 30 miles north of Anchorage. Nancy died at their cabin on December 11, 2008. Jay passed four years later in Anchorage on November 2, 2012.

Harry Brelsford worked for Alyeska Pipeline Service Company for 18 years–eventually becoming the general counsel. He retired in June 1988 and moved with his wife Diane to Seattle, Washington. Following the Exxon Valdez oil spill on March 24, 1989, Alyeska brought Harry back from retirement to represent their interests. He worked for one more year before returning to Seattle. Harry died on May 7, 2003 at the Virginia Mason Hospital in Seattle from congestive heart failure.

Armand felt good walking into the ARCO Land Office after being gone for six years. The Land Office still had five employees–including the new supervisor, Burt Brown. Burt graciously welcomed Armand back, "Armand, great to have you in our group again! Take a few days to get situated. Then I've got a special mission for you."

Armand liked special missions. "What have you got?" asked Armand.

Burt smiled and replied, "ARCO bought a few offshore leases next to Saint Lawrence Island near Southeast Cape. We're sending the Ocean Ranger drilling rig to explore these prospects. The drilling department is thinking about resurrecting the old DEW line site as a base camp. There are still some buildings and an airstrip that we can use to base our operations. I need you to research the land status and find out what it will take for us to lease the facility from the air force. And, oh yes, I need you to visit the site and tell us if it's worth pursuing. OK?"

After working in the pipeline grinder for six years, Armand thought this assignment would be pure fun. "Sounds just fine with me, Burt. I'll get on it within a couple of days."

A few days later, Armand began his research. Through reams of paperwork, he stumbled across a report from a military pilot had who recently flown over the site. The pilot observed that the buildings appeared intact but cannibalized by residents from the nearby village of Savoonga. Windows and doors were missing. However, the port and fuel tank farm facilities appeared untouched and serviceable. Boots were needed on the ground to verify the pilot's observations.

Armand paired up with Bill Penrose, the ARCO drilling engineer assigned to the project, to investigate the site. They flew to Nome, spent the night, and then left early the next morning on a chartered twin-engine Otter to Southeast Cape. As they were flying the 160 miles over the Bering Sea, the captain had a serious conversation with Armand and Bill through the headsets. He handed the controls of the aircraft to his copilot before turning in his seat and addressing the men.

"Gentlemen," he began, "no one has verified the condition of the runway. The gawd-forsaken weather out there could have busted it up or someone might have dragged a couple of seal carcasses across it. We just don't know. So when we get there, we're going fly over it a couple of times and check it out. If it looks bad, we're not landing, OK? I just want to prepare you guys for the possibility of a long flight for nothing." Armand and Bill nodded and tightened their seatbelts.

As they approached the island, the pilots slowly dropped them through the clouds. They emerged at the shoreline and the crew leveled the aircraft a few hundred feet above the cape. The beauty of the Twin Otter was that the pilots could slow it down and safely maneuver it.

The captain decelerated the plane, which allowed the three men time to thoroughly evaluate the deserted camp as they passed over it. They confirmed what the military pilot had reported. The buildings were torn apart with building debris strewn hundreds of yards like spokes of a wheel from each structure. The villagers had removed anything of value–timber, windows, and doors.

After three passes, the captain deemed the runway suitable for the rugged Otter landing gear. He set up for a short landing and touched down between potholes. Then the copilot reversed the props and added power. The reverse thrust shoved the men forward against their harnesses before the plane came to stop. "Welcome to Southeast Cape International Airport," the captain calmly said through his microphone. "We do appreciate your business and hope to see you guys real soon. Please remain seated as we taxi to the main terminal." Armand and Bill glanced at each other in disbelief.

When the pilots shut down the engines, Armand and Bill realized the wind was whistling across the tarmac. The plane began to dance lightly on its gear. "Ah, a typical beautiful day on Southeast Cape," the captain said as he took off his headset and addressed the men. "I guess that I don't have to tell you guys that we have only a short time on the ground. Weather blows in here quicker than the snap of the finger and then it holds tight for days. So do what you got to do quickly. If you see me waving, you guys run back here on the double. Got it?" Armand and Bill nodded. "Good," the captain said as the copilot opened the side door. The wind ripped inside and assailed the occupants. Screaming above the gale, the captain yelled, "Now go get'em."

Bill started running bent into the wind for the tank farm. Armand tumbled toward the barracks. When Armand reached the buildings, he immediately saw that they were useless. Driven rain and snow had ravished the interiors, leaving them structurally unsound. After thirty minutes of wandering and battling the wind, Armand had had enough. He buttoned up his coat and leaned into the wind for the hard trek back to the plane. As he approached the Otter, he saw Bill being blown back. When they met, Bill just shook his head. The fuel system and dock were destroyed beyond repair. There was nothing here for ARCO to utilize.

The men piled into the airplane. The crew needed no further instructions. The copilot checked to see if his passengers were properly strapped into their seats before restarting the engines. Because of the stiff wind, the plane took off using only a few hundred feet of the deteriorating runway.

The trip back to Nome and Anchorage was uneventful. Armand and Bill filed their reports, which ARCO took to heart and decided to base the drilling support from Nome. When the Ocean Ranger arrived on site, ARCO shuttled the crews to the platform by helicopter every twelve hours.

The exploratory hole proved to be dry. ARCO repositioned the Ocean Ranger off the Yakutat Bay. The Yakutat hole was also dry. After these expensive ventures, ARCO sent the Ocean Ranger back to the southern China Sea. Shortly after its arrival, a severe typhoon hit the rig. The storm broke the Ocean Ranger's anchors and it overturned. All hands perished in the storm. The horrible incident reminded the world that oil exploration can be a dangerous and high-risk venture.

In late September 1977, Burt Brown asked Armand to do something unusual–present the Land Department's 1978 budget at the annual Alaska budget conference. Typically, the department heads gave a presentation to the ARCO president and board members. However, this time the president wanted to hear from the department staff. Armand thought it over and finally accepted the invitation.

Armand was comfortable with presenting ordinary personnel expenses and foreseeable project costs, but he had a burr under his saddle about company money wasted on speculative oil and gas lease sales. He decided to go out on a limb and use this rare opportunity to express his feelings about lease sales and propose an alternative.

Without consulting Burt, Armand went to the Geological Department and found a geologist who shared his opinions and vowed to help him. The two dug up costs of past lease sales and follow-up seismic studies and organized the data into realistic examples that could be explained to the conference attendees.

Armand's big day came in early October. The ARCO board members and Thornton Bradshaw, president, sat behind desks with department files organized in front of them. Each presenter was required to walk onto a stage and give a concise account of their department's next year's budget. The budget reviewers had a duplicate file of each presentation.

By sheer luck, the board asked for the Land Department's budget first. Burt introduced Armand to the audience. Most of the board knew or heard of Armand Spielman and recognized his valuable contribution to the new pipeline. Thus, they waited patiently when Armand walked to the podium and organized his files before speaking.

"Gentlemen," began Armand as he looked up from his file, "the first page in your folder summarizes the costs of our five-person staff to provide land services in Alaska. There are no surprises and I'm sure you will find the costs reasonable." Armand watched the men scan the budget table in front of them. He noticed several nod in agreement. Armand took a deep breath and continued, "So, I want to take a few minutes to discuss a situation that I believe is wasting million of dollars." The men's eyes flicked to him with intense interest.

Here we go, thought Armand. "If you turn to the next page you will see cost summaries of money spent leasing oil and gas prospects and then investigating them with seismic programs. The seismic studies determined that these leases had a low potential for producing recoverable product.

"I propose a better approach. Why not drill exploratory wells in our own fields? We have two high-potential fields to choose from—the Swanson River Unit and the Soldotna Creek Unit. An exploratory well can be drilled much cheaper than implementing a seismic study and wells give us realistic snapshots of field potential." Armand nodded for his geologist accomplice to come forward. "Here to give you a more detailed comparison of seismic versus well data is our company geologist."

The geologist gave a simplistic review of data collection and costs. At the end of the presentation, Armand asked if anyone had any questions. Instead of questions, the audience applauded—something they never did during budget reviews. Armand glanced over to Burt and saw him hovering between anger and relief at Armand's gamble.

As Armand was walking out the door, Bill Allbright, ARCO vice president, caught him and congratulated him for such a bold and excellent presentation. "You know, Armand," said Bill as he pulled Armand aside, "we could use a man like you in Dallas. Would you consider relocating to Texas?"

The question surprised Armand. "I hadn't thought about it until now, Bill. The move might do Jacque and me some good. I'll have to discuss this with her. Can I have a few days to mull it over?"

Bill smiled as he replied, "Sure, Armand, no hurry. Let me know your answer."

Armand shook Bill's hand and said, "Thank you, Bill. I will be in touch within the week. Thanks for the opportunity."

Over the next week, Armand and Jacque discussed the pros and cons of moving to Dallas. They discovered that nothing was really holding them back. Their son Terry was working for Fluor Corporation in Valdez constructing the Alyeska Marine Terminal. Their oldest daughter, Lana, was now employed by British Petroleum working on the North Slope. Their youngest daughter, Linda, was married and living in Boise, Idaho. Lana's husband solved the remaining issue about saving the Spielman South Anchorage home. He agreed that they would move into the house and take over the mortgage payments while Armand and Jacque were gone.

With the most pressing issues solved, Armand accepted the offer to relocate to the Dallas headquarters. They moved in December 1977 and eventually found a newly constructed home in a beautiful northern Dallas suburb. They happily settled down and enjoyed the warmer weather.

About a year later, Armand notice Jacque appeared to be in constant pain. "What's the matter, honey?" he asked.

"I don't know, Armand," Jacque replied as she moved slowly down the hallway of their home. "I just don't feel good. I haven't for some time and my pains seem to have gotten worse lately."

Armand was concerned. Jacque seldom complained about her ailments. He said, "Let's get some recommendations, find you a doctor, and get you checked out. I understand Dallas has some good ones here." Through mutual friends, they selected a doctor and he gave Jacque a thorough examination. He found nothing out of the ordinary. He pre-scribed some pain medication and asked her to return in two weeks.

Jacque faithfully followed the doctor's instructions and kept seeing him for two months. After no improvement, Armand found another doctor. He also could not find the source of Jacque's discomfort. Out of desperation, Armand contacted a third doctor who performed a bat-tery of tests and was left baffled as to the cause of Jacque's condition.

After a year of medical examinations, they had nothing to show for all the prodding and probing and false hopes. Jacque had had enough. As Armand held her one night, Jacque turned to him and said, "Armand, I want to go home."

"Home," replied Armand, "home as in California or Saint Louis?"

Jacque shook her head and said firmly, "No. Alaska is home. I always felt best there. Please take me home."

Armand knew something serious was happening to Jacque. Her plea sounded to him like a final request. How could he deny her? Armand nodded yes and held her tighter.

In November 1979, Armand approached Bill Allbright about a transfer. Surprisingly, he found Bill in complete agreement. "Armand," Bill said as he waved his hand around the office, "I've got some major space problems around here. We've got so many landmen trainees right now that we don't have desk space to handle them. I was hoping you would entertain a transfer to our Midland, Texas office."

Armand shook his head and replied, "I was thinking some place farther north."

Puzzled, Bill asked, "You mean Oklahoma?"

"Um . . . no Bill. I was hoping for Alaska."

Bill looked incredulous. "You are kidding me, right? No one wants to go back to Alaska."

Armand looked Bill in the eyes and said, "I'm serious, Bill. Jacque has come down with a serious unknown ailment and we want to go back home. We've got family in Alaska. It's the right thing to do now."

Bill went silent for a moment as he studied Armand. Then he exhaled and said, "OK, Armand. I understand. I didn't realize Jacque was ailing. Sure, we can get you back to Alaska. When do you want to move?"

"Soon," replied Armand. "Very soon."

In the spring of 1980, the Spielmans' family doctor asked Jacque and Armand to come see him for a private meeting at his Anchorage Providence Hospital office. When they saw the doctor walk into the room with a sorrowful and compassionate expression, they knew his prognosis was not hopeful. "Jacque, you have pancreatic cancer," he said holding Jacque's hand. "I'm sorry, but there is no cure. We can extend your life for a few months, but that's all."

The solemn walk back to the car and silent ride home underlined the finality of the doctor visit. They spoke to each daughter about their mother's cancer. Fluor had relocated Terry to Venezuela to reconstruct a refinery. Armand wrote Terry a letter explaining the seriousness of the situation.

Jacque tried to put her best face on her condition, but time slowly sapped her strength and the cancer spread through her body. Surprising her doctor, Jacque managed to proceed with her life for another year and a half until she was finally hospitalized in September 1982. The doctor told Armand to call the family together. Jacque would die soon.

The girls were not a problem because they were readily accessible by telephone. Terry, however, was a different matter. His work site was in a remote part of Venezuela with no telephone service. Armand called Fluor's human resources office in Irvine, California and asked for help reaching Terry. The human resources office relayed the message to their International Relocations Department who finally delivered the news to Terry in Venezuela a few days later.

Unknown to his parents, Terry had a secret that he was now compelled to reveal. He had married a Venezuelan girl, Elba, in June and Terry had not told his parents yet. Without giving it a second thought, Terry told Elba that she was coming with him. Fluor gave Terry emergency leave. They packed their bags and left the next day.

Terry and Elba reached Anchorage two grueling days later during the afternoon of October 11. Lana's husband met them at the airport and brought them to the hospital. Terry walked to his mother's bedside, knelt down, and softly said, "Mom. It's me, Terry."

Jacque's eyes fluttered and opened at the sound of her son's voice. She turned to him smiling and said, "Oh, Terry! It's so good to see you. Thank you for coming."

Terry smiled back as tears welled up in his eyes. "You are welcome, Mom. Took me a while to get here." Then Terry turned and motioned Elba to step closer. When Jacque saw her, a puzzled look crossed her face. "Mom," continued Terry, "there's someone here that I want you to meet. This is your new daughter-in-law, Elba. We were married last June."

Elba knelt to join her husband and reached out her hand to Jacque. Jacque slowly grabbed it and gazed into Elba's eyes. Then a radiant smile broke across her face and she pulled Elba to her. They embraced and, when Elba pulled back, Jacque studied her exotic features as she addressed her. "Welcome to our family, Elba. You are very beautiful. So you are from Venezuela?"

Elba nodded and replied, "*Sí*. Terry and I met in Venezuela."

"Then we have something in common," said Jacque. "We both left our countries to marry Spielmans. You made a wise choice. I am so happy to meet you." They discussed small things of life until Jacque's strength left her and she sank deep into her pillow. Lana took Elba to her home and Armand, exhausted from days of hospital vigils, went home with them. Terry volunteered to stay and watch over his mother for the night.

Through the evening and night, Terry talked softly to his mother. He recalled the fun they had traveling to France to meet her parents and relatives. Terry discussed his life over the years—successes and failures, excitement and disappointment. Jacque sometimes responded, but mostly appeared to sleep. Terry thought she was listening and his voice was comforting her.

During the early morning, Terry noticed his mother was very still and he couldn't detect breathing. He signaled for a nurse. The nurse examined her and immediately summoned help. A second nurse arrived and instructed Terry to stand outside the room. Terry felt helpless as he walked into the hallway. Then he saw an older woman walk towards him with a small bouquet of flowers. She stopped in front of his mother's room and noticed the two nurses working over Jacque.

The woman turned to Terry and said, "Hi, I'm Jacque's neighbor. I thought I'd drop off some flowers and say hi before going to work."

"Oh, thank you. I'm her son Terry and I spent the night with Mom. I think she's real tired, but . . ."

A nurse came out of the room and addressed Terry in a matter-of-fact voice, "I'm sorry to tell you, Mr. Spielman, but your mother has passed. You should summon your family to pay their last respects before we move the body."

The neighbor gasped and dropped the vase. The shattering broke what was left of Terry's reserve. He collapsed in tears.

As Armand looked upon Jacque's body, he realized that all his accomplishments meant nothing. Here was his beautiful wife, whom he had met in battle-torn France. She had left everything she held dear to be with him in the United States. Jacque had loved him without restraint, given him three beautiful children, shared his victories and disappointments, and now she was gone. *Why is it*, thought Armand as he turned to his grieving family, *that we work so hard for other men's dreams and fail to hold on to what really matters?* "I love you," said Armand as he looked intently at his grown children. "We are going to get through this. I'll make sure of it."

After completing his senior high school year in Colorado, Mike Travis entered the University of Alaska at Fairbanks in September 1975. He graduated in 1980 and went to work for Fluor Engineering on the Northwest Gas Pipeline Project. The Northwest project planned to build a pipeline from Prudhoe Bay to the Canadian border. The gas line would roughly follow TAPS from Prudhoe to Delta Junction. Then the route deviated from the Alyeska route and followed the old Haines pipeline to Canada.

Like several earlier gas line projects, the Northwest project died a slow death, but not before Mike gained a thorough knowledge of pipeline construction techniques and close familiarity with the TAPS route.

Fluor employees had to study the successes and failures of TAPS and apply the lessons learned on the Northwest project.

Mike's next employer was the Alaska Department of Transportation and Public Facilities (DOT&PF). He went to work in the Fairbanks DOT&PF Environmental Section on Peger Road in May 1984. A few years later, Mike attended a seminar sponsored by the Arctic chapter of the International Right-of-Way Association (IRWA). During a break, cohorts introduced him to staff from the Anchorage DOT&PF office. "And here's our chief of Right-of-way, Dan Beardsley."

Mike's jaw hit the floor when he recognized Dan. Tongue-tied, all he managed to say was, ". . . uh, Coach?"

Dan smiled and said, "Mike. Good to see you again." If there was ever an example that Alaska was a small town, this was it. Dan pointed to a large man towering above the crowd and continued, "Do you recognize that guy?"

Mike looked bewildered as he gazed upon the huge man and muttered, "Coach Sullivan?"

Dan patted Mike on the shoulder and said, "Mike, you're not in high school anymore. Just call us Dan and Jay."

Mike shook his head and replied, "This is going to take some getting used to."

Mike eventually overcame his shock and developed a close relationship with Dan and Jay that spanned decades. In due course, Dan and Mike entered the consulting world and continued to collaborate with Jay on projects. In the mid-1990s and in 2008, Dan, Jay, and Mike went on a lecture circuit teaching seminars on navigability laws. The proceeds went to the Arctic and Sourdough IRWA chapters to promote right-of-way training.

Dan and Jay introduced Mike to Bob "Silver" Ylvisaker. Bob and Mike enjoyed each other's company at various IRWA functions. Mike and Jay maintained their special relationship up to the time of Jay's death in 2012. After a coincidental set of circumstances, Dan and Mike now work across the hall from each other in the same building in Anchorage—proving once again what a small town Alaska really is. They continue to help each other with projects across their big state.

Bibliography

BOOKS

Berry, Mary Clay. 1975. *The Alaska Pipeline: The Politics of Oil and Native Land Claims.* Indiana University Press. Bloomington, IN. 320pp.

Naske, Claus and Herman Slotnik. 2011. *Alaska –A History.* University of Oklahoma Press. Norman, OK. p295.

Roscow, James. 1977. *800 Miles to Valdez.* Prentice-Hall, Inc. Englewood Cliffs, NJ. 227pp.

Sampson, Anthony. 1975. *The Seven Sisters: The Great Oil Companies and the World They Shaped.* Viking Penguin. New York. 334pp.

Spielman, Armand C. 2012. *A Project that Reformed Alaska and Its Legislature.* Anchorage, AK. 89pp.

ARTICLES

Alaska Bar Association. In Memoriam. *Obituary of Harry Brelsford.* http://www.alaskabar.org/servlet/content/in_memoriam_.html

Joint Pipeline Office. Trans-Alaska Pipeline System Renewal EIS. *TAPS History. Key events in the history of the Trans-Alaska Pipeline System.* http://tapseis.anl.gov/guide/history.cfm.

Passion for the Climb. Jennifer Brice. *Letters from Helenka.* www4.colgate.edu/scene/mar2007/passion.html

River Teeth: A Journal of Nonfiction Narrative. Jennifer Brice. *Angle of Attack.* Vol 6, No. 1, Oct 1, 2004. 17-40pp.

September 12, 1969. *First Pipe Arrives in Valdez.* Valdez – Copper Basin News. First Edition. Valdez, AK. Entire paper.

March 6, 1970. *More TAPS Delays.* Fairbanks Daily News Miner. Fairbanks, AK. p 1.

March 10, 1970. *TAPS Road to Yukon Two-Thirds Finished, Survey Crew Moves Ahead.* Fairbanks Daily News Miner. Fairbanks, AK. p A6.

March 10, 1970. *Alaska Natives Ask Federal Court To Stop TAPS Job.* Fairbanks Daily News Miner. Fairbanks, AK. p A6.

March 13, 1970. *No Pipeline Permits Until After April 1 Hearings.* Fairbanks Daily News Miner. Fairbanks, AK. p 1.

April 3, 1970. *Miller Outlines State Move in Telegram to Sec. Hickel.* Fairbanks Daily News Miner. Fairbanks, AK. p 1 & A7.

April 6, 1970. *New Steps on Pipeline.* Fairbanks Daily News Miner. Fairbanks, AK. p 1.

April 7, 1970. *Road Work Suit.* Fairbanks Daily News Miner. Fairbanks, AK. p 1.

April 7, 1970. *Natives Ask TAPS Damages.* Fairbanks Daily News Miner. Fairbanks, AK. p A-10.

April 9, 1970. *TAPS Still Not Considering Any of Alternative Proposals.* Fairbanks Daily News Miner. Fairbanks, AK. p 1.

April 13, 1970. *Stevens Village Major Roadblock in Start of Pipeline Construction.* Fairbanks Daily News Miner. Fairbanks, AK. p 3.

April 15, 1970. *State May Build Access Road North.* Fairbanks Daily News Miner. Fairbanks, AK. p 1.

April 17, 1970. *Villagers 'Misled'.* Fairbanks Daily News Miner. Fairbanks, AK. p 1.

April 20, 1970. *Committees to Examine Road Action.* Fairbanks Daily News Miner. Fairbanks, AK. p 1.

April 21, 1970. *Construction of Valdez Terminal Awaiting Interior 'Line' Permit.* Fairbanks Daily News Miner. Fairbanks, AK. p 1.

April 21, 1970. *TAPS Gets Miller Proposals.* Fairbanks Daily News Miner. Fairbanks, AK. p A4.

April 21, 1970. *House Committee Airs Stevens Village Snag.* Fairbanks Daily News Miner. Fairbanks, AK. p A5 & A8.

April 23, 1970. *TAPS Injunctions in Way.* Fairbanks Daily News Miner. Fairbanks, AK. p 1 & 3.

May 1, 1970. *Attorney General to Take Up Slope Road.* Fairbanks Daily News Miner. Fairbanks, AK. p. 1.

May 5, 1970. *Governor Asks Funds to Build Road.* Fairbanks Daily News Miner. Fairbanks, AK. p 1.

May 5, 1970. *Judge Based Injunction on Erroneous Conclusion.* Fairbanks Daily News Miner. Fairbanks, AK. p A3.

May 12, 1970. *Natives Hired for TAPS Job.* Fairbanks Daily News Miner. Fairbanks, AK. p A5.

May 28, 1970. *Livengood to Yukon Haul Road Completion.* Fairbanks Daily News Miner. Fairbanks, AK. p 1.

June 9, 1970. *Jap Firm Delivers Pipe.* Fairbanks Daily News Miner. Fairbanks, AK. p A4.

June 9, 1970. *TAPS, State Shift Route of Haul Rd's North End.* Fairbanks Daily News Miner. Fairbanks, AK. p A2.

June 16, 1970. *Federal Attorneys Act Swiftly to Nullify 2 TAPS Injunctions.* Fairbanks Daily News Miner. Fairbanks, AK. pp A1 – A2.

June 16, 1970. *TAPS Terminate Pacts to Build Pipeline Road.* Fairbanks Daily News Miner. Fairbanks, AK. p A3.

June 30, 1970. *Burgess-Houston Meets with TAPS.* Fairbanks Daily News Miner. Fairbanks, AK. p A2.

July 7, 1970. *BLM Reorganizes Pipeline Crew.* Fairbanks Daily News Miner. Fairbanks, AK. p. A1.

July 7, 1970. *Special Session Cancelled.* Fairbanks Daily News Miner. Fairbanks, AK. p A3.

February 26, 1971. *CDFU Takes Stand on Pipeline.* Valdez – Copper Basin News. Valdez, AK. p 3.

March 19, 1971. *Some Progress on the Pipeline.* Valdez – Copper Basin News. Valdez, AK. p 1.

May 6, 1971. *P.W.S. Fisherman File Injunction.* Valdez – Copper Basin News. Valdez, AK. p 7 & 11.

May 20, 1971. *Cordova Fishermen Meet with Admiral Palmer.* Valdez – Copper Basin News. Valdez, AK. p 1.

November 4, 1971. *Egan Advocates State Ownership of Oil Pipeline.* Valdez- Copper Basin News. Valdez, AK. p 1 & 12.

January 13, 1972. *Impact Statement Goes to President and Environmental Quality Council.* Valdez – Copper Basin News. Valdez, AK. p 1.

January 27, 1972. *Alyeska Acquires Terminal Site.* Valdez – Copper Basin News. Valdez, AK. p 1.

July 20, 1973. *First Lathrop Football Team Set.* Fairbanks Daily News Miner. Fairbanks, AK. p 12.

August 18, 1973. *First Lathrop Football Team Launches Season Next Week.* Fairbanks Daily News Miner. Fairbanks, AK. p 11.

August 24, 1973. *Lathrop Football Debut Saturday Against Service at Growden Park.* Fairbanks Daily News Miner. Fairbanks, AK. p 9.

August 27, 1973. *Lathrop Yields to Service.* Fairbanks Daily News Miner. Fairbanks, AK. p 9.

August 28, 1973. *Atmosphere Changes as Prep Football Comes to Fairbanks.* Fairbanks Daily News Miner. Fairbanks, AK. p 9.

September 14, 1973. *Malemutes Ready Final Home Game.* Fairbanks Daily News Miner. Fairbanks, AK. p 14.

September 24, 1973. *Malemutes get Victory No. 1 by Beating Falcons 24-14.* Fairbanks Daily News Miner. Fairbanks, AK. p 10.

October 1, 1973. *West Mauls Lathrop.* Fairbanks Daily News Miner. Fairbanks, AK. p 13.

October 9, 1973. *Malemutes Drop Last Game of Season to Chugiak Team.* Fairbanks Daily News Miner. Fairbanks, AK. p 8.

January 17, 1974. *Preparation for Pipeline begins as Camp Buildings, Site Work Bid.* Fairbanks Daily News Miner. Fairbanks, AK. p 16.

January 23, 1974. *Pipeline Permit Signed.* Fairbanks Daily News Miner. Fairbanks, AK. p 1.

January 23, 1974. *Pipeline Timetable since 1968 Listed.* Fairbanks Daily News Miner. Fairbanks, AK. p 1 & 3.

March 21, 1974. *Gravel Auction.* Fairbanks Daily News Miner. Fairbanks, AK. p 19.

April 25, 1974. *ACV to Cross Yukon.* Oil and Resource Development. Alyeska Roundup. Fairbanks Daily News Miner. Fairbanks, AK. p A1.

April 29, 1974. *Pipeline Construction Gets Under Way.* Fairbanks Daily News Miner. Fairbanks, AK. p 1 & 3.

May 6, 1974. *Wainwright Lease Signed For Alyeska.* Fairbanks Daily News Miner. Fairbanks, AK. p 1.

April 9, 1975. *Legal Notice of Condemnation Proceedings. George Duncan. Raymond Duncan.* Fairbanks, AK. p 19.

May 19, 1975. *Candidates Disclose Financial Interests – John Buthovich.*

July 29, 1975. *Legal Notice of Condemnation Proceedings. John Bullock, Ross Harry, H. Leonard, Les Matson, Guy Rivers, H. Sparks, and Yutana Barge Lines.* Fairbanks Daily News Miner. p 11.

September 6, 1975. *Stolen: One House.* Fairbanks Daily News Miner. Fairbanks, AK.

September 24, 1975. *Legal Notice of Condemnation Proceedings. Estate of Keith Harkness, George Harkness, Walter Harkness, and Katherine Harkness Coon.* Fairbanks, AK. p 14.

November 6, 2012. *Obituary of Paxton Sullivan.* Anchorage Daily News. Anchorage, AK.

September 9, 1975. *Dispute erupts over gravel site.* Fairbanks Daily News Miner. Fairbanks, AK. p3.

September 11, 1975. *Alyeska wins injunction.* Fairbanks Daily News Miner. Fairbanks, AK. p 3.

December 5, 1975. *Disappearing Cabin Found.* Fairbanks Daily News Miner. p 6.

December 23, 1975. *The right way?* Letter to the editor by Ray Duncan. Fairbanks, AK. p 4.

November 24, 2010. *Obituary of Andrew W. Miscovich.* Fairbanks Daily News Miner. Fairbanks, AK.

November, 2014. *Brice Brothers Awarded Alaska's Top Honors in Construction.* Alaska Business Monthly. Anchorage, AK.

SOURCES

Alaska Department of Natural Resources Recorder's Office - Fairbanks. Document 1975-001540-0. Declaration of Taking. Grantor: Harkness. Grantee: Amerada Hess Corporation.

Alaska Department of Natural Resources Recorder's Office - Valdez. Books 67 and 68. Mining Claim Location Notices for P. J. Sullivan. Claims Arctic 1-1 through Arctic 8-148.

Alaska Department of Natural Resources Recorder's Office - Valdez. Book 71, Page 289. Affidavit of Annual Labor filed for P. J. Sullivan. Claims Arctic 1-1 through Arctic 8-148.

Alaska Court System. Fairbanks Office of the Clerk. Alyeska Pipeline Service Company vs John Butrovich, Jr., William Waugaman, William Stroecker, Duane Hall, and Kenneth Ringstad. Civil Action No. 75-418. Complaint in Eminent Domain.

Alaska Court System. The Supreme Court of Alaska. Frank Turpin, Commissioner, Department of Transportation and Public Facilities and State of Alaska vs North Slope Borough and Tanana Chiefs Conference. Case No. 3AN-91-05502 CI. Opinion. Opening the Dalton Highway to Unrestricted Travel. August 26, 1994.

National Archives – Pacific Alaska Region. Record Group No. RG 49 BLM. Box 3 of 169. Patent Case #AA005813. Files, 1966 – 1978, 49-80-0073.

Personal files of Armand Spielman. 1969 – 1975.

United States Department of the Interior. 1972. Final Environmental Impact Statement. Proposed Trans-Alaska Pipeline. Report in Six Volumes.

United States District Court. District of Alaska. Exxon Pipeline Company, et al vs David Burns. Final Judgment in a Civil Case. Case number A82-454. October 22, 1985.

United States General Accounting Office. April 8, 1981. Letter from J. Dexter Peach, Director of Energy and Minerals Division, to James Watt, Secretary of the Interior. *Environmental and Other Problems along the Alaska Pipeline Corridor.* Washington DC. 9pp.

Wikipedia. December 2, 2013. Trans-Alaska Pipeline System. http://en.wikipedia.org/wiki/Trans-Alaska_Pipeline_System

Wikipedia. October 23, 2014. 1973 Oil Crisis. http://en.wikipedia.org/wiki/1973_oil_crisis

Certificates of Appreciation

On August 12, 2014, Mr. Thomas Case, Chancellor of the University of Alaska–Anchorage, presented a Certificate of Appreciation to Mr. Armand Spielman. Mr. Case, a retired Air Force four-star general, held the award ceremony at his beautiful Anchorage home. In attendance were the Spielman family and friends. The certificate recognized Mr. Spielman's six-year service as the Land Acquisition Manager for the Alyeska Pipeline Service Company

The Certificate stated, "The Chancellor of the University of Alaska at Anchorage hereby honors Armand C. Spielman for his service and dedication to the State of Alaska's people and its economy on this date of August 12, 2014, signed be the Chancellor, Mr. Tom Case, of the University of Alaska at Anchorage."

The ceremony began at 4:00 p.m. The attendants presented each lady with a red rose and introduced attendees to the guest of honor. At 5:00 p.m., The Chancellor called the guests into his living room and formally welcomed the crowd, introduced Mr. Spielman, presented the Certificate, and asked him to say a few words.

Mr. Spielman thanked Mr. Case and his wife for the wonderful occasion and then he told the audience how the Chancellor came to read his book, *A Project that Reformed Alaska and Its Legislature*. One morning, Mr. Case was flying to Fairbanks. Mr. Ray Dahl happened to sit next to him and had just finished reading the book. Mr. Dahl showed Mr. Case the book and told him about it. Intrigued, the Chancellor asked if he could borrow it. The book impressed Mr. Case and impelled him to honor the author.

Armand Spielman proudly displays the Certificate alongside another Certificate of Appreciation signed by Mr. Edward Patton, President of Alyeska. This certificate recognized Mr. Spielman's service on the Trans-Alaska Pipeline System from March 1, 1969 to June 1, 1975. The following pages display both Certificates.

Jay Sullivan exchanges an oosik for a gavel with American Right of Way President, Gene L. Land, as Jay's wife Nancy looks on. Picture taken 1972.

Picture taken March 2013. Armand Spielman's 90th Birthday. From left to right: Warren Krotke, Dan Beardsley, Armand, Bob Ylvisaker, and Michael Travis.

Harry Brelsford. Picture taken 1980.

William "King Fish" Arnold and his wife at Ted and Ann Steven's
25th Wedding Anniversary at the Captain Cook Hotel.
Picture taken 1977. Ann died the next year in a plane crash at the
Anchorage International Airport.

Citation for William Arnold Photograph

Accession #: B1990.014.5.Pol.04.670

Credit: "Steve McCutcheon, McCutcheon Collection; Anchorage Museum, B1990.014.5.Pol.04.670"

Additional Information: Stevens' 25th anniv, Bill Arnold & Wife